▲

COALITIONS ACROSS THE
CLASS DIVIDE

Coalitions

across the

Class Divide

LESSONS FROM THE LABOR, PEACE,
AND ENVIRONMENTAL MOVEMENTS

FRED ROSE

Fred Rose

CORNELL UNIVERSITY PRESS

ITHACA AND LONDON

First published 2000 by Cornell University Press
First printing, Cornell Paperbacks, 2000

Printed in the United States of America

Library of Congress Cataloging-in-Publication Data

Rose, Fred.
Coalitions across the class divide : lessons from the labor, peace, and environmental movements / Fred Rose.
p.   cm.
Includes bibliographical references and index.
ISBN 0-8014-3605-2 (cloth). —ISBN 0-8014-8636-X (pbk.)
1. Social classes—United States. 2. Social reformers—United States. 3. Labor move-ment—United States. 4. Peace movements—United States. 5. Environmentalism—United States.   I. Title.
HN90.S6R67   2000
305.5'0973—dc21   99-41669

Cornell University Press strives to use environmentally responsible suppliers and materials to the fullest extent possible in the publishing of its books. Such materials include vegetable-based, low-VOC inks and acid-free papers that are recycled, totally chlorine-free, or partly composed of nonwood fibers. Books that bear the logo of the FSC (Forest Stewardship Council) use paper taken from forests that have been inspected and certified as meeting the highest standards for environmental and social responsibility. For further information, visit our website at www.cornellpress.cornell.edu.

Cloth printing   10 9 8 7 6 5 4 3 2 1
Paperback printing   10 9 8 7 6 5 4 3 2 1

FSC FSC Trademark © 1996 Forest Stewardship Council A.C.
SW-COC-098

▲

To the bridge builders I met along the way

▲

CONTENTS

PREFACE

This book is rooted in my experiences, struggles, and questions as a white, middle-class guy seeking to contribute to social justice and social change. I've spent a good part of the past two decades exploring how I could be effective in this vocation. What follows are the best personal and political answers I've found both as an organizer and as a student of social movements.

Born at the start of the 1960s, the son of two research scientists, I have been both blessed and cursed to have internalized two conflicting sets of values—a professional, middle-class ethic of personal success and a countercultural ethic of living for and in the present. A recurring theme in my life is whether to pursue a traditional professional career or to find work as an activist. This has given me a critical view of middle-class lifestyles, even though I now find myself in one. As a result my analysis of middle-class (and working-class) cultures in this book speaks to some of my own ghosts.

My focus on working- and middle-class coalitions dates back to 1985–87, when I directed a military conversion project with a peace organization in Tacoma, Washington, called Sixth Sense. We built a successful coalition with metal trades unions in the shipyards as Navy contracts dried up at the end of the Reagan military boom. The coalition eventually brought new state ferry contracts to Tacoma by changing restrictive state insurance requirements. The act of summoning my courage, going down to the union halls, and trying to bring workers into the coalition had a profound effect on me. It taught me about the social and physical distances I needed to cross.

I entered graduate school in part out of my frustrations with activism. The day-to-day work of organizing makes it difficult to think critically about strategies and worldviews. I was disturbed to discover that many movements I worked with remained vague about how to promote the changes they sought. I was also concerned about the narrow focus of most organizing, which at times inadvertently contributes to the ills of others.

My research gave me a golden opportunity to look more deeply into the process of building coalitions across class lines. By the time I began my research in 1991, conversion had gained national attention with the end of the Cold War. It was an exciting time of experimentation and change, and I took the opportunity to seek out and learn from people doing the best coalition organizing in the country. I was able to build on the labor and peace movement contacts I had in Washington State as a starting point for this research.

My goal has been to produce a book that will be useful to activists and organizers and also to students of social movements. Although I have emphasized the cases I personally observed, I have placed them in a broader theoretical framework. Throughout the writing I have struggled to strike a balance between concrete and immediate experience on the one hand and ways of understanding politics on the other. My hope is that this book will inspire you, the reader, to redouble your efforts to cross the class divide. I invite you to share your experiences or your reactions to the book with me. I can be contacted through Cornell University Press.

This book is dedicated to the bridge builders I met along the way—those pioneers who take personal and political risks to cross the frontiers of social class to realize a vision of a unified movement for change.

In Washington State: Gordon Baxter and Rob Stern, from Plumbers and Pipefitters Local 32; Rick Bender, from the King County Labor Council; Beth Burrows, from the Washington Biotechnology Action Council; Bob Dilger, from the Washington Building and Construction Trades; Andrea Durbin, from Friends of the Earth; David Fleischman and Bill Patz, from Washington State Sane/Freeze; Nate Ford, from the Puget Sound Metal Trades; Jim Freese and Hank MaGuire, from the International Brotherhood of Electrical Workers Local 46; Mike Gilbert, from the Northwest Conservation Action Coalition; Jack Gilchrist, from Latherers Local 1144; Otto Herman, from Rebound; Jeff Johnson, from the Washington State Labor Council; Ron Judd, from the Seattle Building and Construction Trades; Paul Knox, from the Washington State Department of Community Development; and Darlene Madenwald, Ted

Pankowski, and Joan Thomas, from the Washington Environmental Council.

In Minnesota: Mel Duncan and Janet Groat, from Jobs with Peace; Jeff Farmer, from the Service Employees International Union Local 113; Toby Loppoko, from the Minnesota AFL-CIO; Jim Mangen, from the Working Group on Economic Dislocation; Claudette Munson, from the International Brotherhood of Electrical Workers Local 2047; and Dan St. Clair, from the United Auto Workers.

In Maine: Mike Cavanaugh, from the Amalgamated Clothing and Textile Workers Union; Bill Meserve, from the United Paperworkers International Union Local 14; Charles O'Leary, from the Maine AFL-CIO; Susie Schweppe, from the Peace Economy Project; and Burt and Gail Wartell, from the International Association of Machinists Local 6.

All unattributed quotations in this book are taken from interviews conducted with labor, peace, and environmental activists. Some individuals are identified by their first names only—these are pseudonyms. When both the first and last names are given, this is the speaker's actual identity.

FRED ROSE

Deerfield, Massachusetts

PART I

▲

The Class Divide

Conflicts between labor unions and peace or environmental organizations seem to pit the economic needs of working people against the goals of environmental protection or peace. Two fundamental questions, developed in the opening chapter, frame the remainder of the book: What is the democratic alternative to this struggle for political advantage between two just causes? and, Can an alliance between unions and peace or environmental organizations shift the debate to how to achieve the goals of both movements? The second chapter provides an overview of how these questions might be answered; it outlines the theoretical arguments that later chapters develop through cases and examples.

▲

The Progressive Logjam

Aberdeen, Washington, is a lumber port deep in the heart of timber country on the southwest corner of the Olympic Peninsula. In this working-class city generations of loggers and woodworkers fought timber companies for better wages and safer conditions through the International Woodworkers of America and earlier unions. But times are hard for the Aberdeen union local, which lost 70 percent of its members between 1980 and 1992. Union members attribute their troubles in part to a newer adversary—environmentalists. In many workers' minds environmentalists are a more difficult opponent than the bosses. As one union leader put it,

> The preservationist portion of the environmental movement has taken on fanatical, religious—if you will, zealous—dimensions. . . . These people are pilgrims, religious about environmental protection. They're beyond reasoning. They are attempting to use the owl and some other species as launching pads to advance a philosophy that is outright frightening. . . . None of the environmental groups truly cares about the communities impacted by job loss. They say they care, but that's just public relations.

Two hours by car and a world away, the staff of several national environmental organizations in Seattle find this union attitude maddening. Without a doubt, these environmentalists are extremely concerned about the fate of the Northwest's forests and local endangered species. Out of frustration with the war of words, they have begun to charter flights so people can see for themselves the effects of the timber industry. They point to pictures showing a patchwork of clear-cuts of stumps and debris in the midst of isolated tracts of woods. In their fight to save the last remaining virgin forests, one environmentalist described the unions in these terms:

> We say we're running out of forest, and they say we're not running out of trees. They do not understand the ecosystem. They desire to hunt and fish, but it's not necessary to understand the ecosystem for that. They work from ignorance. . . . Industry needed a scapegoat to conceal what was happening in the industry—automation of the mills, log exports, unsustainable cutting levels on private lands. . . . Labor has been duped. People tell me these timber workers aren't dumb, but they have fallen for a line here.

From Washington State to Washington, D.C., environmentalists and timber unions battled on the national stage in the late 1980s and 1990s. The federal government, it seemed, faced a tragic choice between preserving timber communities and jobs on the one hand and saving spotted owls and old-growth forests on the other. Headlines read: "Jobs v. Owl," "Oregon's Other Threatened Species: The Timber Worker," "Owl vs. Man," and "Saving Spotted Owl and Destroying Families."[1]

Why was the country faced with a choice between two just causes, between the right of people to work and the right to protect the environment? Certainly other choices existed. Timber workers recognized that they "have a vested interest [in the forests], and that interest does not include wiping out or eradicating the resource."[2] And many environmentalists felt that "workers and communities should be marching hand in hand with environmentalists."[3] Furthermore, many compromises could be reached if both jobs and the environment were the most important policy goals. These measures would have required restrictions on the big timber companies and the redirecting of timber profits, choices that never entered the political debate.

In the 1960s, during the Vietnam War, national attention was galvanized by a similar battle between construction workers and peace activists. The most graphic image of conflict between the labor and peace movements came on May 9, 1970, when three hundred "hard hat" construction workers in New York City brutally attacked antiwar protesters in front of a television audience of millions. Unions and peace protesters clashed throughout the Cold War over the size of the military budget and the morality of weapons construction. Even today, some peace activists accuse workers at defense plants of promoting war and destruction by participating in military production. They protest at plant gates to "encourage labor in the military industry to seriously consider the personal, political, economic and legal tasks for us all to create a world secure from the horrors of nuclear weaponry."[4] Defense workers, who are proud of their work, often perceive peace activists as insensitive to their economic needs and violent in their intent to destroy good jobs.

Progressive politics in the United States depends upon reconciling the immediate needs of working people with the social, environmental, and peace-related goals often raised by middle-class movements. Conflicts over these issues have frustrated attempts to build a unified movement for change, dividing people by class, race, gender, nationality, and occupation. They have fueled the present politics of division that confronts the public with tragic choices between protecting economic well-being and preserving the environment or health, or between keeping jobs and cutting unnecessary military production. The vision of a unified movement, particularly of a working- and middle-class alliance, is, in Barbara Ehrenreich's words, "almost the defining dream of the American left."[5] Indeed, these types of coalitions have provided the base of support for the New Deal as well as progressive social and environmental legislation. Working- and middle-class majorities have also elected social-democratic governments in Europe. So long as the left is unable to bring together working- and middle-class movements and to reconcile their issues, it will remain weak and marginal in American politics.

This book is about coalition organizing between working-class unions and middle-class peace and environmental organizations. It asks why these organizations are so often in conflict, and how and when activists can bridge the divisive issues of jobs versus environmental protection or jobs versus military reductions. These issues took center stage in the 1980s and 1990s. Alliances like those examined in this book are learning how to advance an environmentally healthy, peace-promoting, *and* economically secure society.

Is This All There Is to Democracy?

Conflict and miscommunication are not problems just for the left. In many ways they are normal politics in America. Abortion, affirmative action, taxes, health care reform, free trade, the minimum wage, gun control, and myriad other causes polarize the country. Politics in the United States as a whole has become a competition between opposing interest groups lobbying for narrow issues. Social movements have also become narrow advocates for isolated issues such as peace, the environment, or union member benefits—very different from broad, multi-issue movements of the past such as the socialists or populists.

Recreating an inclusive politics that can bridge the many divisions in our society is the political challenge of the day. National politicians consult opinion polls to respond to the public's moods, but much more than that is needed to reconcile people with profoundly different experiences, needs, and values. How can people transcend their differences? How do groups with such divergent interests as timber workers and environmentalists learn to comprehend each other's legitimate concerns and incorporate them without losing crucial political ground to uncompromising adversaries? Isn't there more to democracy than competing factions?

The answer to this problem, at least in theory, is that political participation, even of the most self-centered kind, can teach people to value and incorporate diverse perspectives. That was the vision promoted by such advocates for democracy as Jean-Jacques Rousseau and John Stuart Mill, who believed that even though individuals enter the political process to advance narrow issues or interests, they will be transformed as they negotiate with others who possess equivalent motivations of their own and an equal right to pursue their goals. As people argue their agendas in public, they are forced to explain why their personal interests make good policy for the whole community. "I want" or "I need" must become "I deserve" or "we should." As individuals confront other people's claims about the common good, they learn about their goals and perspectives. As Mill said, "It is from political discussion and collective political action that one whose daily occupations concentrate his interests in a small circle round himself, learns to feel for and with his fellow-citizens and becomes consciously a member of a great community."[6]

But politics in practice hardly lives up to these visionary ideals. Our narrowly competitive interest-group politics seems to discourage just this kind of fellowship and sense of common destiny, so sorely needed today. As they engage in debate, participants in our political process often become more polarized and entrenched in their positions rather than informed by shared understandings. Compromise often becomes a pragmatic trade of concessions, a question of what each side "gave away," rather than a reflection of deeper insights attained through dialogue. Politics as practiced today no longer promises a larger vision worthy of common allegiance. It now connotes corruption, greed, and loss of integrity instead of participation in the "great community."

Stronger communities and families are often prescribed as a cure for our ailing political system.[7] People, in this view, are so focused on advancing themselves and pursuing selfish interests because they have lost their ties with family, civic organizations, religious organizations, local government, and other community institutions. A generation ago people commonly lived in neighborhoods where they knew one another, looked out for each other's children, and felt safe to leave their doors unlocked and walk around freely—all qualities of community that have declined dramatically in recent decades. In Robert Putnam's words, people are more often "bowling alone" than in generations past.[8] The key to rebuilding a sense of common destiny, then, could be to revitalize local associations so that people feel they belong to a community. Involvement in a family, church, community organization, or local government—organizations that serve as intermediaries between isolated individuals and the large, anonymous institutions of mass society—could teach people to care about the needs of others and to work effectively with people with different interests.

But membership within a community organization or church or participation in the peace, labor, or environmental movement has not been enough to bring these different segments of the community together. Narrowly defined advocacy organizations tend to attract or recruit people from similar social backgrounds. Conversations within groups segregated by class, race, interest, or location do little to broaden perspectives about the common good. As a result these movements often find themselves wondering where the "other people" are. The problem is that homogeneous organizations and shared purpose can isolate and separate people instead of integrating them.

If individuals are to develop through public participation, they need to interact in meaningful ways with people who are different than themselves. As William Sullivan says, the root of civic life "is involvement with others: other generations, other sorts of persons whose differences are significant because they contribute to the whole upon which our particular sense of self depends. Thus mutual interdependency is the foundational notion of citizenship."[9] Isolated movements, single-issue interest groups, and political participation based on voting and lobbying do not provide this vital ingredient of "involvement with others." When single-issue movements do interact, it is most often through anonymous forums such as the press, or in public hearings, or across protest barricades that further cement convictions and conflict. Other opportunities for participation in more diverse associations are clearly needed. Could intermovement coalitions provide this opportunity?

Representatives from the Association of Washington Business called a meeting with leaders of the building and metal trades unions in Seattle in 1991 to discuss a business-sponsored bill to weaken the state's growth management law. Management had often relied on the trade unions to oppose limits on construction, and again they argued that the unions shared their interest in passing business's bill. But this time labor was also building an alliance with the environmental community around other issues important to the unions, and they refused to abandon their allies. Instead they argued that controlling growth is a quality of life issue that is important to their members. As a result, labor and environmentalists together defeated the business-sponsored bill.

The politics of division that confronts people with choices between multiple necessities such as jobs and a healthy environment is more than the product of a divisive political system. Powerful interests are served by pitting citizens and their legitimate issues against each other. Military corporations have aggressively argued that job loss is the inevitable and unacceptable cost of military cuts in order to bolster their campaign for sustained military spending. Similarly, big timber corporations have benefited enormously from the conflict between unions and environmentalists, which slowed environmental protections and maintained political pressure for cutting more public forests. Dividing movements and social groups is a well-established strategy for undermining opposition and distracting public attention from issues of power and common interests.

Political and economic elites generally cannot act alone; they require allies from other social groups to advance their goals. How issues are framed depends on the makeup of these alliances, with elites frequently collaborating with the working or middle class at the expense of the excluded group's interests and issues. When workers join with corporate management to oppose environmentalists, the political choice is often framed as economic vitality versus environmental protection. Similarly, when workers join with management to oppose peace advocates, the issue becomes jobs versus peace. When the middle class joins with elites, however, economic efficiency is often promoted at the expense of jobs or wages. Middle-class expertise is frequently used to advance corporate profit making with significant costs for the working class in the form of de-skilling and loss of control over the work process, lower wages, replacement by mechanization, and occupational hazards.[10] This was the case in the timber industry during the 1980s when mechanization increased productivity almost 50 percent, which cost over thirteen thousand jobs.

In contrast, working-class and low-income alliances with the middle class must seek to balance competing social and economic goals rather than advance economic interests at the expense of justice, peace, and the environment, or vice versa. Labor coalitions with middle-class peace organizations are promoting conversion as a way to sustain jobs while cutting the defense budget. Recent alliances between environmental justice organizations and traditional conservation and preservation organizations are working for socially just environmental policies. Many labor and environmental coalitions have formed to promote environmental health in the workplace, environmentally sound jobs, and healthy communities.

Opportunities for collaboration are greater now than they have been for a generation. After World War II, cooperation by some segments of the working and middle classes developed around an expanding high-wage economy and generous government social programs. These policies along with other economic and political changes later helped undermine the New Deal coalition, which could not sustain new demands brought by the civil rights, environmental, and peace movements. Yet the ending of the Cold War, the increased economic insecurity of the working and middle classes, the growth of both environmental problems and ecological awareness, and the loss of community control in a globalizing economy—all are creating new opportunities for cooperation. These trends are encouraging new coalitions at the local level which have the potential to reinvigorate a national coalition as well.

What are labor coalitions with peace and environmental groups discovering about ways to integrate issues of jobs and the environment, or jobs and peace? Could these discoveries serve as models for a progressive agenda? Are these coalitions capable of shifting the balance of power in favor of more progressive policies? These are the larger political questions addressed in this book.

While this analysis focuses on social class, the processes described here are broadly applicable to bridge building across divisions of race, ethnicity, and geography as well. Class is not the only cleavage that divides people. Ultimately, multipartner coalitions that cross diverse social boundaries are needed. Coalitions that bridge each of these different divisions teach their own vital lessons. My hope is that by describing an important relationship that needs to be forged—between working- and middle-class movements—this book will contribute to building a broad-based movement for change.

Five cases of conflict and cooperation between working- and middle-class movements are described in this book. The conflict between environmentalists and unions over old-growth timber protection in the Pacific Northwest illustrates how divisions arise and movements polarize. This was the most prominent national example of labor-environmental conflict in the 1980s and 1990s. While this battle was raging in the forests of the Northwest, construction trade unions were mending relations with environmentalists close by in Seattle after twenty years of conflict. Small trust-building measures grew into increasingly sophisticated cooperation until both sides could publicly agree that, in the words of one labor leader, "We cannot make a choice between economic prosperity and jobs and protecting our environment. We need leaders with the vision, guts and determination to deliver on both counts. Nothing less is acceptable."[11] This successful coalition illustrates how different class movements can find common ground under the right circumstances and with effective leadership and practices.

The three labor union and peace movement coalitions examined in this book joined together at the end of the Cold War to convert military industry in their communities to civilian production. The sudden end of the U.S. arms race with the Soviet Union along with declining military budgets set the stage for defense workers and peace advocates, who had long been in conflict, to find common goals. Coalitions in Maine, Minnesota, and Washington State represent the best practices of labor-peace cooperation, according to national organizations and activists. Despite earlier conflicts, all three achieved significant results, although each pursued a distinct approach to organizing. Their successes and failures during a unique historic period teach important lessons about working- and middle-class movement alliances.

WHAT'S AHEAD

In the following chapters I interweave stories about successful coalitions (and lost opportunities) with the lessons they teach about the reasons for conflict and the prospects for cooperation. From these diverse cases some important patterns emerge, lessons useful for understanding interclass and intermovement coalitions generally. Chapter 2, "Coalition Democracy and Class Politics: An Overview," summarizes the main theoretical conclusions from the case studies. Three observations describe the social context for coalition organizing. First, labor, peace, and environmental movements take fundamentally different forms because they derive from working- versus middle-class cultures. Second, movements face choices about which other classes they will cooperate with as allies, with costs and benefits inherent in each alliance.Third, political decisions about allies depend upon interpersonal relationships and cultural experiences. Three political implications follow: Single-class movements tend to reproduce some existing forms of oppression even as they work for change; working- and middle-class alliances are essential for bringing about progressive social change; and, finally, interclass coalitions provide a means for learning across class lines that is necessary for fundamental democratic change.

These far-reaching conclusions are developed through specific examples in the remaining chapters. Voices of labor, environmental, and peace activists are used extensively, and the case studies are described in some detail so that the reader can see how these conclusions were drawn. Three themes are developed throughout. Part II asks why the labor, peace, and environmental movements are so often in conflict. Part III examines the historic conditions and strategic choices that are necessary for reconciling working- and middle-class movements. Part IV looks in depth at the techniques and practices that contribute to successful coalition building across class lines.

Reasons for conflict are sought through a detailed look at the Northwest timber controversy between labor and environmentalists, and at the history of both cooperation and conflict between labor and the peace movement. Chapter 3, "Battles over Old Growth," explores the most common explanation for these conflicts, namely, that they are the result of opposing interests, in this case interests in cutting trees and preserving them. But a detailed examination of each side's interests reveals that there are costs as well as benefits in fighting each other, just as there are in cooperating. Chapter 4, "When Classes Meet," asks why both sides saw their interests as conflicting. The answer is that significant cultural differences—a complex web of perceptions, organizational practices, relationships, values, and contexts that people use to interpret their interests—divide working- from middle-class movements.

Relationships between groups build on past experiences, and Chapter 5, "History Hangs in the Balance," recounts a legacy marked by both dramatic experiences of conflict and some exemplary coalitions. Labor moved away from its earlier association with the peace movement during and after World War II because of vicious attacks on the left, the rapid growth of the middle class, and the strategies of elites and working- and middle-class organizations. The result was wide cultural gaps between class-based movements, which have taken decades to begin to close.

In the present period, however, coalitions between labor and the peace and environmental movements are on the rise. This reconciliation depends upon changes both external and internal to organizations. Chapter 6, "The Political Moment," examines the conditions that are presently favoring closer cooperation. Global economic and political changes have made collaboration a necessity. Beyond that, developments within each movement are shifting agendas and priorities toward cooperation. Attacks on the labor movement coupled with a new generation of union leaders and the declining power of labor are feeding a broad new interest in coalitions among unions. Environmentalists are also increasingly incorporating social considerations into their conservation and preservation agenda in response to the antienvironmental public backlash and growing discontent among grassroots environmentalists. These trends are visible in the rise in environmental justice, occupational safety and health, and sustainable development organizing. Coalition activity within the peace movement expanded with the end of the Cold War, partially in response to the economic dislocation caused by military cutbacks.

Favorable conditions and creative organizing, however, are not sufficient if working- and middle-class activists don't learn to understand each other in the process. Cooperation requires skillful mediation between different class cultures, perceptions of interests, and agendas. Chapter 7, "Coalition Organizing," describes techniques for building trust and cooperation and evaluates different strategies for interclass coalition organizing. Conversion coalitions in Maine, Minnesota, and Washington all confronted unique challenges, and each began with its own assumptions about how to organize. These cases are analyzed in depth to illustrate the importance of testing trust, building relationships, and agreeing to disagree in the coalition building process. As the Maine case study demonstrates, coalition organizers need to be sensitive to the tensions that often arise within their organizations and movements.

Chapter 8, "Learning in Coalitions," describes the successful transition from hostility to collaboration between environmentalists and building trades unions in Washington State. Some critical lessons about participation, politics, self-respect, and change are inherent in any organizing process. But other lessons can be learned only from coalitions across social divisions, which teach us about trust, the diversity of life experiences, and the place of individual and group interests in the broader society.

Chapter 9, "Bridge Builders," identifies the key role that these unique individuals play in bringing groups together. Each generation, with its specific economic, political, and social conditions, produces its own co-horts of bridge builders: men and women who understand the cultures and politics of both working- and middle-class movements.

Coalitions must also reframe their different agendas to incorporate the issues of separate partners as described in Chapter 10, "Finding a Common Language." The coalitions studied in this book discovered creative ways to integrate working- and middle-class agendas; and they offer lessons for a broader progressive program. To work together these coalitions also developed hybrid organizing strategies that integrated the best of both working-class (interest-based) organizing and middle-class (education-oriented) organizing. Conversion coalitions in Maine, Minnesota, and Washington each experimented with different strategies that provide important models for future organizing.

The concluding chapter explores the implications of intermovement coalitions for building a more unified alliance for change. The democratic promise of intermovement coalitions is that they build political majorities with integrated agendas that are worthy of broad support. In this way coalitions present an opportunity for the deliberation and collective learning that democracy requires. The case studies examined here suggest that through coalition building, social movements have the potential to transcend the limitations of contemporary interest-group politics and to build a broader movement for change. Political conditions are ripe for this collaboration, and many experiments are now taking place at every level of society. Effective organizing can take advantage of these opportunities to rebuild a unified progressive movement. But a darker future is also possible, one of increased conflict that forces people to choose between economic, environmental, and social values and pits classes, races, and communities against one another. What movements learn from the past and how they incorporate these lessons into future organizing will have an enormous impact on the course of history.

▲

Coalition Democracy and Class Politics:
An Overview

How do we make sense of the complex process of cross-class coalition building? What patterns among the cases examined here can be generalized? Understanding any situation requires a framework that identifies the major players and the important behaviors and conditions. In this chapter I outline the conceptual framework developed to answer three fundamental questions: Why are working- and middle-class social movements so often in conflict? When and how do these movements build effective coalitions? and, What role do working- and middle-class coalitions play in advancing progressive social change? This chapter summarizes the theoretical argument; the rest of the book develops these ideas through case studies of conflict and coalition building. Some readers may prefer to begin with the case studies and then return to the theory later.

My conclusions can be summarized in six broad arguments. The first three provide a social analysis of the inner life of working- and middle-class movements and of the people who belong to them:

1. The labor, peace, and environmental movements are class-based movements drawn from the working and middle classes.
2. Class members and class-based movement organizations have multiple competing interests in forming alliances with different classes.
3. Culture and social relationships determine the perception of interests and of allies among multiple possibilities of class alliances.

The second three arguments develop the political implications of these observations:

4. Single-class movements often reproduce the very problems that different class movements organize against, even as they work for social change. This fact is a direct outgrowth of the limited class membership of separate movements.
5. Working- and middle-class alliances are essential for progressive social change, as a historical analysis of competing class alliances and interests demonstrates.
6. Interclass coalitions provide a means for learning that is necessary for fundamental democratic change. This is the political implication of the role that culture and relationships play in shaping alliances.

In this chapter I provide a road map to what follows, outlining ideas and showing the contours of the entire argument.

CLASS-BASED MOVEMENTS

Labor, peace, and environmental organizations are class-based movements. The most visible manifestation of this is that each movement draws its members overwhelmingly from one class. Socially homogeneous membership inevitably results in movements that reflect the practices, lifestyles, language, thought processes, and values—that is, the culture—of that social group. Therefore in both membership and form, the building trades, metal trades, and production unions in this study are, like the labor movement as a whole, working-class organizations in contrast with the peace and environmental organizations, which are distinctly middle-class.

The heart of the concept of class is that people in different economic positions have different levels of access to power and opportunities in society. Various indicators are used to identify people's positions in the class hierarchy, including income and wealth, occupation, education, and level of skill. Members of peace and environmental groups in Washington State and Maine, for instance, had an average income of $57,300 in 1992, while forest industry workers made an average of $29,300 and construction trades workers about $29,000.[1] While 87 percent of peace and environmental members in Maine and Washington had college degrees and 48 percent had graduate degrees, among construction and timber workers degrees are far less common.[2] These statistics reflect the fact that the large majority of members among peace and environmental organizations are professionals or studying to become professionals. Almost 60 percent of the members of the organizations in this study are teachers, doctors, lawyers, engineers, scientists, and other professionals.[3] This pattern has been found in other studies of the peace and environmental movements both in the United States and in Europe.[4]

Working- and middle-class occupations are both culturally and physically different. Working-class work generally involves manual labor that is closely supervised. Aspects of these tasks can often be mechanized, the machine substituting for human labor or reducing it to standard tasks that replace the skill of the worker. So the working-class experience on the job is often one of external control over time, physical movement, the pace of work, and the environment. Skilled craft occupations in the shipyards of Seattle provide a good example of this external regulation. The workforce must either conform to highly regimented rules or face clearly designated punishments. For instance, employees punch a time clock, and the hours at work are precisely counted by both employee and employer. Many shipyards test potential employees for drugs before they hire as well as occasionally on the job. Furthermore, shipyard employees are required to obtain permission from a supervisor if they wish to leave their job due to illness. These examples illustrate how the working class functions within a highly ordered system of rules and regulations.

By contrast, middle-class jobs generally involve some aspect of knowledge or mental work that cannot be accomplished by machines. Middle-class work requires analysis and interpretation of individual situations, which cannot be ordered into mechanical processes alone. Rather, professionals are required to meet standards established by their peers, standards that they internalize as their own values, responsibilities, and personal contributions. For example, teachers are supposed to produce students who are more educated at the end of a school year, where the standards for education are set by occupational associations consisting of other educators. Middle-class workers generally do not punch time clocks, although they may well be bound to rigorous schedules for accomplishing certain tasks. Instead, the emphasis is usually on completing those tasks in the best way possible, and people have significant freedom to organize their time, including when they leave the workplace. Thus middle-class work, especially professional work, is internally controlled through incentives that encourage and reward desired outcomes.

The organization of work outlined above—both the actual content of tasks performed and the ways that people relate as bosses, workers, and colleagues in the work process—order people's lives in profound ways both on and off the work site. The working class must learn the manual skills and discipline to perform often repetitive tasks at a pace and time mandated by employers. This challenge contrasts greatly with the middle class, which must acquire the information, judgment, and discipline to accomplish qualitative outcomes as defined by professional standards. Training for these different roles starts early through tracking for academic versus nonacademic programs in school. Family life also prepares people for the habits and expectations of the workplace: working-class families use external authority to discipline children, while the middle class uses emotional pressures to teach internalized norms.[5] Different classes thus adapt to the demands of their work by developing distinct values, ways of speaking, and patterns of relationships in families, neighborhoods, and workplaces.

Class cultures are both empowering and limiting. They provide people with tools to live successfully within class institutions, relationships, and employment opportunities. The ability to be accepted as a friend, to be trusted by work mates, to handle oneself in social and work situations, and many other capabilities are skills that develop only from direct personal experiences. Competence in working-class culture is a skill distinct from middle-class competency, so that even the best-educated professionals may be at a loss when having to communicate with working-class union members and vice versa. So class cultures both enable people to act within their own limited social settings and erect barriers to functioning in other contexts.[6]

Working- and middle-class members interpret politics and think about change differently as a result of their class-based experiences. These differences are evident in the models of organizing advanced by different-class movements. Working-class people tend to approach social change through organizing around perceived immediate interests, while middle-class movements tend to see change as a process of education and value change. These differences are the products of different class cultures.

In the following analysis I do not mean to imply that working-class people are motivated by interests without values whereas middle-class people act on values devoid of interests. All social groups are motivated by both interests and values. However, labor and working-class community organizers themselves tend to frame their approaches to politics and social change in the language and logic of interests. Middle-class organizations, on the contrary, tend to conceive of their organizing in the language and framework of values and education. These different approaches to organizing are also reflected in the issues that working- and middle-class movements pursue. Working-class labor and community organizations generally focus on economics and the interests of members, while middle-class movements tend to address universal goods that are noneconomic. These differences are direct outgrowths of the cultural and economic experiences of each class.

Working-Class Organizing: Advancing Common Interests

External authority confronts working-class individuals with rules and regulations that are defined by management, parents, government, or others, as described above. A person's desires and needs often appear in conflict with the expectations of those in power. So working-class people experience their own interests as in opposition to the interests of others. These others set the rules and ensure that workers conform, that they accomplish goals or fill needs according to rhythms or in locations not of their own choosing. To further their goals or assert their interests, workers must confront this external power. This conflict is inherent in the organization of externally regulated society.

Consistent with their class experience of social regulation, working-class movements also tend to interpret politics in terms of competing interests. External authority produces a clear sense of individual and group interests in relationship to authorities. The opposition that this creates centers on immediate, tangible needs and desires: the quality of life on the job—health and safety, working conditions, respect and fair treatment—as well as the pay and benefits that determine the quality of life off the job. Community organizers also emphasize the need to identify issues of immediate self-interest and to motivate people to make tangible changes in their lives.[7] They organize around both the physical and psychological needs for human growth. This includes meeting not only survival needs such as food, shelter, and safety but also the need for meaningful work and fulfillment, for self-respect, for control over one's life, and for the feeling that one matters in the human community.

In working-class organizing, other groups are also assumed to be motivated by self-interest. The organizing goal is to unite sufficient numbers of people with common interests against these other groups. As a result, working-class organizations place considerable priority on discerning friends and foes as part of a calculation of relative power. As one organizer put it, "Now, we all know there are only two parties: there are the bosses and there are workers, and when workers unite they have a union and there still are two parties—there are bosses and there are workers who are now united."[8] Thus, organizing is often likened to a war between opposing sides.

Most labor organizations do include some values as well as interests among their goals. For example, one union aims "to cultivate feelings of friendship among those of our industry" and "to elevate the moral, intellectual and social conditions of our members, their families and dependents, in the interest of a higher standard of citizenship."[9] These goals are also conceived of in terms of the interests of the group. For example, solidarity and a sense of camaraderie are promoted as qualities that build the organization and increase its ability to act collectively to achieve specific benefits.

Middle-Class Organizing: Educating about Values

In contrast with working-class experiences with external authority, internalized regulation requires that individuals embrace agreed-upon goals and willingly use their special expertise to achieve needed tasks. Professionals are assumed to have adopted the values of their trades, which generally include honesty, integrity, service to the public good, and quality work. No simple formula can determine how these goals can be achieved, since each situation—the needs of each student or the circumstances of each legal case—requires considered judgment. Thus professionals must develop their own techniques, which are continually honed, but never perfected, through experience and further learning. A commitment to ongoing development of one's skills is expected of a professional. Newly gained ideas and understandings can produce substantial change in how one carries out one's job. Certainly personal interpretations of values, goals, and priorities have significant implications for how one works, and changes in these can alter one's practices. Engineers welcome the chance to work more efficiently or incorporate new techniques, just as teachers alter their lessons to accommodate different goals.

Because action, for the middle class, is the product of ideas and values, it follows that social change is likewise viewed as the product of changes in consciousness, that is, a product of education. The environmental, peace, and feminist movements have generally sought to teach people new values, raise their consciousness, and alter their attitudes about how they live and relate to others. Often middle-class activists believe that "if people only knew about the problems being raised, then they would be more likely to act."[10] This assumes that people share similar values, but that some fail to act on them due to lack of information, avoidance, fear, ignorance of alternatives, or some other reason. In some cases, organizers seek to instill the public with new values or new appreciations. Thus the environmental movement has worked hard to impart a greater appreciation of the impacts of behavior and lifestyles on the earth, and the women's movement has changed public perceptions of the roles of women. The peace movement's agenda has long reflected this sense of needing to "think in a new way" about violence, conflict, and particularly war. The problem, in this view, is that people accept war and violence as ways to resolve conflict, and the challenge is to alter this way of thinking.

Middle-class movements explain their positions in the language of strong moral arguments. Even the most pragmatic middle-class organizations frame their issues in broad ethical terms, and never in terms of advancing the interests of a particular group. Indeed, one of the defining features of these movements is that they advance universal goals and not the interests of their class, despite the fact that these movements emerge from within a particular class.[11]

Political activity for the middle class is a direct outgrowth of personal and professional development, and multiple affiliations are common. Young people are encouraged to pursue their own ideas and interests, which can easily lead to activism. Individuals generally join peace or environmental organizations from a sense of personal conviction. At times the issues derive from a personal interest or need, such as industrial pollution of a nearby ecosystem or conscription by the military, but often participants will not immediately gain from the changes they promote. Usually the change relates to a universal good that individuals can only realize if everyone else does too. The personal motivation for participating in these movements derives from the feeling that one is contributing to a worthwhile cause, such as reducing air pollution or stopping a conflict overseas.

MULTIPLE COMPETING INTERESTS

The recognition that working-class movements and middle-class movements take different forms and reflect different motivations is critical for understanding the relationships between them. Do these differences lend themselves to cooperation or to conflict? The second conclusion suggests that there are valid reasons for both:

Multiple competing interests exist for all classes, and thus movement politics is complicated by debates about which strategies and alliances to pursue. Each interest pulls in different directions: toward competition among members of the same class, toward collaboration with management, toward solidarity within a class, or toward coalition building between nondominant classes. This choice of strategies confronts labor, peace, and environmental organizations every day.

Class position does not determine any particular strategy relative to other classes. Rather, members of each class can choose among four different strategies that reflect different interests inherent in the organization of society.[12] First, people have an interest in outcompeting others who share the same class position and seek similar gains in the market. Here competition results from similarity, with each side trying to distinguish itself as measured by a common standard. Second, individuals have an interest in cooperating with others who possess complementary skills and abilities in the division of labor, which generally means collaboration with the owners and managers of companies who control resources. Segments of society specialize to cooperate in a shared task. Here difference is the source of interclass collaboration. Third, conflict takes place over the organization of the division of labor and the distribution of benefits and resources throughout society. This antagonism, which unites those with a similar class position against other classes, is based on differential access to power and resources. A fourth strategy, that of coalition building between classes outside the division of labor, is the major subject of this book. Working-class employees and middle-class professionals generally work separately in work processes organized by owners and managers of businesses, organizations, and government. Coalitions between the working and middle classes, therefore, often must forge new relationships that haven't developed in the day-to-day workplace.

Competition, collaboration, and solidarity are all evident within the labor movement. At the first level, workers with similar skills compete in the labor market. Merit, experience, reputation, and friendships affect one's standing in this competition, as do personal attributes such as gender, race, age, family background, and class. This competition is managed by employers who make the final decisions about the combination of personality, experience, and skills that they will hire.

Within the division of labor, workers throughout an industry share a mutual interest with one another and with their employers in collaboration for the overall prosperity of their sector. Industrial unions seek to join workers of all trades within a workplace, thus uniting those who labor in different aspects of the same production process. If this cooperation across the division of labor is extended to management, employer and employee share an interest in the well-being of their industry as a whole and especially their particular firm or plant. In this sense, the adversarial relationship between labor and management is also bound in a common destiny.

At the level of class solidarity, workers share a common class interest that can be defined with different shades of militancy. On the socialist end of the spectrum, it is in the interest of the working class to alter the organization of the production process so that workers and not private individuals (the owners) control the fruits of their labor. More immediately, labor as a class shares an interest in increasing unionized work and ultimately union bargaining power vis-à-vis employers in general. The AFL-CIO explains that "workers formed unions so that they could have some say over wages, hours, working conditions, and the many other problems that arise in the relationship between a worker and employer."[13] Furthermore, unions have a broad interest in achieving a "family wage" for all workers. If companies have access to cheap labor alternatives, it undermines the union's ability to bargain. Thus the labor movement has also favored national social legislation requiring such things as a higher minimum wage, health insurance for everyone, and family leave.

Just as competition, collaboration, and class solidarity compete for the allegiance of labor in the case of the working class, so, too, do these three levels coexist for the middle class. Middle-class individuals with similar skills compete for limited employment opportunities just as working-class individuals do. Because specialized training and skill define many middle-class jobs, these are highly differentiated by merit as measured by standardized examinations. Despite efforts to depersonalize hiring practices, however, management retains ultimate discretion over who will win the competition for jobs.

Professionals and managers also frequently have an interest in collaborating with both owners and workers as complementary occupational groups in the division of labor. Technical and managerial staff within large corporations share an interest in the advancement of their sector and firm, just as workers do. Although middle-class careers are not often bound to specific companies or firms to the same degree as production workers, they are served by the success of the firm during their period of employment.

Middle-class interests in solidarity take several forms. The middle class is in some ways part of the working class and shares its interest in organizing against upper management and corporate owners. Some professional and middle-class employees have unionized—most notably teachers, nurses, and government employees, who are less specialized than other professionals. The middle class also unites through professional associations to control credentials and standards. Often that means passing legally sanctioned licensing rules that control entry into the professions and limit competition for existing members.

In addition to interests in competition, collaboration, and solidarity, the working and middle classes have interests that are served by working together in coalitions. Very often single-class movements find that they need to build additional power to accomplish goals that a group is not strong enough to achieve by itself. Given the greater economic and political power of those who are wealthy and who control capital resources, lower-class groups frequently find themselves in need of allies. Sometimes organizations with very different agendas have an interest in joining against a common enemy who obstructs both their goals. Finally, coalitions are sometimes built upon shared values and common moral purpose. People have an interest in promoting fair treatment throughout society, and moral outrage can be a strong basis for uniting with other groups who have limited power to stand up for their own interests. For all these reasons, working- and middle-class groups have interests in cooperating.

CULTURAL PERCEPTIONS OF INTERESTS

If people have multiple competing interests that could be served by different strategies of class alliance, then why would an individual choose one strategy over another? My third conclusion argues that cultural processes shape people's perceptions of interests and allies:

People have valid reasons for pursuing strategies of competition, collaboration, solidarity, or coalition building, and each strategy serves some interests that are inherent in the organization of society. The strategies that people select depend on their values, past experiences, understandings, and relationships. Culture determines perceptions of interests, and differences in class culture and segregation between classes create barriers to identifying common interests.

Most studies of coalitions explain alliances in terms of rational calculations by each side about power and interests. In this view groups cooperate when they can attain benefits together that they could not win alone. But since people have many different competing interests, and since potential risks and benefits are inherent in pursuing any of these interests, they face real choices about how to better their fortunes. Rationality alone cannot distinguish among these different competing interests. The interest that any individual chooses to pursue will depend on that person's perspective—on his or her values, goals, and loyalties. Furthermore, perceptions of interests depend fundamentally upon how a person interprets the meaning of events and their likely outcomes, including interpretations of other people's motivations, assumptions about people's rights, expectations about the behavior of different players, and interpretations of past events. Thus people reason within a cultural context.

Since calculations are also generally clouded by uncertainties about outcomes, people must rely on convictions and instincts to guide their decisions. For instance, the power of a social movement is developed through the process of organizing; it is not a fixed or calculable quantity. Rational calculations are also difficult for movements because their activities do not take place within institutional forums, nor are they limited to established techniques, although this is less true for organizations that confine themselves to traditional avenues such as collective bargaining or legislation. Many movements seek long-term changes in broad social problems through processes that are not clearly known ahead of time. Thus alliances cannot be assessed in terms of any single, narrow goal. Furthermore, a struggle can enter many different spheres, from the economic to the political to the cultural. When the forum and goals are not set, calculations become difficult if not impossible.

Since people apply different frameworks to make sense of their circumstances, debates about interests are highly contentious. There is a long history of divisions within the labor movement between those who conceive of management as a natural enemy with different class interests and those who see labor and management as sharing a mutual interest in the industry's prosperity. Similarly, peace and environmental activists are divided over the merits of cooperation versus confrontation with government and corporations. The endless debates demonstrate how subjective the process of identifying interests can be.

Class cultures provide one lens through which people make sense of their experiences. Working- and middle-class cultures lead to different frameworks for interpreting events. For instance, the working-class experience of physical labor teaches people to trust the practical knowledge gained from personal experiences, while middle-class mental labor depends on people trusting abstract knowledge learned through written documents and "impartial" research. This results in different bases for interpreting events, with consequences for how people will perceive their interests.

Social relationships also strongly influence one's framework for interpreting events and one's definition of interests. Stories told by friends, relatives, and respected public figures shape one's point of view. The influence of these relationships depends upon the degree of trust. The ideas, interpretations, and experiences of those who are visibly concerned about one's best interests will be especially important in shaping one's thinking. Shared contexts and experiences can also be sources of trust that bridge gaps in relationships.

People from different classes or other social groups often lack both the direct relationships and common experiences that are critical for trust. Such groups are therefore unlikely to have opportunities to influence each other. Different cultural contexts also produce disparate interpretations of events and opportunities. Social segregation therefore erects barriers to perceiving common interests, thus hindering alliances.

REPRODUCING CLASS SOCIETY

What are the political consequences of movements that are based on class and interpret their interests within culturally limited perspectives? The fourth conclusion is that these movements tend to reproduce aspects of society about which they are culturally blind:

Social reproduction happens when individuals, acting in their own interests, unconsciously reinforce and recreate the structures and conditions that make up society. Working- and middle-class movements, like all political agents, reproduce aspects of class society even as they work to change other aspects. These movements are prone to exacerbating the oppressions against which other movements rebel when they choose strategies of competition, collaboration, or solidarity. If movements do not become aware of the unconscious ways in which they reinforce existing divisions in society, they are likely to encourage them.

Participation in social reproduction is largely unintended, and people generally do not consider the broader social consequences of their actions. If society continues in its present form over time, however, people's actions must be effectively contributing to that order. And if class divisions are among the stable characteristics of society, then these must also be reinforced through daily practices.[14]

Social reproduction is particularly ironic for social movements which seek to change society. Movements working for peace or environmental protection or workers' rights may even be ideologically opposed to the idea of reinforcing class divisions. But activists inevitably bring their own cultures with them, and reinforce their own class-cultural forms of identity, relationships and motivations. In so doing they also reproduce class divisions in society overall. As Charles Chatfield and Peter Van Den Dungen observe about the history of the peace movement, "While peace advocates favored policy changes in their societies, they also shared the social values and assumptions which underlay established politics. . . . Their choice of goals and strategy reflected not only their as-

sessment of their societies but, as well, their subjective and often culturally given assumptions."[15]

In other words, individuals and movements can participate in reinforcing and reproducing aspects of society even as they work to change
other aspects. Organizations devoted to social change confront a complex system that is deceptively moving and shifting all the time, even as
it maintains its basic form. Indeed, change is among the defining characteristics of capitalism, but many dramatic changes such as the rise and
fall of product cycles, sectors, and companies take place within the ordinary functioning of society (ordinary change). Some kinds of change replace one powerful group with another without shifting the organization of power (redistributive change). These achievements paradoxically
also serve to reinforce essential parts of the existing order. Fundamental
change, change that transforms the organization of society (transformative change), can only be understood in contrast with those changes that
reproduce the existing order.[16]

To complicate the picture, ordinary, redistributive, and transformative change are not distinct, and quantitative shifts at one level can lead
to qualitative differences. The development of new technologies through
ordinary processes of development can have dramatic implications for
the balance of power between classes. Certainly new forms of automation or transportation make it easier for capital to replace labor in the
workforce. Such changes are partly responsible for the current decline of
the labor movement. Changes in the distribution of power can also eventually alter the organization of production itself, a strategy advanced by
the social democrats in Europe who hope to move toward socialism
through the ballot box. Certainly changes at a higher level have implications for lower-level change. Thus a reorganization of social institutions
through implementing socialism, for instance, would also alter the distribution of power in society and change the ordinary functions of the
system as well.

Historically the middle class has played a role in reproducing class divisions through the three strategies of allying with capital (collaboration), regulating competition through the state, and institutionalizing
professional practice (solidarity). The Progressive Movement active at
the turn of the twentieth century exemplified these middle-class strategies. Progressives brought about reforms in education, municipal government, public health, medicine, conservation, and labor laws and
sought to curb the worst excesses of corporate abuse. But they accomplished these changes in ways that advanced the power, opportunities,

and interests of the middle class. Progressives acted collectively to institutionalize rational processes as the only legitimate means for decision making. They succeeded in implementing merit-based employment practices in government and business where the advantages fell to those who were educated and articulate, namely, to the growing middle class.

Progressive reforms inadvertently served to reproduce the subordinate role of the working class in society and the economy.[17] They excluded folk practices of healing, teaching, working, political activity, and other crafts by establishing educational and licensing requirements in the name of protecting the public and applying the advances of science. Members of the working class were forced to purchase and utilize services instead of providing them themselves. They increasingly viewed the growing class of professionals as experts, educators, and disciplinarians. Furthermore, experts, collaborating with capitalists, used machines and scientific management to remove skills from the working class and control its work. While some aspects of society were reformed, class divisions and power inequities were reproduced, expanded, and reinforced.

In a similar vein, during the 1990s the environmental justice movement has been particularly critical of the role of middle-class environmentalists in reproducing the oppression of low-income communities and communities of color. Large environmental organizations have frequently imposed their solutions to problems at the expense of indigenous and low-income communities, despite these organizations' claims of expertise and collective benefit.[18] For example, wealthier communities have been able to resist the siting of toxic facilities in their communities, with the unintended consequence that these facilities shift to communities less able to resist and more in need of the economic compensation. Poorer urban communities also suffer as industries abandon environmentally hazardous sites rather than pay cleanup costs. In these and other ways environmentalists have inadvertently contributed to the reproduction of class and race inequalities.

Working-class movement strategies to control competition through trade unions, to collaborate with capital through business unionism, and to unite as a class through industrial unionism have likewise reproduced class society. The strategy of controlling competition between workers with the same skills has long dominated the American Federation of Labor (AFL) and the craft unions. Craft unions have often been exclusive clubs that maintain a unique relationship with employers to funnel economic benefits to existing members. This approach produced a tier of better-paid workers while reinforcing the subordinate position of the less skilled, who were not included in union protections.

This model of class collaboration and protectionism has long been rejected by class-conscious labor radicals. The Congress of Industrial Organizations (CIO) was founded on the idea of solidarity among all workers in an industry regardless of craft. CIO organizers promoted "social unionism," a version of reform where unions, in addition to advancing the standard of living of their members, promote the social and political interests of working people as a whole. They have sought to do this by pushing for legislation for full employment, welfare, universal health care, and public housing, often working through the Democratic Party's liberal wing. But by shifting the focus from economic negotiations with employers to the sphere of politics, social unionism reinforced the existing order. Unions accepted the principle that owners would retain control over investment, the organization of work, and corporate policies, while workers would focus on narrow economic concerns. This preserved the basic organization of class society.

Union collaboration with management and government after World War II led to labor's opposition to the peace, environmental, and other middle-class movements during the 1960s. Craft unions at times joined construction employers to oppose environmentalists and peace activists, who they perceived as threatening their jobs. The AFL-CIO's link to the Democratic Party brought tensions as the peace movement opposed Vietnam War polices and the politicians responsible for them. A few CIO unions did seek alliances with emerging social movements in the 1960s and 1970s, but such alliances were exceptional, as unions continued their strategy of close collaboration with management. (See the history of labor and peace relations in Chapter 5.)

These examples illustrate how single-class movements reproduce the existing organization of society and politics. These strategies reinforce class divisions by collaborating directly with the interests of capital, by accepting the existing social rules and distribution of power, by magnifying divisions in their own class, by replicating hierarchical organizational forms, and by defining issues narrowly.

TRANSFORMATION THROUGH INTERCLASS COALITIONS

The fifth conclusion is that whereas movement strategies based on competition, collaboration, and class solidarity have a limited capacity to transform society, interclass coalitions with other nondominant classes are far less vulnerable in this regard:

The fourth strategy, forming coalitions with other nondominant classes, is far less likely to reproduce forms of oppression in society. Working- and middle-class coalitions have formed the constituencies for progressive governments in the United States and Europe. These alliances have the potential to build majorities for fundamental change.

Socialist and left political movements during the industrial revolution proposed that the working class alone would become a majority that would promote radical transformation of society. Marx believed that capitalism would force more and more people to become working-class wage earners in the expanding industrial economy. As a result society would be increasingly polarized between the working-class majority and the owners and managers of business. Mechanization and competition would concentrate wealth, while working people would become increasingly poor, overworked, and insecure. Workers were expected to organize as a class against their common conditions and form trade unions to improve their economic lot and then working-class political parties.[19] The early communist, labor, and socialist movements and parties in Europe therefore appealed primarily to working-class voters and members, although the question of alliances with the middle class was often a divisive one, pitting one faction against another.[20]

Contrary to these predictions, a stable and growing middle class emerged over the past century, while the working class has not supported the transformative politics that it was expected to. Estimates of class size vary depending on the definition, but the working and middle classes each presently comprise on the order of 35–40 percent of the population.[21] Furthermore, although economic conditions vary widely in the working class, the uniform misery anticipated earlier never arose.

Since the working class has neither become a majority nor a unified voice for change, successful movements have relied on interclass coalitions. Class alliances supported the parliamentary reform movement in England and the European revolutions of 1848.[22] Socialist parties in Europe recognized early on the need to build working- and middle-class coalitions to achieve majorities, and successful social democratic parties in Sweden, Norway, and Denmark relied on coalitions between the working class and farmers or, later, between the working and middle classes.[23] Working- and middle-class electoral coalitions have also provided the basis for liberal reform governments in the United States, particularly with Roosevelt's New Deal.

Divisions between the working and middle classes have consistently undermined progressive politics in the United States. The New Deal coalition split apart over the civil rights and the antiwar movements of the 1960s, which led to the defection of the white working class, the lower middle class, and southern voters. According to Steve Fraser and Gary Gerstle, these movements

> delivered the final blow to the New Deal order by opening up a gaping hole between two vital Democratic party constituencies: on one side stood a coalition of blacks and middle-class whites committed to an agenda of racial and sexual equality, social welfare, and moral modernism; on the other side gathered working-class and lower-middle-class whites, largely Catholic in the North and Protestant in the South, calling for a reassertion of such traditional values as patriarchy, patriotism, law and order, hard work and self-help.[24]

The absence of a sustained working- and middle-class alliance has been critical to corporate domination of politics in the United States as well as in Britain and continental Europe. This became particularly evident in the 1980s when the conservative swing in American politics reached its zenith. Ronald Reagan was elected with strong support from most white, middle- to high-income constituencies with at least high school education. This upper-income bias resulted in part from the withdrawal of increasing numbers of low-income people from voting altogether. Reflecting his constituency, Reagan supported policies that favored high-income and socially privileged groups: tax cuts that redistributed wealth upward, cuts in unemployment and welfare payments, and expansion of military spending.

The labor movement and middle-class movements for peace and the environment are important class segments for building a working- and middle-class political majority. Organized movements play a vital role by placing new issues on the public agenda, which influence the behavior of broader segments of the population. As noted above, divisions between labor and middle-class movements undermined the New Deal Democratic coalition, most dramatically in the 1972 presidential election when the AFL-CIO refused to endorse the "peace candidate" George McGovern. Divided over protection of the spotted owl, labor and environmental antagonists paralyzed Congress for a decade. By contrast, united working- and middle-class movements have passed important legislation for civil rights, social welfare, occupational safety and health, clean air and water protection, and national environmental protection.

If indeed working- and middle-class coalitions are critical for progressive social change, how can movements from different cultural perspectives build trust, relationships, and a common perception of interests? The final conclusion is that learning to bridge class differences is essential to the coalition-building process:

Working- and middle-class coalitions provide a context for class-segregated movements to learn from their differences and to develop a common agenda worthy of broad community support. These coalitions have the potential to overcome the narrow limits of issue politics and to create a broad, inclusive movement for social change.

The combined power of working- and middle-class movements could be formidable, but the many differences in class culture, issues, and actors constitute barriers to such coalitions. Indeed the history of such cooperation is mixed at best. Single-issue, single-class movements have important missions of their own: raising unrecognized issues and developing power for underrepresented groups. Neither the working nor the middle class alone, however, can transcend the limitations of the existing political economy of which both classes are products.

Social movements therefore confront two systematic problems. First, they need to build working- and middle-class alliances if they are to create a majority for progressive change. Second, they need to transcend the limitations of their class perspectives in order to develop an agenda that can transform society. These challenges are linked, since movements must learn to develop a more inclusive conception of the common good as the basis for building broad support. Conversely, they need to involve broad participation in order to develop an inclusive agenda.

Movements need to learn from their differences to build a diverse constituency and develop an inclusive agenda. While pragmatic needs for power often motivate coalitions to come together, coalitions built on self-interest alone are inherently unstable as organizational priorities shift, sides compete for resources, and perceptions of issues diverge. Coalitions persist on the basis of their internal politics—trustful relationships, shared values, negotiated strategies, and alliances of opinion—not just their common interests. If cooperation is to be sustained, the process of working together must deepen understandings of the other side, strengthen relationships, and develop an inclusive sense of purpose. The promise of interclass coalition building is that it can provide a context for this learning.

Learning is integral to all activism, and movements provide a process for citizens to learn the skills and values of self-government in a society that fails to provide for political education. But interclass coalitions provide a particularly rich opportunity for learning because participants are forced to reexamine their own prejudices and assumptions if they are to continue to work together. Each side encounters activists who share their desire for social change but who enter the political arena with very different cultural perspectives, expressing qualitatively different kinds of goals and ways of meeting goals. Working- and middle-class movements have much to teach each other about their experiences of class society, their perceptions of interests, and their strategies for survival. Differences in class culture thus present opportunities as well as barriers, for they indicate the kinds of changes required by a movement if it is to appeal to members of the other classes.

As interclass coalitions learn to work together, they are simultaneously learning important lessons about structural change. Participants learn to trust and understand people who they previously perceived through stereotypes and media images. More substantively, cooperation with different class groups helps each side develop a more sophisticated understanding of the place of its concerns in society. Middle-class organizations learn to think about the economic and practical implications of their goals for vulnerable groups, and working-class organizations come to perceive the social, environmental, and long-term implications of their immediate interests. Ultimately, participants come to better understand the democratic process of dialogue and compromise as they also come to appreciate the limitations of the present distribution of power. This learning process is largely unconscious, but it is one of the most valuable consequences of cooperation, breaking down stereotypes and integrating segregated groups.

Nevertheless, the lessons of coalitions continue to differ for each class as coalition builders from the labor, peace, and environmental movements develop qualitatively different ways of reframing a common agenda based on their different class-cultural backgrounds. Labor begins with the language of interests and must find ways to speak about values, whereas middle-class movements begin with the language of values and must learn ways to speak about interests. Reconciliations between the two continue to reflect these class differences even as they converge on a common agenda.

Ultimately the lessons of these local coalitions could provide the framework for a new national progressive agenda and alliance. Intermovement and interclass coalitions are experimenting with new ways to bring together divisive issues of jobs and the environment or jobs and peace that could appeal to both working- and middle-class constituencies. They therefore are developing models for rebuilding an alliance between the working and middle classes broadly. What these coalitions are learning at the local level has much to teach about the future of progressive politics in this country. This prospect and promise are examined in the chapters that follow.

▲

Why the Conflict?

The next two chapters move from the global questions introduced in Part I to the concrete experiences of working- and middle-class movements when they meet face to face in real life. Conflicts provide an ideal opportunity to observe what is at stake for the adversaries. A close look at the timber wars of the 1980s and 1990s reveals much about why conflicts develop between working- and middle-class organizations.

▲

CHAPTER THREE

Battles over Old Growth:
The Problem of Multiple Interests

No controversy so dramatized the costs of polarizing issues of jobs versus the environment in the 1980s and 1990s as did the conflict over protecting old-growth forests in the Pacific Northwest. Timber workers and management formed an alliance to battle environmentalists in the woods of California, Oregon, and Washington State and in the halls of Congress. The issue divided and paralyzed government as the courts sought to enforce the Endangered Species Act. And even when presidential compromise finally broke the congressional stalemate and met the letter of the law in 1993, the resolution was rejected by both sides, and protests in the woods escalated to new levels.

At stake in this conflict are the remaining old-growth forests of the Northwest—the giant redwoods, cedar, spruce, fir, and hemlock west of the Cascade Mountains in California, Oregon, and Washington, which continue up the coast into British Columbia and Alaska. These trees are from two hundred to a thousand years old and often tower over three hundred feet above the forest floor, making them the oldest and largest trees in the world. A visitor to a stand of these ancient giants enters a time and space so beyond human scale it is awe inspiring. Old-growth forests provide unique habitat with their high but open canopy, snags or standing dead trees, and slowly decaying fallen logs. Among the rich diversity of species dependent on old-growth forests are several that are endangered and threatened, including the northern spotted owl, flying squirrels, northern three-toed woodpeckers, and the marbled murrelet.

Also at stake in this conflict are the timber communities that dot the Northwest forests. These are complex "occupational communities" organized around the tasks of logging, milling lumber and other wood products, trucking and shipping, and providing services to these industries.[1] Over the past 150 years, a distinct culture developed in these communities, steeped in stories of strength and bravery as well as appreciation for the power and abundance of the surrounding natural world. This culture predominates in the rural communities in the region where timber is the primary industry. However, it often clashes with the urban, more cosmopolitan culture of Portland and the population centers around Puget Sound, as well as with the higher income new settlers pushing into rural communities from California and across the country.[2]

By far the most common explanation for the timber controversy, shared by observers, academics, and people involved directly in the struggle, is that it is a straightforward conflict of interests. In this view, the benefits that timber workers gain from cutting trees have come into conflict with the benefits to environmentalists of protection. But what benefits are these? What are each side's interests? Do we simply ask timber workers and environmentalists what they want or need, and accept their own perceptions as accurate statements of their interests? People may say one thing and do another—for reasons they may or may not admit in conversation. So should we take people's actions as real indications of their interests rather than just their stated goals? How can we decipher actions when interpretations differ? And what if people are deceived about their own interests, so that both self-understandings and actions are not accurate representations of real interests? If so, a person's interests could only be identified by clarifying the costs and benefits inherent in their conditions. But identifying real conditions is also open to debate and interpretation. In what sense is the timber controversy a conflict of interests? And whose interests are served by the conflict between timber workers and environmentalists?

EVOLUTION OF THE TIMBER CONFLICT

The timber wars of the 1980s and 1990s were fought in the courts, in the media, in Congress, and on the front lines in the forests themselves. Protesters in the woods spiked and sat in trees to prevent timber harvests and sabotaged millions of dollars worth of logging equipment. Almost nine hundred activists were arrested at the largest protest of six thousand people in 1996 to protect some of the last remaining redwoods in California.[3] National, state, and local law enforcement officials including the FBI have been used to restrain protesters. Loggers have fought back with their own protests, impressive rallies of logging trucks sometimes stretching miles along the roads as they traveled to gatherings of up to several thousand people. Casualties resulted on both sides: tree sitters were hurt when their trees were felled; workers were injured by saws that shattered when they hit a spike; and an activist, Judi Bari, had her pelvis shattered when a bomb exploded in her car during the beginning of Earth First's Redwood Summer campaign.

The timber industry and environmentalists had been on a collision course for decades prior to these open battles, particularly with regard to the use of public lands. The federal government manages the majority of its timberland for multiple purposes, including recreation, wildlife habitat, timber, and water quality protection. Cut levels in the public forests rose dramatically after World War II as demand for lumber increased, reaching deeper into the Pacific Northwest woods. This region provided one-third of the nation's timber in 1988. Pressure to cut on public lands is particularly high at present because the large corporations, which own 25 percent of the timberland for their own use, have overcut from their holdings. Thus for the next twenty or thirty years these companies, like the smaller enterprises that do not own their own timber, are hoping to harvest trees from federal lands. Cut levels on national timberlands are therefore hotly contested, particularly in the remaining old-growth forests.

Prior to spotted owl set-asides, federal lands supplied five to six billion board feet of timber per year in the Northwest. This is something on the order of 110,000 acres (about 170 square miles) of public land cut a year. Of the approximately thirty million acres of original forest that existed in the Pacific Northwest prior to white settlement, estimates of remaining old growth vary from less than 10 percent to 25 percent. Virtually all of these ancient forests are on federal lands. These trees are the most valuable for timber because of their size and the quality of their wood. As many as seventy thousand acres of old growth were cut each year until 1991, when the federal courts halted logging in the national forests until a plan was devised to protect the spotted owl.

Research in the 1970s and 1980s began to demonstrate the value of old-growth forest for habitat and nutrient cycles. This altered earlier assumptions that second-growth forests were ecologically equivalent to old growth. In 1982 the Forest Service chose the northern spotted owl as an indicator species for the health of old-growth forests in Washington and Oregon. It was in the early 1980s that scientists began to become concerned about the possible extinction of the owl.

The Reagan administration accelerated the environmental threat to old-growth habitat through its pro-cutting policies after the 1980 election. The new policy was to liquidate old-growth forests and replace them with faster growing and more productive plantations of younger trees.[4] This conflicted with the Forest Service's own policy of cutting for sustainable yields, and dissent grew within the agency as well as in the broader environmental community. Timber corporations profited enormously from large harvests of low-cost federal timber that they could export at high prices particularly to Japan.

Environmentalists responded with direct action and legal challenges to prevent cutting. Sporadic protests were followed by the Sierra Club Legal Defense Fund's three lawsuits starting in 1987 to protect the owl and its old-growth habitat. The first suit, filed by twenty-six environmental organizations, was against the U.S. Fish and Wildlife Service for failing to list the spotted owl as an endangered species. In 1988 a federal court ordered Fish and Wildlife to reconsider its decision and allowed it until May 1989 to act. Fish and Wildlife did propose to list the owl in 1989; and in June 1990 the northern spotted owl was designated a threatened species under the Endangered Species Act.

Fish and Wildlife's designation came only after a series of court injunctions that forced the Forest Service and the Bureau of Land Management (BLM) to protect the owl. In 1988 the federal court found that the BLM had been "arbitrary and capricious" in not considering the threat to the spotted owl in its management of timber. Temporary restraining orders on the BLM halted timber sales in spotted owl habitat in 1988 and 1991, followed by a 1992 injunction blocking all logging in old-growth forests until the BLM could prove that it had followed the National Environmental Protection Act when planning its sales. The National Forest Service's practices were similarly rejected in 1989, when a federal court halted timber sales until a full consideration of the owl protection case could be heard. An injunction in 1991 set aside 11.6 million acres of forest land for owl protection and ordered the National Forest Service to develop a permanent plan by March 5, 1992. Harvest levels in the national forests dropped dramatically because of the court injunctions from 5.3 billion board feet (bbf) sold in 1987 and 5.6 bbf harvested to .4 bbf sold in 1995 and .88 bbf harvested.

The federal government responded to the courts by assembling its Interagency Scientific Committee (ISC) to develop a conservation plan for the owl. In 1990 the committee reported that existing Forest Service and BLM policies would lead to the extinction of the owl and proposed the creation of large habitat conservation areas to preserve the species. The

ISC's recommendation was to protect about 50 percent of the remaining owl habitat.

Congress countered the court injunctions with its 1990 appropriations bill requiring the Forest Service to sell over a billion board feet of timber in spotted owl habitat. This was one in a series of riders attached to appropriations bills since 1986 that overruled judicial review of timber sales. The Bush administration further reduced the level of protection from 11.6 million acres in 1991 to 2.8 million acres one year later. Bush also intervened to allow thirteen additional sales on BLM land protected by the courts by convening the Endangered Species Committee, nicknamed the "God Squad." A federal court later found that the Bush White House had illegally sought to influence that committee in favor of the sales. The Bush administration along with industry also promoted amending the Endangered Species Act to include consideration of the economic impacts of protection. Forest Service sales, however, remained blocked by court injunctions.

Spotted owl protections came at a time when timber workers and communities were already suffering from significant job loss. Rapid automation during the 1980s meant fewer jobs despite an increased harvest. Output increased almost 50 percent between 1980 and 1987, while nine thousand jobs were lost.[5] To preserve remaining jobs, labor unions made an alliance with the timber industry and introduced legislation in 1991 called the Forests and Families Protection Act, which would ensure a higher minimum cut level on national lands. The International Woodworkers of America and the Carpenters Union led this initiative with the support of the national AFL-CIO. Labor also recognized the need for some protection of old-growth forests and for compliance with the Endangered Species Act, a compromise which they convinced industry to accept as politically necessary. With the country in the midst of a recession, this initiative halted momentum for environmental legislation to permanently protect old-growth forests. Protectionist bills like the Ancient Forest Protection Act lost sponsors to the labor initiative. This deadlock paralyzed Congress, and no legislative solution to the controversy was found.

In his 1992 electoral campaign, presidential candidate Bill Clinton promised to resolve the dispute between timber communities and environmentalists by personally convening a roundtable conference of all participants to find "the truth, common ground or something in between." With the vice president and the secretaries of agriculture, interior, labor, and commerce, President Clinton convened a high-profile timber summit in Oregon on April 2, 1993. The timber industry and workers testified in favor of renewed logging, and thousands of timber workers were given the day off to participate in demonstrations. Environmentalists testified for protections, joined by representatives of the salmon fishing industry, who also opposed excessive lumbering because of the destruction of salmon habitat.

Clinton charged his cabinet with proposing a new national policy within sixty days. On July 1, 1993, Clinton made public his plan, which would permit harvests of old-growth timber averaging 1.2 billion board feet per year. Spotted owl reserves were to be set aside, in which logging would be limited to salvaging dead or dying trees and thinning new trees. To compensate for the jobs that would be lost because of the restrictions, Clinton proposed to provide $1.2 billion over five years in economic aid for development, retraining displaced workers, and river restoration. These funds would support over fifteen thousand new jobs carrying out tasks like repairing streams and roads. On February 23, 1994, the Clinton administration reduced the proposed harvest levels down to 1.1 billion board feet per year in order to provide wider buffer zones around rivers and streams.

Both loggers and environmentalists attacked the plan for conceding too much. The timber industry predicted devastating regional job losses and a rising cost of lumber. Environmentalists opposed the salvage logging allowed in old-growth reserves and continued to fight for greater protection. In May 1994 the Sierra Club Legal Defense Fund sued the federal government for not adequately protecting wildlife, and the timber industry filed a suit arguing that the federal government violated open meeting laws by developing its management plan in secret.

To end the injunctions, Clinton's plan was submitted to the federal courts for approval. In June 1994 the courts allowed old-growth timber sales to resume despite pending lawsuits. In December 1994, after considering both environmental and timber company arguments, the court determined that the government's plan did fall "within the bounds of the law" in protecting endangered species. In the judge's view, however, the plan represented the maximum legally allowed level of timber sales. With court appeals pending, opposing sides continue to reject both the government's and the court's solution. Salvage logging spurred a new round of protests by environmentalists in the Northwest as the conflict continues.

Opposing sides have regularly predicted very different economic consequences from spotted owl protections. In 1991 environmental groups estimated between 8,900 and 12,930 direct jobs, or between 31,600 and

45,900 total jobs, were at risk in the next twenty years. But from three to four times as many direct jobs (33,600) could be lost, they claimed, due to automation in the same period.[6] By contrast, the timber industry projected much higher job losses due to owl protections. They estimate that over 100,000 total jobs could be lost due to owl set-asides in addition to the 44,500 total jobs lost due to modernization over the next decade. The federal government's Scientific Panel on Late Successional Forest Ecosystems released a report in 1991 estimating a loss of between 30,000 and 56,000 jobs from moderate protection of the owl. In 1995 estimates of job loss from owl protection still varied greatly. President Clinton estimated that 9,500 jobs would be lost from his plan. The timber industry said that 85,000 direct and indirect jobs would be lost.

PERCEIVED INTERESTS

Timber workers and environmentalists approached this conflict from very different points of view. Workers defending their livelihoods and environmentalists defending an endangered ecosystem were both fighting for causes they perceived as morally right and honorable. These perceived interests have three dimensions. First, each side has a statement of interests. Second, each side makes an argument for the legitimacy of these interests based on some claimed reality (often conceived as human nature or some other absolute principle). Third, each side directly and indirectly identifies a social geography, that is, a set of allies and enemies, or "insiders" and "outsiders," who either share or oppose the interests of one's group.

Labor's Perceived Interests

Unions and union members generally claim that their interests would be served by limiting environmental protections and allowing stable cut levels on federal lands. Although jobs have diminished throughout the industry for a variety of reasons, they see the greatest immediate threat to jobs as the reduced timber supply in the national forests. As the AFL-CIO states, "The issue is . . . preserving the jobs and communities that depend on the continued harvesting of timber on public lands in the region." Hence unions have sought both to defeat legislation that would set aside old-growth forests and to convince Congress to override judicial barriers to cutting.

To accomplish their goals, unions must redirect political attention away from environmental preservation to its social and economic costs. The unions, for instance, have pushed hard to incorporate economic considerations into the Endangered Species Act. "You need to think about the economic impacts of protecting species," they argue again and again. "Look at the human side of the equation."

These interests are valid, timber workers claim, because they are economically necessary, environmentally beneficial, and socially correct. Timber workers provide a valuable service producing necessities for society, "wood fiber for everything from toilet paper to vanilla and all points in between." Furthermore, they argue, they are the real environmentalists who care about the forests in their day-to-day work and decisions. They love the outdoors, but nature is not something sacred to be left to its own devices. Humans can improve on nature in a way that serves society's needs—and doing so is human nature. They claim that sufficient land has already been protected for environmental purposes and that it is possible to preserve the forests and the owl while sustaining harvest levels.

This view also identifies a social geography, a set of allies and enemies. Labor clearly identifies with industry, which they claim has a shared interest in preserving the harvest level. "Let's face it," one union member explains, "this is one of those issues where the industry and the force employed by them will go hand in hand to a large degree because they have very similar interests." Although unions have had many conflicts with timber companies, they are perceived as honorable and explicit about their intentions. Companies are not blamed for fighting hard for their interests because competition forces them to do so. But companies have "gotten greedy" in the past and overcut the resource. Unions present themselves as the voice of reason in contrast with corporate overcutting, always seeking a balance between cutting and preserving the resource. Indeed, labor introduced legislation that, in its view, "takes the entire scope of owls, timber supply, set-asides, and people and puts it all into one hopper."

Environmentalists are seen as the enemies. They have different interests and do not care about communities or workers. They are presented as manipulative, untrustworthy, dishonorable, fanatical, and misguided. Their desire for protection is irrational and religious. Environmentalists do not understand the timber industry, and they react to clear-cuts without appreciating the nature of timber as a managed crop that regenerates itself. Environmentalists fail to see that cutting improves natural processes by maintaining a youthful and vigorous forest, and salvages useful wood instead of allowing it to rot or burn. They are

devious, exaggerating the environmental problem to serve their own ul-
terior motives, which are beyond reasonable environmental goals. In
one union leader's words, "These people are pilgrims, religious about
environmental protection. They're beyond all reasoning. They are at-
tempting to use the owl and some other species as launching pads to advance a philosophy that is outright frightening . . . to see to it that the
Olympic Peninsula is precluded to human habitat."

The boundaries of friend and foe are drawn in other ways as well.
Geographically, environmentalists are seen as largely east coasters who
have destroyed their land and are imposing their problems on the West.
Environmentalists are generally believed to be urban residents who
want to protect vacation lands at the expense of rural communities. They
are seen as different occupationally as well because they don't make a
living by their hands. They are ignorant of the Northwest and suscepti-
ble to the false stories told by environmental organizations.

Environmentalists' Perceived Interests

In contrast with timber workers, environmentalists perceive their interests as upholding the court injunctions in Congress and winning final
protection for the remaining old-growth forests by legislative action. To
accomplish their goal, timber supply from federal lands would need to
be dramatically reduced and jobs lost. The environmentalists have an interest in helping displaced workers find new jobs or otherwise get compensation so that they don't complicate the debate over protection. One
avenue they have pursued to increase local jobs is to decrease log exports to make more timber available locally as a replacement for the loss
in supply from federal lands.

These goals are justified as environmentally necessary, socially inevitable, and morally and politically right. Environmentalists make the
case that dramatic new protection is necessary immediately. With 90
percent of the ancient forests gone, they argue, the country must act
now to protect what's left or the ecosystem will be destroyed. The
choice is not between protection or stable levels of supply but between
reduced supply now or later. If we wait, the resource will be depleted
and jobs lost anyway, but at the added cost of the extinction of many
species and entire ecosystems. Job loss is not the fault of environmentalists but the result of mismanagement by the Forest Service, which has
allied itself with timber companies to favor cutting over protecting
wildlife habitat. Thus environmentalists are protecting the public interest in clean air, clean water, and biological diversity. As one environ-

mentalist says, "We're constantly vindicated and validated as being in the right."

Given the recession in the early 1990s and broad concern about protecting jobs, environmentalists have an interest in appearing sensitive to the social and economic costs of protection. They argue that they are the real advocates for the long-term interests of workers who have mistakenly allied themselves with industry. Industry doesn't care about jobs and workers, but is using labor to fight its battles in exchange for some possible short-term job gains. The real job loss has come mostly from industry automation and overcutting. With the resource depleted, rural communities have to develop economic alternatives. Our society doesn't guarantee jobs, and people are often displaced by restructuring in the economy. One environmentalist notes, "Helping communities hasn't become accepted in forestry, in the steel industry, etc." But still they support trying to offset these economic hardships with worker retraining, economic adjustment assistance, and economic development programs in the communities. As another environmentalist explained, "We are promoting work in the forests other than with dead trees—closing roads in the forests, restoring watersheds and other environmental work."

In the environmentalists' view, the major social division is between themselves and the timber industry coupled with the industry-dominated National Forest Service. "Industry controls the Forest Service and Fish and Wildlife," said one environmentalist, "so they've basically ignored the goal of protecting species. If the forest service had done its job to protect the owl, we wouldn't have this situation requiring draconian measures." Environmentalists claim that they receive broad support across the country and that they represent the national interest against the special interest of the timber industry. They see the timber industry as entirely self-interested, always protecting only its "bottom line." Environmentalists perceive industry as lying to the public and government, manipulating government agencies behind the scenes, mismanaging the resource, and callous about the human costs of its policies. Industry would destroy the country's natural heritage for short-term profits while blaming environmentalists for the resulting social problems.

In the environmentalists' view, unions are misguided, ignorant of the science of forest ecosystems, shortsighted, unsophisticated and simplistic in their concerns, and destroyers of nature. Loggers as a group are caught in an outdated past and face the inevitable demise of their industry. They have been duped into allying with industry, but they could be allies of environmentalists.

The subjective statements of timber workers and environmentalists about their own interests hide as much as they reveal about the conditions and choices facing each side. Three important areas of misperception and misrepresentation are common. First, each side's interpretation of its interests denies basic facts that are central to the other side. The union view is based on an unwillingness to admit that the forests are as devastated as the environmentalists say. This denial continues despite the fact that these environmental claims were largely vindicated by the ISC. The unions need to deny these findings in order to sustain their belief that the environmentalists are really plotting something more devious than spotted owl protection. They can then label environmentalists as extremists and vindicate their own position that cutting should continue.

Environmentalists, similarly, refuse to accept that the timber communities will be devastated by ancient forest set-asides, despite the report of the federal government's Interagency Economic Effects Team. Instead they attribute most of the future job loss to automation, that is, to industry actions. Environmentalists need to deny that protection causes hardships to sustain their argument that the corporations are the real villains and communities and labor should join in opposing them. To accept that they are harming communities, just as industry is, would detract from their claim to follow a higher moral standard than corporate managers.

Second, each group's perception is based on demeaning the other side in some fundamental way. Environmentalists argue that unions are misguided about their own interests. The unions, they claim, have been duped into aligning with industry, whereas their long-term interests are actually being advanced by environmentalists. They are shortsighted, tying themselves to an industry that makes short-term profits at labor's expense. Management has proven that it is willing to destroy the unions and abandon the workforce. Labor should see through the propaganda of industry, which blames environmentalists for its own misdeeds. Industry is the one that has diminished the resource and made it necessary to drastically reduce harvest levels, and it has tricked and bribed labor into working with it.

On the other hand, union members believe that environmentalists are lying about their real interests and that they are underhanded in their political actions. They claim that environmentalists aren't really motivated by CO_2 levels and global warming or endangered species, and that their arguments are erroneous. Preservationists are not like normal people who want to make a living and enjoy life. They are fanatical about this one idea of preserving nature. They are urban easterners who have destroyed their own forests and natural areas; they want natural places to visit, but ask others to pay the price of protection. Their unspoken goal is to ruin the timber industry in the Northwest, and to achieve this, they have sought to divide industry and unions, to get them fighting among themselves. And they want to remove decision making from local communities, where people experience the issue firsthand, to the halls of Congress, where they can manipulate voters. They want to force others to live according to their view of what is right. Thus they are not only dishonest but politically devious as well.

Third, neither side presents a coherent view that accounts for the needs or concerns of the other. One government observer explained,

> It isn't the environmentalists goal to take jobs away, nor is it industry's or labor's goal to destroy ecosystems. They're by-products of their primary agenda, which is the problem of single-issue politics; you're not responsible for the by-products of your agenda. It's someone else's problem. The industry says, "We're not in the ecosystem business. You want to make ecosystems? Buy 'em from us." That's what they say. Environmentalists say, "Job losses? We're not in the economics business; we're in the ecosystem business. If you have an ecosystem, come to us. If you want to protect jobs—sorry, we can't help you."

This political one-sidedness persists despite each side's claim that it presents a balanced view that accounts for the concerns of the other. Environmentalists claim to be looking out for the best interests of workers and communities, and workers claim to be protecting the environment.

These claims and counterclaims have escalated as each side sought the political high ground. Increasingly polarized opponents have "mirrored" each other's rhetoric by framing issues in favorable ways, vilifying the other, interpreting statistics to their advantage, and oversimplifying and dramatizing the issues.[7]

When one side or the other reached some wrong belief or understanding—when, for instance, environmentalists did not recognize that the spotted owl decision had pushed beleaguered timber unions into a corner in which they were fighting to survive, or when timber unions did not understand that there really are as few old-growth trees left as the environmentalists have said—its stated goals did not accurately represent its interests. Each was basing its understanding of its interests on false information. As the debate became more heated and the sides became more fixed in their views, their positions departed farther from their real interests.

Hidden Agendas

If environmentalists and timber workers do not present accurate statements of their own interests, it may be that they have unarticulated interests that they are acting upon. Possibly they are not able to express their real interests due to fear or calculation about political consequences or some other reason. Shrewd observations about actions or more intimate knowledge of real motivations could reveal interests that are not stated publicly.

Each group has organizational interests that it doesn't speak about openly. In both the environmental and labor situations, popular grassroots sentiments are being expressed in the political system through interest groups. These environmental and labor organizations serve their own interests by servicing their members, increasing their funding, and building their political influence. But even while an organization makes strategic calculations about how to advance its organization, in public it argues its case on principles. For example, one observer argued confidentially that

> Labor knows that it can't trust industry to look out for it; they fight with these guys all the time. They know that industry overcut the resource; they were writing reports in the '70s predicting timber shortages in the '90s if harvest levels didn't change. The same guy who wrote those reports is lobbying for the labor and industry bill now. But who was going to look out for the communities and labor? No one. The environmentalists weren't doing it. Labor had to hook up with someone or they'd never be heard. So it made good sense for them to work with industry; at least they got a hearing. The unions are desperate; they only have a few years left. They were looking for any way to save some union jobs. It really wasn't until they started to attack the Endangered Species Act that they got any attention. Before that, the enviros were ignoring them; they didn't care. But when they started talking about amending Endangered Species, that got them looking. It was a good tactic for labor.

"On the other hand," this confidential observer continued,

the environmentalists are tacitly cooperating with big industry despite the fact that they are presented as the enemy. Environmentalists have agreed to restrict their efforts for protection to public lands. This leaves the large, private timber owners free to cut on their lands, and able to profit from the higher prices that will result from the reduced supply.

[I've had environmental lobbyists tell me] that they have nothing to gain from working with the small mills and labor who are dependent on public lands. The deal they cut was with Weyerhaeuser, because Weyerhaeuser says, "You can deal with public lands, just stay the hell away from us." These are the big guys; they're the ones with the money and the clout. And the problem is nobody believes they can win against them. They'd rather take their chance just fighting with the communities rather than taking on what they see as a bigger enemy.

Labor unions and national environmental organizations are undoubtedly making strategic calculations about their agendas. Both movements' organizations have been harshly criticized for compromising their principles in the pursuit of short-term gains. As a public relations consulting firm reported to the AFL-CIO about improving its image, "Many Americans consider unions to be bureaucratic institutions. . . . They see unions' priorities coming from the needs of leadership as much—or perhaps more than—the needs of members." Unions are "narrowly focused on their own bureaucratic goals rather than their members."[8] National environmental organizations face very similar criticisms for becoming centralized bureaucracies focused on pragmatic compromises with government and industry and guided by calculations about raising funds from national donors and mass mailing appeals.

But although the labor and environmental movements often act like interest groups in the political process, they represent much broader public mobilizations. Though the environmental movement has powerful lobbying and legal organizations focused on strategic calculations, efforts to protect the spotted owl predate the involvement of major environmental organizations by as much as two decades. Scientists researching the owl at universities and government agencies first appealed to the BLM about protection in 1971. In 1985, Haida Indians in Canada brought world attention to the issue of logging old growth when they physically blocked logging trucks. Dozens of local organizations have joined the cause using everything from direct action to lobbying. Earth First's "monkey wrenching" has included protesters pouring sand in gas tanks of bulldozers, chopping down billboards, chaining themselves to machinery, and spiking trees. Other grassroots efforts include the Western

Ancient Forest Campaign and the campaign to pass California's "Forests Forever" initiative. These movements were not acting on expedient political calculations. They were leading the fight to protect old growth long before deals were cut in Congress.

Unions are more than interest groups as well. They are the major voice for timber communities that have no other organized political voice. Anger and resentment against environmentalists is widespread in the timber towns. There have been several large rallies against the "greenies," with over 500 logging trucks and 3,500 participants from Washington, Oregon, Idaho, Montana, and California. Signs saying "This Family Supported by Timber Dollars" are seen throughout the region. Cars sport bumper stickers: "Save a logger, kill an owl," "I love spotted owls . . . barbecued, fricasseed, baked, stir-fried." The outpouring of protest against old-growth set-asides was not orchestrated by the unions, which provided the organizational resources for this protest. In these communities dependent on the logging industry, maintaining the economic base represents a broad public interest as well.

OBJECTIVE INTERESTS

If the hidden agendas of political organizations do not represent the interests of the broader publics active in the timber controversy, then possibly each side has been deceived by the rhetoric, misinformation, and political and economic pressures about their real interests. By stepping back from the immediate conflict and analyzing the conditions under which each side is acting, one can, perhaps, identify interests that people caught in the fray may have lost sight of. Labor unions, environmentalists, and timber industry management face different conditions as a result of their distinct class positions.

Conflicting interests between labor and management are clearly illustrated in the timber case. Management efforts to maximize profits in the face of competitive pressures come at the expense of workers' wages and control over the work process. The unions forfeited considerable ground to management in the 1980s, losing wages and benefits, representation, and overall jobs. Corporate strategies to rid themselves of unions altogether and to realize a complacent workforce continue. By shifting production overseas and to the unorganized South, by replacing labor with machines, by contracting out to nonunion loggers, and by substituting profitable exports for production, management has increased its power relative to the unions and working people. Many of the remaining organized workers are in small and medium-sized mills that depend on public lands, so the big corporations would be glad to see these firms go out of business. This would reduce competition and destroy the unions at the same time. Furthermore, timber workers have a long-term interest in sustainable yields from the forests, which big corporations, with holdings throughout the United States and the world, do not share. Overcutting on private lands played a major role in the current crisis, and overcutting on public lands could exacerbate the problems for workers. Thus workers and timber industry have many conflicting interests.

As suggested previously, however, labor and management also objectively share some common interests. Both depend on the prosperity of the timber sector and the well-being of particular companies. These interests have brought together labor and management as environmentalists have attacked the timber sector as a whole. Middle-class environmentalists do not have economic interests tied to timber harvesting, as workers and management do. The economic well-being of the upper middle class derives largely from professional and service sector jobs. The core of the environmental movement and the people who staff environmental organizations are professionals—lawyers, lobbyists, academics, teachers, health professionals—or their children. Their power as a class derives from controlling knowledge and information, not from material production, and their incomes often depend upon local, state, and federal taxes and provision of necessary or legally required services such as education, medical care, or environmental services. They remain relatively unaffected by the declining manufacturing base of the economy. Thus the interests of the middle class in environmental protection are distinct from the economic interests of labor and management in the timber sector.

Nevertheless, workers and environmentalists do have interests in common as well. Protection of the environment ultimately depends upon the practices of the people who use it, and timber workers make choices every day that have important consequences for the ecology of the forests. Even when regulations exist, they depend on people implementing both the letter and the spirit of the law to protect the environment. Thus environmentalists have a significant interest in ensuring that timber workers understand and apply good environmental practices. However, environmentalists have political as well as practical reasons to ally with timber workers. They lost considerable congressional support for the Ancient Forests Protection Act by failing to address the social and economic consequences of their bill. Failure to involve workers and communities in decisions about resource use has fed the antiprotection-

ist "Wise Use" movement, which seeks to limit environmental regulations in the name of property rights. Thus progress on the environment
is increasingly tied to meeting community needs as well.

At the local level, communities also have significant environmental interests. A healthy environment is necessary for a sustainable economy,
and species such as the spotted owl are indicators of the health of the
forests. Overcutting timber on private and public lands is undermining
the economic and environmental base of timber communities. Politically, timber workers need allies if they are to counter the power of the
timber industry. Corporations are making profits at the expense of both
workers and the environment, and timber workers implicitly recognize
their common plight with the owl when they argue that they too are an
endangered species.

Many alternative programs would benefit both labor and environmentalists if these two had defined their interests in common. One possibility would be to protect old growth on public lands and redistribute
the gains and losses more evenly through political means. If the big companies make large profits, some of this windfall could be redistributed to
the small and medium mills and their workers. This could be done in a
variety of ways; for example, smaller companies could be given access to
some private lands to replace public set-asides. A second approach
would be to reduce log exports and ensure that more of the logs from
private lands are available to the smaller mills. Both options would help
to preserve jobs and the way of life in timber communities. Another approach, which has been the focus of the Clinton administration's policy,
is to use taxes to redistribute costs of protection by funding retraining
and alternative jobs. For environmentalists, the advantage of protection
along with redistribution is that it would reduce the backlash that would
come from protection at the expense of the workforce. For communities
and working people, redistribution would mean that they would not
feel the brunt of change as severely.

Although their conflicts have received more publicity and national attention, environmentalists and timber workers have succeeded in developing collaborative agreements and alliances in some situations. The
United Paperworkers International Union (UPIU) strike in Jay, Maine, in
1987–88 demonstrated just how mutable perceived interests and alliances can be. People in town had long accepted polluted rivers, a high
cancer rate, overwhelming smells, and toxic waste from the paper mills
as part of life. The UPIU local president Bill Meserve observed, "Quite
frankly, back a lot of years ago, the company was a good company to
work for and we tried to help the company rather than hurt her by dis-

regarding a lot of things, overlooking a lot of things." But two disasters during the strike dramatized the link between the company's environmental and labor policies of cutting pay, intensifying work, reducing jobs, exposing workers and communities to toxic substances, and trying to break the union. A malfunction in the mill's waste treatment system resulted in sixteen million gallons of waste dumped into the Androscoggin River, and then a chlorine dioxide leak at the mill forced the town to evacuate and could have killed thousands of people if it hadn't been for the cold weather. In response, the union local developed an alliance with Greenpeace and passed the first environmental ordinance in the state which empowered the town to monitor and enforce state and federal environmental standards. Although the national union ended the strike in 1988 against local wishes, the labor and environmental alliance remains intact, and the town of Jay continues to enforce environmental regulations against threats that the company would shut down its plant. This and other examples of cooperation demonstrate that timber workers and environmentalists can be allies, and that issues can be framed in ways that are beneficial for both sides.

The timber controversy illustrates how people have multiple, conflicting objective interests defined by the conditions in which they find themselves. Workers, environmentalists, and corporate management each have interests that could be served by allying with other classes. Workers do benefit from their alliance with management to sustain jobs, especially union jobs. They also have real interests in cooperating with environmentalists when environmentalists are committed to policies that meet their needs. But such alliances have risks and costs. A labor-management alliance polarizes the issues of jobs versus the environment, so that compromises that meet the interests of both timber workers and environmentalists are less likely. Ongoing protests, with their political and economic costs, will result from such a standoff. Environmentalists risk diluting their environmental proposals if they collaborate with labor. And workers have no guarantees that good, stable, well-paid economic alternatives would replace lost timber jobs if they did cooperate with environmentally needed changes. Thus choices between these different alliances and ways of perceiving interests are inevitably controversial and divisive.

People's perceptions of their interests are plagued by misperceptions, misrepresentations, and biases that exaggerate the benefits and minimize the costs of the chosen alliance. Each side justifies its alliances and positions in principled terms that overstate the environmental, economic, and social benefits while ignoring the costs. This self-deception makes the present configuration of alliances seem more set, more inevitable than it is, while it masks other ways of perceiving interests. In the timber case, labor's alliance with management is based on a denial of the environmental costs of continued logging of old-growth forests, just as environmentalists' position is based on ignoring the economic costs to unions and communities and the long-term windfall to the large timber companies. As long as both sides remain fixed in their present positions, they are unable to admit their other objective interests.

The important political question is: Why, out of the numerous objective interests people face in any situation, do they choose to perceive their interests in one way over another? Why did timber workers and environmentalists come to perceive their interests as opposed when they could have seen them as shared? An analysis in terms of interests cannot answer that question. But it does provide an understanding of the choices that people face and the consequences of pursuing different interests. The next chapter seeks to unravel how people choose from multiple, structurally given competing interests and alliances.

▲

CHAPTER FOUR

When Classes Meet: Class-Cultural Lenses

You rarely find labor and peace groups at the same place at the same time. I feel when I deal with these groups, I'm totally schizophrenic. They seem to have very little understanding of each other and very little interest in understanding each other. . . . There's a whole different culture between labor and the traditional peace movement constituency which is largely white and middle class and upper middle class and university based, not exclusively so, but largely that's the case and certainly the perception.

—A Maine labor and peace activist

When people from my union walk into a room with the Washington Environmental Council, they immediately don't feel comfortable. They don't like those people. That's a big gulf.

—A Washington labor activist

How many people here do not live in North Seattle? Don't own a pair of Birkenstocks? Don't use National Public Radio as their primary news source? Don't have European ancestry? How many people join Sane without being pro-choice? Do we push people like that out because they don't accept the whole ideological range of issues?

—Introductory remarks at Washington State Sane/
Freeze annual meeting in 1992

Is business an ally to workers in managing and developing the timber sector, or is management exploiting workers to make profits at their expense? Workers in Oregon and Washington answered this question differently when they first settled these rich timber lands. Timber mills developed earlier in Oregon, beginning in the 1820s with small mills that shipped logs down the coast to San Francisco. Farmers from preindustrial Germany brought their values of self-sufficiency and a feudal social order with them to their new home. They worked part-time in the mills and set up farms on cleared land. Conservative craft unions developed, which became affiliated with the American Federation of Labor. These unions reflected the values and experiences of these farmer–timber workers, who saw it was in their interests to work cooperatively with management in the mills.

In Washington the deep-water ports of Puget Sound encouraged sizable logging operations, and Weyerhaeuser and others capitalized large mills. Significant waves of immigration came later than in Oregon, including large numbers of industrial workers from Britain and Scandinavia. These workers brought to Washington State their experiences with harsh working conditions in their native countries, and many had already developed an anticapitalist ideology. This growing population of unskilled workers was looked down upon by those organized in the skilled trades. As a result Washington's settlers joined more radical unions like the Industrial Workers of the World (IWW), which perceived organizing in terms of class conflict.[1] These unions clashed with the AFL craft unions that vied for the loyalty of timber workers in the region.

The cultural experiences of German farmers and Scandinavian and British industrial workers clearly shaped the kinds of unions these workers built and their interpretations of their interests. Conditions in Oregon and Washington also influenced settlers' experiences as they worked in the mills and forests in the new country. Culture and conditions combined to shape immigrant interpretations of their interests. Loggers and environmentalists in the present period also draw upon their cultural heritages and economic conditions to make sense of their situations. This chapter considers how logging and environmentalist cultures contributed to each side's interpretation of its interests.

WHEN CLASSES MEET

The cultural barriers between unions and members of the peace and environmental movements become apparent when activists from both sides sit down together to work out differences. Union members and middle-class activists talk, meet, and communicate differently. Workers are frustrated with the time and energy that middle-class movements devote to process, while peace and environmental activists find the formality and hierarchy of unions difficult to accept. One labor attorney explained his experience:

I probably had twenty different unions that I was counsel for over the years that I worked as an attorney. I don't think that I can think of an instance when I went to a union meeting or an annual convention or a conference of labor people in which we sat around and waxed philosophic about the direction of the labor movement. I mean we might do that in private conversations over coffee, but as a group culture, it's not something that is really customary. People are much more focused on, "OK, tell me what I need to know in order to work within my plant or my industry."

Labor activists frequently find the meeting styles of middle-class organizations difficult and tedious. A union activist in Maine who is very supportive of the peace movement described the problem in these terms:

Some of the issue of class is how it colors what you're used to in terms of meetings—like this whole retreat process. I'm just really glad I had an excuse not to go [to the coalition retreat]. It was just—I'm used to conventions. I'm used to Robert's Rules of Order, not consensus. And I prefer those, because if we're making a decision then I want a decision. Whether my position wins or loses, I prefer having the decision made by the group rather than not. And it's what we're used to in the labor movement.

A colleague continued,

Liberal groups, peace, ecology-minded groups, they look at things more intellectually. They have to have structure. We in labor put on our football helmets and run into the issue. We've been in the issue so long, our structure is there. [Peace organizations are] too long and slow just trying to get the structure together.

Working-class participants often find that peace and environmental organizations are not attuned to the immediate needs that motivate their activism, nor are they organized to achieve short-term goals. One union member whose union recently survived a decertification vote describes a typical experience working with a peace organization:

These peace people don't understand that it's a war out here. The union just went through a major fight over decertification and development of an independent union. It was bloody, and people who were good friends before now won't talk to each other. It split fathers and sons. The contrast between giving people hell at a bar over the union vote and then going to a conversion meeting where people sit around and eat cheese and sip herb tea is really frustrating. Those people seem like they're from a different solar system. I'd love to get three or four of them down here to spend six months in this office and then see what they think.

The peace people are too intellectual and always wanting to work on the structure of the organization. I was at a meeting recently where they talked about the structure of committees and subcommittees again. The shipyard could be closed by the time they get the structure together. The union is used to getting down to work and getting things done. They wouldn't talk to the governor more than once, and if he wasn't listening the first time then he'd read about it in the paper next. This is a war, and you can't be nice about it. We face 350 new people out of work and need to tell them something. I feel a sense of urgency about it that I don't get from the peace people.

Peace and environmental organizations, reciprocally, find the labor movement's lack of attention to group process is limiting. An environmental participant in a coalition with labor observed,

Labor groups don't process. In environmental groups sometimes you can stop a meeting and process what's going on and talk about different levels of needs and styles. I've never felt that that could happen in this coalition, indeed I thought they'd all spit up if I even suggested it. The need to do that would be a need coming from me. It might help them understand me and maybe myself, but they weren't wanting it, I didn't ever pick up on that.

Middle-class organizations also find the hierarchy and formality of the union structure foreign and distasteful. Unions demand levels of privacy that are alien to peace and environmental organizations. These middle-class groups not only welcome but actively recruit all comers to their deliberations. Peace and environmental organizations have few if any formal rules about membership or participation. New arrivals are often asked and expected to take part in the discussion and decision making along with people who have worked with the program for some time. Participation and equality are fundamental values.

By contrast, unions are closed organizations that do not share names of members or open their meetings to outsiders. One coalition builder from labor comments on this difference:

We'd try to get someone [from the coalition] to talk at the union meeting—well, that's fine, but you can't be at the union meeting. You have to come, say your piece, and then leave before the business starts. That's just the way it is. The difference is the adversarial role that you play with the company, and you have to protect that at all costs. That's where it comes from, and the way it will always be. The union is quite closed. When it came time to call people to support or whatever, well, it's against union by-laws to give out home numbers. [Environmental/peace organizations feel like] "That's silly. You can come and be on our phone bank any time." There's a difference.

One environmental activist described her experience learning to work with the formal structure of the labor movement in these terms:

You've got to kiss the ring. That's my shorthand for paying deference. If I thought it was something especially made up for me personally or enviros per se, I might take it differently. It comes out of a different generation, a different educational experience. They had to fight a kind of fight where those kinds of things mattered, and it's understandable. Labor for the most part belongs to a very formally structured organization in which they do kiss each other's rings and it does matter who does what first and who calls whom first and that you go through the proper channels. We're kind of flying by the seat of our pants, a lot of us [environmentalists]. We're not used to doing that. There's all these things that are very different, enough to make people edgy. So they go to the mechanisms that they're used to working with, for the formal structure.

Why do working- and middle-class activists have such different styles of organizing and working? A closer look at their different experiences can help make of sense these two realities.

LOGGING CULTURE

Logging in the Pacific Northwest was originally a nomadic life led by independent-minded men who moved from logging camp to logging camp as they pleased. As much as half the workforce was foreign born at the beginning of this century—British, German, and Scandinavian. The camps were originally shacks in the woods and evolved into car camps or semipermanent villages on railroad cars for easy movement to the next timber stand. Loggers moved often if they grew dissatisfied with the conditions or food in a camp or just to assert their independence. As a result, the turnover rate in camps was as high as 55 percent a month in

1917.[2] Up to 90 percent of loggers were unmarried and without ties to any permanent settlement.

As roads made logging operations more accessible, loggers abandoned the camps for towns and cities. The federal government supported this process through policies to ensure a stable supply of timber for communities to harvest. Yet despite these efforts at stability, the timber industry remains largely seasonal work with regular, cyclical downturns. Thus loggers periodically experience unemployment and the need to move from job to job.

In addition the work is strenuous, dangerous, and demanding, requiring constant vigilance. If the trees do not fall as planned or the logs are not moved with care or the equipment not properly maintained, loggers suffer major injury or even death. According to a study of the hazards of the industry,

> From 1970 through 1979, in California, Oregon, Washington and British Columbia, . . . 1,372 timber industry deaths took place. The men were killed in routine fashion: they did not look, or jump, or get out of the way, or run fast enough. The grisly fact of their 1,372 deaths reinforces our statistical conclusion that logging is the most dangerous business of all and the most "unforgiving" of carelessness; a job which requires a man to be alert constantly like a soldier in combat; a business where, on guard every moment, the logger had better be ready to run for his life.[3]

Logging is a team effort with one goal: to get the logs to town. To achieve this requires coordination and cooperation. Loggers work in crews to accomplish their tasks. The fallers and buckers cut down the trees and chop them into small enough logs to move. A choker setter fastens cable around the logs so they can be skidded to the landing. One or more "Cats" (bulldozers) move the logs to the landing. A landing chaser unhooks the chokers and trims extra branches. The loader operator then loads the logs on trucks.

Logging is a way of life that has been handed down from father to son. Youths used to enter the woods in their early teens, and even today many young people do not finish high school before beginning work. Training happens on the job, and a good logger must be competent at many skills. In a day he may be called upon to operate heavy equipment, set the choker cables, trim logs, or even repair equipment. A young logger begins at the bottom of the social hierarchy as a choker. Here he must prove himself to be quick and efficient. He may move up to become a landing chaser or, if he applies himself to learning to use equipment, to a

Cat operator or loader. Fallers and buckers have the highest status among occupations.[4]

A skilled logger can use his reputation to advance in his career or locate new work. No certificates prove one's level of skill, only reputation recommends one for future work. The qualities that make a good reputation include hard work, competence in diverse skills, inventiveness, independence, dependability, and common sense.

As a tangible, task-oriented activity, logging produces a culture that places particular value on getting things done. This is central to loggers' work lives, in which the emphasis is on accomplishing tasks under any circumstances. Logging requires considerable initiative and creativity when the work site is isolated far out in the woods. This attitude of getting things done is reflected in leisure activities as well. Hunting and fishing are both practical, goal-oriented forms of leisure that, like logging, use the natural world to meet human needs and wants. In their political activities, timber workers also emphasize activity and results, and are impatient with abstract conversation.

The close bonds among loggers and their dependence on reputation combine to produce a strong sense of personal identity with their occupation. A person's sense of self is tied to being a good worker, being independent, having a good reputation, and being skillful and innovative when the need arises. Mathew Carroll and Robert Lee describe two consequences of this strong occupational identity: "One is to foster what is often a very intense attachment to the occupation; the other is to provide the individual with an identity and its accompanying sense of empowerment."[5]

Loggers and timber communities have also always felt that they are contributing to the welfare of society by providing a necessary raw material. In the Pacific Northwest they can be particularly proud of the value of their products,which derives from the unique quality of timber from the region. Timber workers, then, see themselves as the intermediaries between nature and society, as people whose work makes these magnificent forests useful for society.

Loggers develop a strong affinity and respect for the woods and the natural world they come to know so intimately. They learn to understand trees and their environment in a tangible way—their manner of growth, their unique qualities, their mass and texture. Nature is something they touch every day. It is stubbornly solid and concrete. Nature is also something they actively change through their labor. It is not separate from humans, but something to be shaped and used for survival, a resource to be understood and applied. Its haphazard ways can be enhanced by skillful human intervention. Thus loggers not only save some of the bounty of the woods for human use, but also feel that they improve on nature's own designs by increasing its productivity.

Furthermore, the logger's experience of nature is one of regeneration and renewal. Since childhood they have seen woods progress through a succession from clear-cuts to brush to trees. This process is aided by clearing and planting, which are part of the logger's trade. They see forests in various stages of regrowth all around them.

A logger's sense of nature is highly experiential, and members of this trade generally value direct experience as the basis for knowledge and the standard for truth. Since survival in the woods depends on wits and awareness, these people learn to trust themselves and their senses. Experience is also the way that people develop skills and become competent, capable woodsmen. For these reasons, people learn to trust the knowledge gained from experience over "book learning" and abstraction.

Overall, loggers interpret behavior in terms of self-interest. As one timber worker explained, to gauge the legitimacy of what someone says "you ask him where he's from and what vested interest he has truly in what he's advocating." With regard to the owl set-asides, they clearly perceive their own tangible losses in terms of jobs and income. This is a direct question of their personal interests, since, as they say, they "live—and will probably die—in timber communities." Workers have had to defend their interests vigilantly against threats to their livelihoods on many occasions. For example, in 1986 timber workers ended a bitter month-long strike against Weyerhaeuser which cost them $4 per hour, a 20 percent cut in pay and benefits. The union was forced to settle when Weyerhaeuser threatened to replace striking workers with permanent new hires. With corporate profits up 21 percent for the first half of that year, workers had reason to see their interests as in conflict with management's.

Close community ties within the working class produces a clear division between members and outsiders, which reinforces a sense of interest competition. While members expect others within their peer group to make relating to others more important than accomplishing goals, they learn at a young age that outsiders do not share this value. The common interests which apply within the group are often violated by outsiders who place their interest in profit or their goals (such as protecting owls) over the well-being of their community. Thus working-class members distinguish their behavior toward members of their own group from attitudes and behavior toward outsiders.

The unions that loggers create are expressions of their conditions and cultural experiences, which share important characteristics with other members of the working class. Workers join unions to protect and advance tangible interests in pay and benefits, safety, and treatment on the job against the interests of outsiders. To accomplish these goals, union meetings focus on the practical details of tasks that need to get done. Because the interests of the union and management are in competition during contract negotiations, each side expects to be held strictly accountable by the other. This has benefits but also places limits on workers, since the ability of unions to negotiate contracts derives from their capacity to provide a disciplined workforce. In collective bargaining, the union promises that workers will comply with the rules and demands of management in exchange for guaranteed wages, benefits, and conditions. This requires discipline within the organization, so unions must have defined structures and leaders that command significant respect. These patterns of pragmatism, hierarchy, interest competition, and allegiance are familiar features of working-class life.

ENVIRONMENTALIST CULTURE

Diverse environmental organizations seek to protect the ancient forests of the Pacific Northwest. The Sierra Club Legal Defense Fund has spearheaded legal challenges, while the Sierra Club, Audubon Society, Wilderness Society, and National Wildlife Association have dominated national legislative efforts. Local grassroots organizations have been formed to protect specific stands of forest from cutting, often using direct action tactics, protests, legal challenges, and media campaigns. Numerous other local, state, and national organizations have joined to support old-growth protection. These different organizations pursue a wide variety of strategies and appeal to different kinds of people—from professional lobbyists and researchers to concerned citizens responding to direct mail campaigns to rebels joining the protests by Earth First! and other grassroots organizations.

The Washington Environmental Council (WEC) provides one snapshot of the membership of these organizations. The WEC is the primary voice for the environmental movement on statewide issues in Washington. An umbrella organization of over ninety local environmental groups as well as state and local chapters of national organizations, the WEC has an active lobbying presence in the state capital, participates in state regulatory and oversight processes, and has sponsored several statewide ballot initiatives. The average WEC member is about fifty years old, is equally likely to be male or female, and has been a resident of the state for a little over half of his or her life.[6] WEC members almost always have a college education, and many have a master's or doctoral degree. They mostly work in the professions and in 1992 had an average income of $67,000. Over half of them are lawyers, professors or teachers, scientists or engineers, doctors, or government-employed experts. One out of ten also works for upper management in a large company or owns a business.

Despite the diversity among environmentalists, these people's lives follow some common patterns that distinguish them from the lives of timber workers. Although they grew up in different parts of the country and pursued different careers, they share some common values, ideas, expectations, and assumptions that helped them become successful professionals. They generally have a level of economic security that enables them to make choices about their careers, send their children to college, and travel to natural preserves. In short, they share a common cultural and economic heritage—they are middle-class.

Middle-class culture encourages diverse opinions and motivations. For instance, environmentalists within the WEC have a range of opinions about protecting old-growth timber. Some have very sophisticated analyses of the industry and the need for protection, while others know little about the issue. Some emphasize a sense of responsibility to all species, some want a compromise between saving jobs and protecting forests, while some even believe that the government has done too much to protect the owl already. People come to the WEC with different motivations as well: some to be involved in legislative efforts, some to help people connect spiritually to the earth, some to educate the public about environmental problems, and others to put their personal values into action. Some don't have well-defined reasons for joining the organization at all. As one activist put it, "I'm active in this because I want to be involved in something positive. I do not have any specific ideas I'm trying to push, I'm just here to try to help out, contribute to something I believe in."

This diverse mix of personal motivations is typical of middle-class organizations. Environmentalists differ from their union counterparts in that they have chosen to concern themselves with old-growth timber issues rather than being compelled by personal needs or threats. The vast majority of environmentalists will rarely set foot in an old-growth forest, and may never even see a spotted owl or marbled murrelet. Protection of endangered species is likely to be one of numerous issues they are concerned about, and active involvement with this issue may ebb and flow depending on shifts in personal priorities and interests. As a result, their participation in these organizations is likely to shift over time, and an organization's membership will consist of individuals who have joined for a number of different but overlapping personal purposes.

Environmental organizations are therefore fluid and temporary communities, particularly compared with timber workers, who are likely to know one another for long periods of time both on and off the job. Relationships and friendships for the middle class frequently develop as an outgrowth of pursuing their personal goals. People meet each other through their professional associations, work sites, and organizations often based on shared interests in common topics, concerns, or activities. So relationships too are chosen, just as interests and organizations are. As interests or activities shift, so do relationships. These breaks are particularly decisive as people move from place to place for school and jobs, which is likely to happen several times in a person's adult life. As a result middle-class individuals must create their own communities, and joining an issue organization provides an important way to meet other people who share similar concerns.

Environmentalists therefore continue to act very much as individuals even as they work together in organizations. They are expected to follow their own values, goals, and understandings as they pursue environmental ends. Two brief biographies of environmental activists will illustrate some of the patterns of their middle-class lives.

Jane is an activist who has developed her pursuit of environmental goals into a career. She grew up in Seattle, the daughter of an airline pilot. In college she became active in the campus chapter of the Public Interest Research Group. She traveled to Europe to learn more about her family's heritage. When she returned she trained as an organizer, but didn't continue because she didn't like the philosophy of the organization. At the time growth in Seattle was booming, and she became heavily involved in organizing a city campaign to cap building size as a way to control growth. She then worked as a lobbyist for an environmental organization, but moved on because she felt it compromised her values. Frustrated with what she saw as the ineffectiveness of many organizations, she developed her own consulting firm to help train nonprofits in strategic planning and organizational development. Now she consults with many different environmental and other groups in addition to volunteering for particular causes.

Jane's story has some common features with that of Dave Foreman, one of the most controversial contemporary environmentalists.[7] After college Dave led packing trips into the wilderness and became alarmed at the destruction he saw of the national forests. He returned to graduate school to study biology with the goal of helping to protect the environment, but he dropped out when he saw that biologists mistreated the animals they used as specimens. He went to work for the Wilderness Society and became their chief lobbyist, but he became disillusioned with the ineffectiveness of large national environmental organizations, which he felt were too willing to compromise and too timid about confronting environmental destruction. He and other national environmental staff decided that more dramatic tactics were needed, which led to the founding of Earth First!—for "unapologetic, uncompromising wilderness lovers with a bent for monkey wrenching and direct action."

Middle-class organizations are designed to accommodate individualism, and even encourage it as a fundamental value. They tend to emphasize egalitarian decision making and allow people to express their own ideas and evaluate arguments for themselves. Attention to group process is important for allowing individuals time for self-expression. Since people are expected to follow their own priorities and ideas, individual initiative often determines which programs the organization will pursue. Membership implies no particular responsibilities or duties, and individuals are primarily beholden to their own conscience or sense of responsibility. Meetings tend to be open to anyone who wants to join rather than restricted to members of a particular community like a work site. Middle-class politics is therefore an extension of personal development.

The middle class teaches its children individualism and a focus on personal development to prepare them for professional work. To attain a middle-class job, people need to develop a keen personal interest in some topic such as the natural world. Children are taught to develop their curiosity and affinity for a subject and to discover their talents for mastering it. They learn to be "object oriented," that is, motivated by the achievement of some moral, material, or cultural goal that they adhere to for personal reasons.[8] These interests and goals become the basis of a career, but because career paths may take many decades to develop they are originally valued as part of personal development. Professionals must endure long years in college and graduate school to acquire the necessary skills and credentials to be accepted in high-status occupations such as doctors, lawyers, and academics. They also must internalize a sense of striving to accomplish, so that personal self-worth depends on their ability to perform at work. Many jobs require ongoing learning to keep up with new ideas, and personal development remains an important value for professionals throughout their careers.

Just as with their careers, middle-class activists may be passionate about a cause and have enormous personal investment in its success. Because middle-class members define themselves through their accomplishments and activities, they have a strong stake in the projects they get involved in. The activism of environmentalists identifies who they are, establishes a community to which they belong, and gives focus and purpose to their lives. Through identifying with some larger whole, the natural world, environmentalists find personal meaning. Middle-class movements thus tend to advance broad or even universal goals and values that can inspire a sense of mission.

CULTURES AND INTERESTS

The cultural context helps explain why timber workers have interpreted their interests as they have. Timber workers have a strong cultural basis for drawing social boundaries between insiders and outsiders. Workers share much with their employers in contrast with environmentalists. Employers are known commodities with whom the unions have long experience and ongoing relationships. Employers and employees know what to expect from each other and have a clear idea of each other's motivations. They speak a common language in the industry and have a common set of reference points on the job site. They share a set of production goals and take pride in their product. Thus workers and employers have a broad context in which to build a political alliance.

The labor-management relationship is further reinforced by interdependence. Management has significant power over the lives of employees, from work rules to quality of life on the job to the power to hire and fire. Although these powers are modified in the presence of the union, they remain largely management decisions. But management depends on the quality of its workforce as well as its honesty and integrity on the job. The ability of a company to accomplish its tasks depends on the efforts of the people it hires. Interdependence provides a basis for workers and employers to cooperate politically as well, from a combination of respect and fear of retaliation on the job.

Union and management cooperation derives from the historic ascendance of conservative unions in the past half century. In 1937 the International Woodworkers of America (IWA) was founded as an industrial union within the CIO. The AFL did everything in its power to crush the new union, as did the mill owners. Once established, it was the object of a concerted anticommunist campaign by federal and local government as well as the CIO itself. In 1941 the IWA voted to ban communists after a bitter factional campaign by the national CIO. In the 1950s another major struggle developed over CIO efforts to reorganize the union in a more hierarchical, centralized, and undemocratic way. The result was "control of all levels of the union through appointment by the international office; an organizing program that put dollars ahead of principles; substitution of collective bargaining techniques for class struggle at the point of production; and a shifting of the locus of power from the local level."[9] These characterize the business unionism of the woodworkers today.

Business unionism reflects both cultural changes and interest calculations in the post–World War II political climate. In an earlier period, radical industrial unions fought for a set of interests that they could assert against employers, provided that labor throughout the industry were organized as a class. But the success of government and management in containing the union movement severely limited what workers could attain. Achievable gains were restricted to a context dominated by management. At the same time, union culture was diminished by the purge of radicals from the labor movement. Conservative craft union culture was both reinforced by the dominance of the AFL nationally and imposed by the AFL's and later the CIO's antiradical purges. For both material and cultural reasons, therefore, labor unions began to identify more with the interests of management and the needs of the timber sector as opposed to the interests of the working class.

The collective bargaining process further reinforces both the cultural sense and material reality of common interests. Laborers have the experience of working together with management, even after violent conflicts. At some point in any conflict they are able to sit down and work out their differences "like adult professionals." Furthermore, unions were able to make significant wage and benefit gains through the 1960s and 1970s through collective bargaining. Union workers still generally command higher wages than nonunion workers, so they have reason to identify their interests with the gains attainable through collective bargaining.

Labor's relationships with management contrast with its contacts with environmentalists, who are foreigners from "back East" or from the suburbs. They work through anonymous, distant institutions of power and are rarely directly seen despite their impacts on timber workers' lives. The only environmentalists that local communities encounter are the hikers and tourists that tramp through, and the more militant antilogging groups engaged in direct action protests in the woods. Every now and then environmentalists set up meetings with community leaders, perhaps create a committee, and then go home. Their motives are far less clear, and there is no ongoing relationship upon which to build an understanding between environmentalists and timber workers.

Environmentalists bring a view of nature that is alien to that of wood-workers. They see nature as something to preserve in its present form, as sacred and beneficial in its pristine state. Timber workers, on the contrary, believe that they can improve the work of nature through their labor. They see change and destruction as part of the natural process that goes on with or without humans. Since no one can stop that process, they see the environmentalists' efforts to protect nature as unrealistic.

Furthermore, timber workers have long ago come to think in terms of sustainable-yield forestry. Sustainability has been the stated goal of the Forest Service since its founding, and segments of private industry have been talking about sustainability almost as long. Loggers have seen (and seeing is believing) crop rotations on timberlands their whole lives. Thus they have come to expect that their logging practices already accomplish the goal set forth by environmentalists. But sustainability means different things to each group, and this difference contributes to labor's distrust of the actual purposes sought by environmentalists. They are cynical about the real goals of environmentalists because their stated goals do not seem to justify their actions.

Given their pride in their work and their sense of social identity, timber workers balk at being characterized as destroyers of nature. Such a view runs directly counter to their own perception as improvers of nature and contributors to social welfare. The popular perception of loggers has changed dramatically, and this rapid transformation has been very difficult for timber workers to accept. Today, "people who cut trees are seen as fat, beer-drinking tree murderers, rapists of the land, and so on. So first the workers [were doing what was] the right thing to do, producing commodities that people are seen as having a demand for, and then they are blamed and rejected for having done that. And there is very little extension of sympathy for any suffering that results from that sudden moral exclusion."[10] To accept the new characterization would require demeaning the purpose around which people and communities have organized their lives.

Economic change does not just mean changing jobs for loggers; it entails interrupting their life cycle and life expectations with only uncertainty as a replacement. As a specialist in occupational trauma puts it, "It's not just a job. . . . It's the loss of an entire way of life. It takes a whole different level of 'recovery,' if you will. It's a complete dislocation—a major assault on your world view."[11] Although the timber industry suggests that the way of life that workers have become accustomed to can be retained, environmentalists say that change is not only inevitable but desirable. Even the most generous programs of job retraining and adjustment assistance do not begin to address the loss of investment in logging equipment, experience, or reputation. They do not replace the status and social positions attained through the ordered process of advancement in timber communities. Economic adjustment programs tagged onto environmental bills do not address the broad range of social costs incurred by altering the economic base of community life.

Furthermore, environmentalists propose a very different standard of knowledge than the direct experience trusted by timber workers. They claim that direct experience of the woods is deceptive, and that people need to rely instead on scientific studies. These are performed by distant people in universities or government agencies who have no particular care about the lives of people in the affected communities. Timber workers, especially the more educated, do quote scientific studies at times to support a point, but these are secondary to claims based on experience in the woods as loggers, hunters, or members of a timber community who grew up in the woods.

Environmentalists also propose a different set of criteria for action, which are moral as opposed to economic. Workers and communities claim that their community's needs and interests should take precedence. In a broader sense, they argue for the primacy of human well-being as determined by economics. Against this, environmentalists make a moral claim which underlies their scientific arguments: protecting ancient forests or a species like the spotted owl is a moral imperative. Secondarily, they make an economic argument about the long-term value of old-growth forests in providing as yet undiscovered benefits to society, such as the recent discovery that Taxol from yew trees is useful in fighting ovarian cancer. But even if there were no such possible benefits, the moral arguments sufficiently motivate the environmental movement.

Unionists do recognize that environmentalists seem to be acting on some set of principles other than self-interest. Since environmentalists do not live in timber communities, they do not seem to be personally impacted by the outcome of the timber conflicts. Timber workers attempt to attribute interests to the environmentalists, such as trying to protect land in the West after destroying the land in the East. But more than that, environmentalists seem incomprehensible and fanatical. So workers perceive them as religious, by which they mean impractical, unreasonable or unwilling to negotiate, not interest focused—qualities that are quite the opposite of what timber workers value in themselves. What is clear is that environmentalists do not follow the same principles and standards as loggers.

Environmentalists also work through different political processes than those that timber workers are accustomed to. In the collective bargaining process, conflicts are brought directly to the source without any intervening institutions. Only if direct negotiations or confrontations fail is a mediator or arbitrator possibly called in. Workers and local unions do not trust efforts to settle issues in the distant forum of Congress or the anonymous courts. They see environmentalists as underhanded because they do not participate in face-to-face negotiations with those who will be affected most directly.

Because middle-class movements consist of individuals pursuing their own ideals and values, these organizations are not accountable in the same way that unions are. The environmental and peace movements consist of many organizations without any movementwide structure, and so negotiations with any one organization can be undermined by the actions of other groups in the movement. By contrast, unions are accustomed to working through negotiated contracts to which they expect to be held strictly accountable. They expect to be able to do the same with other groups they negotiate with, and organizations that cannot ensure that their members will follow do not seem credible. Furthermore, labor unions tend to have clearer lines of accountability to membership, and usually they must return to their members and councils for approval before taking positions. Middle-class activists, however, often speak for themselves, and their organizations do not have well-defined constituencies, or have memberships that contribute money but remain otherwise aloof from the activities of the organization. Unions and environmentalists are therefore likely to bring divergent expectations to their discussions.

Working-class timber workers and middle-class environmentalists interpret their interests as conflicting because of cultural barriers reinforced by divisive conditions. Loggers and environmentalists come from alien realities, and each side misinterprets the other through its own cultural framework. Timber cutting means much more for logging communities than environmentalists recognize, both psychologically and economically. And protecting species and ecosystems means far more for environmentalists than timber workers perceive—psychologically and in terms of personal interests. These different meanings follow class patterns.

Working- and middle-class lives are regulated and disciplined differently. The working class inhabits a world of necessities imposed by outside powers and authorities. Laborers must conform to work rules and the pace of production. Unions confront this external power by organizing workers' ability to deprive management of their labor. The issue of old growth follows the same pattern of a conflict of interests against the imposition of changes on timber communities and employment. While the working class is regulated by externally imposed rewards and punishments, the middle class internalizes the rules that regulate their lives. Personal goals and ambitions to succeed are developed early and pursued without supervision. In the workplace, outcomes are rewarded rather than tasks being monitored. People choose to work for causes that provide a sense of identity, purpose, and value. For middle-class individuals, protecting old-growth timber is a continuation of their internally motivated actions.

Timber workers and environmentalists also define their identities and social relationships in different, class-specific ways. For the working class, being a member of a timber community with a good reputation defines who one is. Identity comes from being accepted and known, so that stable friendships and work relationships are important. These relations with family members, peers in school and work, and neighbors tend to be inherited in working-class communities. By contrast the middle class defines itself by its activities and accomplishments. Most important, professionals choose their careers, but working for a cause can also be an important source of identity. Nuclear families are mobile to allow people to pursue their careers and interests, so friends and colleagues are chosen often for shared activities and goals.

Because of these class-based cultural differences, working- and middle-class movements have difficulty perceiving their common interests and working together. The middle class is prone to seeing the working class as rigid, self-interested, narrow, uninformed, parochial, and conflict oriented. The working class tends to perceive the middle class as moralistic, intellectual, more talk than action, lacking commonsense, and naive about power. Each side has a different standard for evaluating information, with the working class trusting experience and the middle class believing in research and systematic study. The result is a wide gulf in understandings of nature, sustainability, economics, and human conduct. Worse yet, working-class unions and middle-class environmentalists seek change differently. The working class seeks to build power to confront external threats, while the middle class hopes to change people's motivations, ideas, and morality. When each side feels its options are limited, as in the case of old growth, there is fertile ground for conflict.

▲

PART III

Historical Context

Strategic choices, the focus of Part II, are placed in historic context in this part of the book. People make choices under inherited conditions, and opportunities for coalitions vary over time. While individuals occasionally make heroic choices to venture in new directions, most people reconsider their interests and alliances only during times of significant change and transition. Furthermore, the legacy of cooperation or conflict between organizations and groups tends to inform people's decisions. New alliances must overcome historic inertia.

The following two chapters shift from the old-growth timber conflict to the broader history of relationships between the peace, environmental, and labor movements. Peace and environmental issues differ in many ways, and these movements have different origins and histories. But the class-cultural dynamics are similar, and the differences between the peace and labor movements parallel those between labor and environmentalists.

▲

History Hangs in the Balance:
Peace and Labor Relations

History depends on the balance of strategic alliances. President Wilson understood this as he moved the country toward joining World War I. The war effort would need a reliable supply of materials, which in turn would require a cooperative workforce. But the labor movement was opposed to the war at the outset, particularly labor radicals such as the IWW. But President Wilson and the American Federation of Labor leadership under Samuel Gompers made a historic alliance. Wilson accepted the AFL as labor's official representative and appointed Gompers as his labor advisor on the Council on National Defense. The government recognized the right of labor to organize and bargain collectively for the first time in exchange for a no-strike clause and dispute settlement by the government's War Labor Board.

Debate over entry into the war dramatized two competing strategies for advancing labor's interests, marked by competing interpretations of the issues. One strategy was for the working class to join in an international peace movement against capitalists and their government allies. Socialist leader Eugene Debs argued, "The workers have no country to fight for. It belongs to the capitalists and plutocrats. Let them worry over its defense, and when they declare wars as they and they alone do, let them also go out and slaughter one another on the battlefields." The alternative strategy of the AFL was to ally with the national government and arms industry against similar nationalist alliances of the enemy Central Powers in Europe. Here the issue was framed in terms of patriotism in the war effort and national expansion rather than the international working class.

Throughout history the choice of strategy—whether solidarity with one's own class, alliance with those in power, or alliance with other classes—has shaped the course of events. An alliance with a powerful group can clearly be of benefit; it can be used to win advantages such as union recognition when labor's cooperation is needed. Similarly, such an alliance can be beneficial when timber companies need allies to further their access to profitable national forests. Has history shown that movements for change succeed better when they have been able to seize the moment, form an alliance with a powerful group, and gain some benefit? Or is there a real alternative to such collaboration, one of class solidarity and alliance with a broad peace or environmental movement, as represented by the Socialists and the Industrial Workers of the World? What can be learned from the history of interclass relations about the consequences of choosing either strategy?

Labor and Peace as Allies: The Legacy of Class Solidarity

Pacifism and opposition to war have a long history in the labor movement, particularly among class-conscious unions. Most of labor opposed American military adventures during the Spanish-American War, and even the American Federation of Labor stated in 1887, "The demands of the working people will never be fully heard in all their strength and nobility of aspiration until the nations of the world mutually agree to refrain from the fratricidal strife that has so often brought misery and dislocation into many millions of happy homes. The working class, the class that always has to bear the brunt of war, has the most profound interest in the establishment and maintenance of peace."[1] When World War I began, unions strongly opposed American participation, as did the nation as a whole. AFL president Samuel Gompers was a strong peace advocate until 1914 when he became an outspoken advocate of the war effort.[2] When the Congress for Industrial Organizations (CIO) was formed in the 1930s, it followed a progressive foreign policy, opposing fascism in Spain, Japan, and Germany; supporting Mexican expropriation of American oil companies; favoring relations with the USSR; and supporting international independence movements. Organized labor in general opposed participation in the Second World War in Europe in its early years until several events convinced labor to join the war effort including the growing preparation for war, Roosevelt's inclusion of labor leaders in war planning, improved labor standards to prepare for the war, and Hitler's attack on the Soviet Union.

The labor movement as a whole opposed conscription after World War II. Labor opinions at the time echoed themes that the peace movement would repeat for the next forty years. For example, a statement from the CIO opposing conscription said, "Money which should go into homes, clothing and food would continue to go into tanks and planes and guns. Taxes to maintain unproductive armaments programs would go up. Simultaneously, living standards would decline. Tensions would increase. Reaction would set in. Our democratic institutions would receive severe shocks from the unbalance of our economy."[3] Both within the AFL and the CIO, the draft was seen as a tool to be used against labor. As the United Auto Workers argued, "We are convinced, from the records of Congressional sponsors of this proposed legislation, and of many of its public sponsors, that one of its unstated purposes is to regiment our youth on a mass basis for use as a military strike-breaking, union-busting force."[4]

Peace movement support for labor also has a strong history. For instance, a significant labor-peace alliance emerged in the most effective organization of the interwar period, the National Council for Prevention of War (NCPW). Founded in 1921, its goal was to substitute international law for war as a means for resolving conflict. The NCPW established a labor department that emphasized the relationships between peace and the interests of working people. A statement prior to World War II titled "Labor's Stake in Peace" explained the organization's understanding:

> In time of war labor has everything to lose and nothing to gain, not only in loss of life and limb but in money. Who is it that pays the bill in the end if not labor? . . . War upsets the rational evolution of our economic life because it diverts the attention and study by the workers from their social welfare problems. And that is why dictators in power today are going out of their way to keep the spirit of conquest alive and holding that up to their people as the noblest and loftiest thing in life. They have failed to meet the economic needs of their people and in order that they might continue to rule, resort to war and to the primitive in man.[5]

Support for the labor movement continued from the older peace organizations that survived the world wars. A. J. Muste exemplified this tradition until his retirement as the executive director of the Fellowship for Reconciliation in 1953. Muste led strikes in the textile mills of Massachusetts and directed the Brookwood Labor College in the 1920s. A devout pacifist, he provided a link between the labor and peace movements.

The AFL's alliance with government and military industry began intermittently with the Spanish-American War and continued during World War I and II, but it became the governing regime only when the country moved to a permanent war footing during the Cold War.[6] This war regime had economic, military, and ideological dimensions. Economically it tied prosperity to the expansion of national markets and access to resources overseas. This linkage was imposed by a combination of military and political strategies that protected long- and short-term economic interests, and was rationalized by a virulent procapitalist, anticommunist ideology that justified suppressing political opposition in the name of national security.

Beginning with the Spanish-American War, the AFL used support for American foreign policy to gain government recognition and economic benefits. This pattern, pursued by Gompers in World War I, was repeated during World War II. Sidney Hillman from the Amalgamated Clothing Workers became labor's representative to the National Defense Advisory Commission and headed the Labor Advisory Committee that oversaw wartime labor policy. That commission established union standards for defense contracts and created labor-management committees in plants during the war. In exchange for no-strike pledges and limited demands, labor negotiated union shops in the defense sector.

The demobilization after World War II raised new fears of unemployment and another depression. The transition was cushioned by the GI Bill to assist individual soldiers, by macroeconomic policies, and by the withdrawal of millions of women, youths, and older workers out of the workforce. Strong civilian and business demand and the position of the United States as the major remaining industrial power eased the transition as well. However, some sectors of the economy declined dramatically after the war. Within a couple of years aircraft sales shrank to under 10 percent of the wartime level, and employment in that industry dropped to 25 percent.

The political economic system constructed by the United States after World War II linked economic prosperity with the Cold War. Europe's economy lay in ruins, and the Soviet Union threatened to remove other countries from capitalist development. Furthermore, communist parties had strong popular support in many countries because they led the resistance to fascism and because the Soviet Union played a key role in winning the war. The Cold War justified anticommunist campaigns in Europe and containment of Soviet influence through global military alliances and a massive arms race. In 1949 the brief war demobilization was reversed, and military spending began its upward trajectory that characterized the Cold War era. The military budget grew from $18.7 billion in 1948 to $63 billion five years later.[7] These levels grew almost without interruption in the 1949–89 period, with a dip following the Korean War and a minor decrease after the Vietnam War. Military spending consumed 50–70 percent of federal outlays between 1950 and 1990.[8]

Organized labor continued to identify its interests with economic expansion tied to American military power. World War II convinced a generation of laborers, businessmen, and policymakers that war is good for the economy. Labor prospered during the war, and subsequently often favored belligerent foreign policies throughout the Cold War as a source of jobs. This attitude was captured in the *Wall Street Journal* in 1970: "Full employment, with the unemployment rate under 4%, for this country at least has been a phenomenon of war periods. We had it in World War II. We had it with the Korean War. And we had it with the Vietnam conflict prior to the recent throttling down of defense expenditure. But these are the only times we have had it."[9]

The AFL and government used the antiwar position of radical labor during both world wars as a weapon in their drive to defeat militant challengers and integrate the labor movement into mainstream society. During World War I, socialists were suppressed in the AFL, solidifying Gompers's own position. The Espionage Act of 1917 made it a crime to criticize the armed forces or interfere with recruitment of troops. And the Sedition Act of 1918 made criticism of the government during war a crime as well. Syndicalism was outlawed in many states. The Industrial Workers of the World and the Socialist Party were the main targets of raids, deportations, and legal persecution because of their opposition to the war. Eugene Debs and thousands of others were publicly tried and jailed, essentially destroying the IWW. Antiwar newspapers were banned as well, with Wilson's approval.

This same pattern of using patriotism to suppress class-conscious unions was repeated after World War II. The AFL joined the anticommunist witch-hunts of the Dies Committee and later supported the House Un-American Activities Committee. When Congressman Dies singled out the CIO for investigation, the AFL joined the hysteria against the "rising communist conspiracy." President Truman lent his administration's support to bring the CIO into the Cold War anticommunist consensus. Between 1947 and 1950 communists and radicals were purged from the CIO with the support of the federal government, the AFL, conservative forces in the CIO, and right-wing organizations. In 1949 the

CIO banned communists from national office in its unions and changed its constitution to allow a two-thirds majority of the executive board to expel unions for communist activities. The CIO conventions in 1949 and 1950 expelled eleven unions with a million members for their refusal to adopt anticommunist policies. By the end of the 1940s, the CIO's foreign policies were in concert with the AFL's Cold War anticommunism, and the AFL and CIO were reunited in 1955.

Without union membership, the peace movement became increasingly middle-class after World War II. This tendency was always present in the peace movement. For example, a staff member of the Fellowship of Reconciliation (FOR) wrote in 1945: "It has become almost trite to point out that the FOR remains entirely too white and white collar. . . . The preponderance of upper middle-class persons . . . in our leadership and general membership make me seriously question whether the FOR as now constituted can ever accomplish a wholesale scaling of the racial and especially class walls which now enclose it."[10] The new generation of peace organizations formed after World War II, however, had even fewer affiliations with the labor movement and less understanding of working-class issues. The Committee for a Sane Nuclear Policy exemplified this pattern. In 1957 Norman Cousins, editor of the *Saturday Review*, and Clarence Pickett, executive secretary emeritus of the American Friends Service Committee, founded Sane to "lead mankind away from nuclear war and toward peace and justice."[11] Severed from the working class, this peace movement no longer spoke of international solidarity, nor of building power, but of a middle-class approach to social change through public education and persuasion. One observer summarized Sane's political philosophy in this way: "Sane was founded on the basic liberal premise that mistaken U.S. policies could be remedied and set right; and that in order to do so, the imperatives are effective communication, dialogue, public education and direct political action. Given certain facts on an issue, Sane liberals believed the government had the intelligence, courage, and willingness to change."[12]

Anticommunism was also used by the government to contain the peace movement and other progressive activities. For example, Sane's growth was stymied by anticommunist attacks, and the leadership's handling of this issue tarnished the organization's prestige and led many peace activists to abandon its ranks. Norman Cousins had always feared communist infiltration of the organization, and he approached the FBI in 1958 for help in identifying subversives in Sane. Senator Thomas Dodd called on Sane to purge its ranks of communists, despite the respectability of its leaders. Dodd's committee subpoenaed Henry

Abrams, cochair of Westside New York Sane, to question him about his communist affiliations. When Abrams refused to tell Sane that he was not a communist, the organization asked him to resign. Many in Sane were appalled that the organization would succumb to Cold War pressures, and several board members and organizational sponsors resigned, including A. J. Muste, Linus Pauling, and Bertrand Russell. Sane did condemn the House Un-American Activities Committee in a statement in 1966 calling for its abolition, but this debate consumed enormous resources in the organization.

This middle-class peace movement was no longer hospitable to even antiwar members of the working class. For instance, during the Vietnam War, opinion polls consistently found the working class to be more critical of the war than other classes.[13] In 1968, 43 percent of rank-and-file union members felt the Vietnam War was wrong, and in 1970 blue-collar workers supported an end to the war in higher proportions than white-collar workers and above the national average. Nevertheless, working-class members generally rejected the peace movement, and polls at the time show that the white working class resented both the war and the protesters.[14] As a result, the membership in the peace movement as well as in the mainstream environmental movement is at present disproportionately middle-class, and especially professional middle-class.[15]

Confrontations between antiwar protesters and labor opposition during the Vietnam period convinced many in the peace movement that labor represented the establishment and was not an ally in the cause of peace. During the 1965 AFL-CIO convention, protesters' calls for debate about the war were met with Meany's retort to "clear these kookies out of the gallery."[16] In 1967 Thomas Gleason, president of the International Longshoremen's Association, led a prowar march in New York of thousands of union members. In May 1970 construction workers in New York City attacked antiwar protesters. It was later revealed that these actions were supported by employers who paid workers to take part in the violence. When between one and two hundred thousand (some say as few as sixty thousand) construction workers and others held a prowar rally on May 20, 1970, President Nixon called the president of the New York Building Trades Council, Peter Brennan, to thank him personally for the support. Nixon invited Brennan and Gleason to the White House to express his thanks and pose for pictures. These events were widely covered in the national press and created an indelible impression of the labor movement's support for the war.

Throughout the Cold War, local peace activists confronted workers in defense plants and weapons facilities through nonviolent protest. These groups engaged in direct action to draw attention to the production of weapons that they considered immoral and illegal according to international law. A dramatic early action that exemplified the spirit of these groups was the effort by four Quakers to sail a ship, the Golden Rule, into a nuclear testing zone in 1958. During the Vietnam War direct action groups destroyed draft files. Since then they have participated in such acts as throwing blood on models of weapons at the Pentagon, damaging nuclear weapons at production sites, and blocking train deliveries of weapons components. In many communities, these nonviolent protesters established ongoing vigils at weapons plants and sought to speak to workers about their participation in the preparation for war. Some went as far as calling on workers to leave their jobs for reasons of moral conscience. These kinds of activities reinforced the divisions between the peace and labor movements at the local level.

THE COSTS OF COLLABORATION

Labor's collaboration with government and industry proved to be only of short-term benefit. After World War I, government repression against radical labor continued and extended to the AFL as well. Federal troops crushed the Seattle general strike in 1919 as well as the first national steel strike. State militia had long been used to suppress worker revolts, but such actions came under federal control with the formation of the National Guard in 1916. AFL strike efforts in many sectors were blocked by management with the help of the courts and government forces.

During World War II the federal government's support for organized labor lasted only as long as labor peace was needed also. After the war the federal government once again enacted repressive legislation that rescinded many of the gains made by labor during the New Deal and the war. The Taft-Hartley Act of 1947 allowed employers to wage antiunion campaigns, forbade secondary strikes called to support other workers, outlawed sit-down strikes and permitted state right-to-work laws. Furthermore, it banned certification of unions if their leaders refused to sign an anticommunist oath.

Anticommunism proved to be an effective weapon against the growth of organized labor and the CIO. With the purge of radical members, the CIO stopped its Southern organizing drive and devoted its resources to raiding members from expelled unions. National unions in the CIO asserted greater bureaucratic control over locals in the name of protecting unions against communism, and membership participation declined. The federal government perceived blacks and Puerto Ricans as security risks and further harassed them in the CIO.

As allies in the Cold War, the AFL and CIO worked with the U.S. government and CIA to undermine independent labor and political movements throughout the world. Early on during the Cold War, the U.S. government used the AFL to combat militant and communist unions in Europe. Particularly in France, Italy, Greece, and Germany, the AFL cooperated with the CIA to undermine communist unions and build "free" labor organizations modeled after the AFL.[17] The AFL funneled money to noncommunist opposition labor groups, circulated propaganda, and worked with the American government to consolidate its influence in Western Europe. Some of these funds for conservative labor organizations came directly from U.S. corporations operating in Europe by way of the AFL. The result was a weaker, more divided European labor movement.

As agents of the government during the Cold War, the AFL-CIO undermined unions and democratic governments in Latin America, Asia, and Africa. It intervened in union politics, participated in strikebreaking, and assisted with assassinations of radical labor leaders. Beginning in 1954 it cooperated with CIA covert operations to overthrow democratically elected and legitimate governments in Guatemala, British Guiana, the Dominican Republic, and Brazil. Many of the military governments that came to power repressed labor unions, eliminated land reform, and imprisoned or killed thousands of people. In Latin America many of these activities were carried out through the AFL-CIO's American Institute for Free Labor Development (AIFLD), which was formed in 1962 by the Kennedy administration after the Bay of Pigs disaster to counter the development of radical labor organizing in Latin America. Major corporations such as ITT, Exxon, Shell, Kennecott, Anaconda, IBM, and others doing business in Central and South America contributed to the effort. These campaigns were extended to Africa in 1964 and Asia in 1968, including efforts to build pro-Western unions in Vietnam. Corporations sat on the board of AIFLD until 1981, when it finally became solely union run. The bulk of AIFLD's foreign activities, as with all of the AFL-CIO's foreign policy adventures, have been supported by the federal government—as much as 98 percent federally funded in 1985.[18] Under Reagan AIFLD continued to serve government foreign policy against the Sandanistas in Nicaragua, in El Salvador, and in Grenada. Over eleven million dollars were channeled to AIFLD and the AFL-CIO's parallel "free labor" operations in Africa and Asia in 1984–85.

The U.S. government also used unions to weaken the peace movement and counter opposition to its military policies. AFL-CIO president George Meany vocally favored escalating the Vietnam war and made clear that no opposition within the ranks of labor would be tolerated. Throughout the war, the national organization condemned the antiwar movement and suppressed criticism within unions. The AFL-CIO supported deployment of MX missiles and legislation that would use defense spending as a jobs program.[19] Although public opinion favored a mutually verifiable freeze on the production, testing, and deployment of nuclear weapons by a margin of two to one in 1982, the AFL-CIO's executive council rejected a freeze resolution. Instead it endorsed the Reagan administration's alternative START proposal.

REVIVING COMMON GROUND: THE COALITION IN OPPOSITION

The peace movement confronted the difficult task of countering the economic, military, and ideological framework of the Cold War, and disillusioned and progressive segments of the labor movement increasingly joined in. The seeds of a broader labor and peace coalition developed through this growing opposition to the war regime. Ultimately, changed economic conditions and the end of the Cold War created the opportunity for a revived peace and labor coalition.

It was the Vietnam War that raised serious opposition to the militarism of the Cold War in the ranks of labor, as it did in the country as a whole. As early as 1962, Labor Action for Peace formed in New York "to rally working men and women to combine their economic and social aims with the aims and requirements of peace."[20] However it was United Auto Workers (UAW) leaders Walter and Victor Reuther in 1966 who charged the AFL-CIO with collaborating with the CIA on covert operations and then attacked the executive board's prowar statement as "intemperate, hysterical, jingoistic and unworthy of labor." While the Reuthers were anticommunist, they favored strong social programs against poverty to dissuade radicals, rather than CIA-style campaigns of destabilization. In 1969 the UAW withdrew from the AFL-CIO and sought to create a new liberal-labor alliance with the civil rights, peace, and other movements within the Democratic Party. To this end, the United Auto Workers contributed significant sums to the Students for a Democratic Society and the Student Non-violent Coordinating Committee.

Reuther's split with the AFL-CIO's Vietnam policy encouraged the growing union opposition to the war. A trade union division of Sane was formed first in New York and then in other cities. In 1967 a meeting in Chicago of the National Labor Leadership Assembly for Peace drew labor leaders from fifty international unions in thirty-eight states and proclaimed its opposition to official AFL-CIO policy. Antiwar labor activists were increasingly prominent in major protests organized by the peace movement as well. The invasion of Cambodia in April 1970 and the murder of students at Kent State spurred greater grassroots cooperation between unions and the student antiwar movement. The Labor-Student Coalition for Peace, the first such effort in the country, organized for a joint day of protest in New York in May 1970. The largest antiwar labor gathering was held on June 23–25, 1972, when a thousand people assembled from thirty-five international unions representing about one-fifth of organized labor.

After the 1968 national election, a significant segment of the New Left recognized that students alone could not end the war, and many began to look to labor as a necessary ally in the struggle. Student activists on many campuses turned their energies to supporting labor struggles as extensions of their own ongoing battles on campus. For example, in 1969 radical students in the San Francisco area and elsewhere helped the Oil, Chemical and Atomic Workers win a strike against Standard Oil, and in return the workers supported a strike by the students and faculty at San Francisco State. In 1969–70 chapters of Students for a Democratic Society across the country helped electrical workers win their first negotiated agreement in twenty years with General Electric in a national strike.

The AFL-CIO hierarchy and the growing peace forces within labor divided again during the 1972 presidential bid of George McGovern. Although the AFL-CIO had opposed Nixon prior to the election and despite McGovern's strong prolabor record, the executive council decided to remain neutral during the campaign because of McGovern's position against the war. In opposition to this official policy, the National Labor Committee to Elect McGovern-Shriver united thirty-one international unions, most of them representing those in Labor for Peace. Election polls show that half of union families voted for McGovern while 48 percent supported Nixon.

After the Vietnam War, peace forces in labor continued to press for a change in AFL-CIO policy. When the national leadership endorsed the Reagan administration's policies in Central America, hundreds of unions issued statements in opposition. In 1983 the National Labor Committee in Support of Democracy and Human Rights in El Salvador forced the national convention to support restrictions on military aid until human rights abuses stopped. At the 1985 AFL-CIO convention, critics of U.S. policy in Nicaragua forced "the first floor debate on foreign policy in the history of the AFL-CIO."[21] More and more national unions distanced themselves from Reagan's militaristic policies as the 1980s progressed. Reagan's program to shift funding from social services to military priorities produced an outcry from labor, particularly unions in the service sector. Eight national unions also endorsed the national Jobs with Peace campaign. In 1983 an AFL-CIO survey of state and local leaders found that 60 percent would not support higher military spending and 80 percent believed the federal government spent too much on the military.

With the rise of the national Nuclear Weapons Freeze Campaign, a labor outreach coordinator was hired to educate local Freeze groups about labor's concerns and to organize labor support for the freezing of nuclear weapons development. The Freeze sought to appeal to labor in part through economic arguments, claiming that a freeze would save over $200 billion over the next decade, which could be transferred to economic and social needs. By 1984 there were twenty national labor organizations that had endorsed the proposal for a bilateral freeze. In 1984 unions and the peace and environmental movements joined forces in an unsuccessful effort to defeat Reagan. Reagan's reelection marked the end of the Freeze in national politics, and his administration continued one of the most ideologically antilabor, militaristic, and anti-environmental administrations since the Cold War began.

During the Gulf War in 1991, a visible minority in the labor movement spoke against war even before the actual fighting. The AFL-CIO's executive council in California passed a resolution opposing the Bush administration's plans for war in favor of economic sanctions. In February 1991, over two hundred local and regional union officials wrote in a *New York Times* advertisement, "It was a grave error to commit our nation to war." They demanded that the bombing of Iraq stop.

UNRAVELING THE WAR ECONOMY

Peace and labor activists developed a critique of military-led economic expansion as they opposed the extremes of Cold War militarism. Rather than accept that economic prosperity depends upon military spending, advocates promoted conversion to civilian employment and production. They recognized that workers and communities were hostage to the military economy in the absence of policies that provided alternatives.

Within the labor movement, Walter Reuther was an early supporter of the conversion of defense industries. After World War II the UAW supported reconversion to civilian production to forestall economic stagnation and meet urgent national needs for transportation and housing. In 1969 Reuther offered a conversion plan for the end of the Vietnam conflict that would invest part of every defense contractor's profits in civilian production. Reuther explicitly denied the stereotype that defense workers favor militarism. He said, "To say that millions of Americans want work and steady income is not to say they want perpetual war. . . . What they really want is peace and full employment."[22] Yet, he argued, defense workers live with the insecurity that stems from the lack of alternatives to defense employment.

Sane has played a leading role among peace organizations promoting conversion over three decades. In 1964 Sane issued its first policy statement on conversion calling for a reduction in military spending to be reinvested in consumer industry, health care, education, scientific research, and housing. The organization argued that "if military spending is reduced, advance planning will be required to ease the economic transition and provide adequate employment."[23]

The end of hostilities in Vietnam had significant economic consequences, but without any advanced planning for conversion. The Johnson administration anticipated a peace dividend that never materialized, and unemployment rose from 3.5 percent in 1968 to 5.9 percent in 1971. Altogether 1.3 million military industrial jobs were lost in sectors such as aircraft, tank production, and ordnance.[24] Demands for economic conversion from both the peace and labor communities gained new momentum with the economic stagnation of the 1970s. When President Carter continued to increase the military budget, a coalition of labor, peace, and justice organizations joined in calling for new budget priorities to meet human needs. In 1977 the Industrial Union Department of the AFL-CIO unanimously adopted a resolution stating that "the military budget is growing even faster than the rate of inflation—and the human needs of the American people, particularly the residents of the cities, will not receive the needed share of national resources until there is a reorganization of budget priorities."[25] George Poulin, vice president of the International Association of Machinists (IAM), stated at a press conference, "We can cut back armaments without damaging our defense posture. The savings could go toward creating jobs in the domestic sector so that our members aren't out of work."[26]

Sane established a labor conversion project beginning in 1977 to counter union support for military spending as a jobs program. Their premise was that "no progress toward reducing defense dependency is possible without addressing the job security needs of military workers."[27] IAM president William Winpisinger joined Sane's board because, as he said, "I'm tired of going arm in arm with the enemy to beg for jobs. ... The Pentagon opposes conversion because it fears the loss of labor support for new weapons."[28] Sane went on to recruit other unions to the conversion program, establish a labor working group on legislation, and provide workshops and publications to educate peace activists about working with labor. The national Sane organization also promoted the formation of local labor-peace alliances to initiate alternative use planning around defense facilities.

In 1977–79 several national peace and labor organizations cooperated to promote conversion legislation. The UAW, the International Association of Machinists, the United Electrical Workers, and the Oil, Chemical and Atomic Workers Union worked with Sane to develop Reuther's 1969 conversion proposal into legislation. McGovern revised his earlier bill into the Defense Economic Adjustment Act, which he and Senator Charles Mathias introduced into the Senate, and Representative Ted Weiss introduced into the House. Labor, peace, and church groups all cooperated in this campaign. Conversion amendments sponsored by Congressmen Dodd and McKinny passed both houses of Congress in 1979 attached to public works legislation, but died in conference committee.

From 1981 to 1986 conversion legislation was not seriously considered in Congress as the massive Reagan military buildup more than doubled the defense budget authority. Conversion advocates focused their attention on opposing Reagan's economic policies and the massive transfer of federal spending from social to military programs. In 1981 Sane joined with sixty national organizations including the Steelworkers and National Education Association to form the Budget Action Campaign. Its goals included maintenance of public services, more equitable taxes, and lower levels of military spending. Efforts to build coalitions around new budget priorities continued throughout the decade and beyond.

Opportunities for a New Peace and Labor Alliance

The postwar period created the social and economic conditions for the division between labor and the peace and environmental movements. World War II had brought the United States to a new level of global economic and political power. Driven by the specter of depression on one side and socialist, labor, and communist challenges to capitalism in Europe and at home on the other, corporate and government interests converged around the Cold War. Within a few short years the wartime alliance with the Soviets reverted to prewar hostilities. Radical movements in Western Europe were contained, and the Left was purged from national institutions, particularly labor. Corporate America made an agreement with the remaining labor movement to share the benefits of growth in exchange for predictability on the job and acceptance of managerial prerogatives.[29] The U.S. economy prospered, spurred in part by military spending and the reconstruction of Europe and Japan.

The labor movement bought twenty-five years of unprecedented prosperity at the cost of its broader social agenda and international solidarity. By allying with business and government, unions undermined their long-term development. A narrow economic agenda made the labor movement politically and organizationally unprepared for the hostile environment of the 1980s. The American labor movement had contributed to weak unions and hostile governments overseas and thus to the ability of corporations to produce more cheaply outside the United States. The national movement had also severely weakened its own ranks through purging radical unions and many of the most energetic activists of a generation. These decisions by the labor movement, combined with a more antilabor and economically less competitive environment, led to the decline of U.S. labor since the 1970s.

Before the consequences of labor's policies became evident, the affluence of the 1960s produced a new wave of middle-class movements. Record numbers of young people attended college, which produced the new phenomenon of the youth culture. From this cohort came the seeds of a New Left, distinctly middle-class in its agenda of personal expression, peace, equality, and protection of nature. These movements explicitly rejected many of the tenets of the older socialist and labor movements including its formal structure, attention to economic goals, and concentration on workplace and electoral organizing. Although some segments of the New Left sought an alliance with labor, their confrontations were far more dramatic and better publicized.

During the second half of the 1980s a political earthquake was in the making as the end of the Cold War transformed the global landscape. The demise of communism in the Soviet Union undermined the ideological rationale for American militarism. But by now the economic world had also changed dramatically from the war-torn days when the Cold War was implemented.

At the dawn of the new political-economic era, labor's old alliance with government and the military was badly frayed. Union critics of official AFL-CIO policy were increasingly vocal and organized. Opposition to the bloated military budget was on the rise. And some segments of the peace and labor movements had reestablished ongoing relationships. The Cold War had no doubt left a legacy of distrust and misunderstanding, but the makeup of political alliances was back in question for the first time in over a generation. Conditions are now ripe for a new realignment of political players. The alliances that prevail in this new political moment will determine the course of history.

▲

The Political Moment: Opportunities for Coalitions

The labor movement skipped a generation and most organizers and leadership are now part of that skipped generation. Some are just getting by, some are careerists, and some are business unionists. They're not fighters, not conscious. The new, young guys are open to different ideas. Labor and socialism used to be inseparable, but they were separated in the 1940s and '50s. Now labor people are more interested in the environment, peace ideas. They came around to that because of societal changes, and also the new generation sees that business unionism isn't working; they're getting destroyed. They see the working class going backwards. They and their kids won't have rental or second houses like their parents. And the peace movement, environmental movement, civil rights movements have been effective.

—A union activist in Washington State, 1991

At the dawn of the new century, the political landscape is in flux and alliances are being renegotiated at the grass roots and among national organizations. What was taken for granted during the predictable years of the Cold War is no longer true. Superpower competition is gone, national economies are fast disappearing, welfare systems are being dismantled, people are working more hours with less job security, unions have lost significant power, communities and families are more unstable, the government's right to protect the environment is under attack, and political parties are losing adherents—in short, loyalties are being redefined. In this transitional time, the opportunities for coalition building between the labor, peace, and environmental movements are greater than they have been in over half a century. This in no way guarantees that a working- and middle-class alliance will prevail, for the countervailing conditions are significant; but recent shifts present significant opportunities.

The economic, military, and ideological realities that defined the Cold War regime are giving way to a new political constellation based on free trade. The old ideology of anticommunism that justified global military intervention to protect markets and access to resources is being replaced with a new ideology honed for the global economy. Superpower alliances are being superseded by a new currency: trade agreements that give legal standing to the power of corporations to move wealth and resources extracted from one country to any other country free from national trade regulations. Enforcement is now more antiseptic than the military coups and destabilization campaigns of the past, imposed by the International Monetary Fund, the World Trade Organization, and global investors that demand fiscal responsibility as the price of credit and investment. So government budgets are cut, social programs are dismantled, economies are opened to global competition, good business climates are enforced—without political debate or bloodshed.

When Congress approved the General Agreement on Tariffs and Trade (GATT) in 1994, it agreed to give away sovereignty over many internal policies to a three-judge panel at the World Trade Organization. As a first glimpse of this future, Mexico and then Europe challenged U.S. restrictions on importing tuna caught by countries that do not protect dolphins. According to GATT, the Marine Mammals Protection Act passed in 1972 is a barrier to free trade. This led to a 1997 congressional compromise that allows for "dolphin-deadly" tuna to be imported, placing the onus on consumers to choose tuna marked dolphin-safe. The agreement also put into place a review process that could undermine dolphin-safe labeling by allowing more questionable fishing techniques to be included under this designation. Similarly, in 1997 Venezuela challenged a regulation negotiated by the Environmental Protection Agency and the oil industry to eliminate toxic contaminants from gasoline as a trade violation. The World Trade Organization ordered the United States to change its standards or pay Venezuela $150 million in damages. Labor, health and safety, and numerous other regulations could similarly be designated as trade violations. The Multilateral Agreement on Investment being negotiated at the end of the 1990s would further cede rights to control the flow of money and production facilities out of the country.

In this free trade regime, the role of U.S. military power in concert with the United Nations and NATO is to ensure stability for the unhampered development of the global economy. The new enemies are countries like Cuba that refuse to integrate into the world trade system, and local dictators like Saddam Hussein and Slobodan Milosivic with national military ambitions that hinder the free flow of the economy. The United States has become the global policeman that still justifies military spending at Cold War levels. But at the same time the United States has also become the biggest global arms merchant, responsible for 70 percent of international arms sales. In the free marketplace where the United States has sustained a trade deficit since the 1970s, weaponry is an important export niche. Through its indiscriminate exports, the United States feeds an arms race with itself, as the Pentagon develops more sophisticated weapons to counter threats from countries acquiring American-made weapons. Thus a sizable arms sector remains part of the new regime.

Globalization of the economy has devastating consequences for workers and the environment. Corporations can now export production and pollution overseas to escape unions and protections—so that North American workers and communities must now compete with poor living standards in every corner of the world. Federal trade policies accelerate these trends by further undermining both worker and environmental protections. This development is not without its ambiguities. Deindustrialization has shifted polluting factories to other countries, leaving cleaner service sector industries in this country. At the local level, exporting pollution may improve the local environment while doing worse damage overseas. Similarly, wealthier countries are specializing in more highly paid work that requires more education, and they are exporting the less desirable, low-wage work to poorer countries. The global economy threatens to exacerbate inequalities while pressuring wealthier countries to meet lower global standards.

THE EMERGING CRISIS

The Reagan administration presided unwittingly over the last gasps of the old regime. Reagan precipitated crises for many when he declared war on the labor, environmental, and peace movements—blaming overzealous environmentalists, overpaid union workers, and the "evil Soviet empire" for many of America's problems. Environmental opponents were placed in charge of government agencies. The arms race accelerated, and politicians talked of winning a nuclear war. AFL-CIO support for U.S. foreign policy no longer translated into political favors for even conservative unions in the 1980s. Reagan's defeat of the air traffic controllers in the Professional Air Traffic Controllers Organization

(PATCO) strike in 1981 heralded the new antiunion political environment.

The Reagan military buildup disrupted the pattern of prosperity that the labor movement experienced during the period of high military spending from 1940 through the Vietnam War years. Union membership did not revive with the buildup of the 1980s. Reagan's staunch antiunion policies extended to the defense sector. New defense procurement contracts went disproportionately to nonunion areas of the country. Increased subcontracting meant that more defense production was carried out overseas. In 1983 the Department of Defense explicitly called for wage concessions from unionized workers. An emphasis on high-tech weapons development and automation meant that growth in the military budget translated into fewer jobs. Reagan's cuts in social spending also hampered union growth in the service sectors, where much of the new union membership has come from in recent decades. Large government deficits and the overvalued dollar made American goods more expensive and contributed to the worsening trade balance, which devastated basic American industries such as steel, automobiles, and rubber.

Then in 1986 the feeding frenzy caused by Reagan's lavish military spending came to a close. The Cold War had bankrupted the Soviet Union, and the U.S. military budget began its first sustained decline since the Second World War. Military spending fell by one-third in real terms from its peak in 1985. An estimated 1.8 million private sector jobs were lost between 1987 and 1997 from cuts in defense purchases. Military and civilian employees at the Department of Defense declined by another nine hundred thousand jobs over the decade. However, the military budget is projected to rise after 1998.

Simultaneously, resource depletion was creating crises in many communities dependent upon extracting wealth from the environment. As the old-growth timber conflict in the Pacific Northwest illustrates, these communities increasingly confront devastating choices between their economic welfare and the health or even survival of the local ecology. Similar stories are unfolding about depleted fish stocks on the east and west coasts, water for growth in the Southwest, open space versus development in many urbanized areas, and global warming versus fossil fuel use internationally. Corporate mobility makes regulating destructive behavior even more difficult because of the real threat of disinvesting.

Industrial pollution and disposal of toxic waste are also sources of crisis especially for low-income and working-class communities and communities of color. Occupational hazards continue to seriously injure three or four out of every hundred workers a year. Each year about ten million tons of hazardous waste are disposed of in landfills, incinerators, treatment plants, and injection wells that are disproportionately placed in vulnerable communities. An even larger amount of hazardous chemicals, mine tailings, and radioactive wastes are unregulated as they leach into the environment and damage human and environmental health. Government military and nuclear weapons facilities are also the nation's largest polluters, contaminating groundwater and soils at over 1,800 sites around the country.[1]

In these evolving and threatening circumstances, the labor, peace, and environmental movements are in the midst of their own transitions—ones that provide the context for new alliances. These alliances respond in part to changing political and economic conditions in the country and in part to developments within the movements. The conditions favoring coalitions within each movement will be examined in the rest of this chapter.

The Labor Movement's Search for New Allies

Labor organizing since the beginning of the Cold War has followed a strategy of "pure and simple unionism," dedicated to winning the right to bargain with employers without pursuing larger political or social change. This strategy reflects the dominance of the craft union tradition of the AFL, which historically perceived unions as an aid to employers rather than a challenge to them. Craft unions organize workers with high levels of skill, the "aristocracy of labor," across job sites to bargain for better conditions for members of their crafts. By contrast, industrial unions organize all workers within a workplace or industry regardless of skill level, occupation, or experience. This more inclusive approach characterizes the CIO, which emerged from the mass organizing drives and sit-down strikes of the 1930s. Having formed within the AFL, the CIO pursues a similar organizing goal, to build sufficient power to negotiate contractual agreements with employers. Both the AFL and CIO perceive collective bargaining within the present system of wage labor as their purpose.

Unions during the Cold War lacked the larger vision of social change that characterized the labor movement when it first emerged. The harsh working and living conditions brought on by industrialization motivated workers to transform rather than just manage the abuses inherent in an economic system in which workers are subordinate to profit-seeking owners and managers. Even the most conservative national union, the AFL, declared in its founding constitution in 1886, "A struggle is going on in all the nations of the civilized world between the oppressors and the oppressed of all countries, a struggle between the capitalist and the laborer, which grows in intensity from year to year, and will work disastrous results to the toiling millions if they are not combined for mutual protection and benefit."[2] The earlier Knights of Labor (1869–1902) promoted solidarity among all workers and sought to replace private ownership with worker-owned producer cooperatives. The IWW was founded in 1905 to establish worker control over production through direct actions such as general strikes and mass work stoppages. Socialist and communist activists brought a vision of international working-class solidarity to transform the economic system from private to public ownership of the means of production.

By the 1950s union activists seeking worker or social control of production were brutally purged from the labor movement, which settled into a passive pattern of "business unionism." Prosperity and repression combined with conservative leadership to produce unions run like businesses, dedicated to servicing existing members, maintaining the financial solvency of their organizations, and advancing the personal wealth and status of their leadership. Militant organizing threatened these goals, and most unions became extremely cautious about strikes and organizing that involved significant risks. With power and control centralized, some union leaders, such as Teamster president James Hoffa and United Mineworkers president Tony Boyle, used union resources to serve their own interests at the expense of their members and the wider labor movement.

Business unionism brought benefits during the prosperous 1950s, 1960s, and 1970s, but at the cost of member disengagement. Cooperation with management brought labor higher wages and benefits. In this social contract, labor promised discipline and stability in exchange for recognition and acceptance of unions. A large segment of the organized workforce attained "middle-class" incomes and lifestyles during these years. This material comfort undermined labor solidarity. One labor leader views the consequences of this change regretfully: "It's hard to get people out to a Labor Day picnic now because people are all off taking vacations like middle-class folks do."

In the 1970s, however, the economic foundation of business unionism disintegrated, which loosened labor's ties with management in many companies. Economic stagnation motivated corporations and the federal government to restore profits at the expense of workers. The result has been an increasingly hostile environment for labor unions. Global mobility—made possible by new technology and free trade policies—enabled corporations to relocate rather than negotiate with organized workers. Union busting has become a multibillion dollar industry, with consulting firms that teach management to intimidate, attack, or fire union activists. Investment in antiunion politics also paid dividends as the government shifted appointments to the bureaucracy that oversees labor-management disputes, the National Labor Relations Board, in management's favor. Government policy and labor law followed and at times led the corporate antiunion agenda, and Reagan's election in 1980 moved the attack on unions into high gear. As one union activist summarized the changing environment for the labor movement,

> There used to be respect, mutual respect at the bargaining table especially. Since PATCO, the respect is gone. They now know that the threat of a strike is not the weapon it used to be for bargaining for the union. And they still have the threat of overseas competition and moving out. And because so many plants have closed, many companies have moved out, you have to take it a little more seriously than you used to. I'm not saying take them at their word, [but] you have to look at it every time. It's changed, and it's not for the better.

Business unionism has proven disastrous for the labor movement in the face of this corporate and government onslaught. The organized share of the workforce reached its peak in the United States at the time of the AFL and CIO merger in 1955, with 25 percent of the labor force unionized. By 1997 it had shrunk to 14.1 percent, while in the private sector only 9.8 percent of workers were unionized.

This crisis, which is forcing change in the labor movement particularly among the younger generation, raises questions about collaboration while creating opportunities for other kinds of coalitions. One young organizer observed, "The younger generation in the unions don't have the pension plans that their older colleagues do. The 'me generation' is past. The 'me generation' is the older unionist who has everything, has a good pension and wages, and doesn't care about helping others. But the younger unionist doesn't have those things and has to think about organizing, has to build coalitions, and has to work with others for change. I see a 'new union member': the younger people, not afraid of coalitions and new ways."

Growing up in the 1960s provided younger union activists with a willingness to challenge and change, in sharp contrast with the experience of their parents' generation. The hierarchy and rigid rules of the older generation are giving way to more informality. Some attribute this directly to the experience of the 1960s. As one union leader said, "People who went through the anti–Vietnam War movement learned they couldn't trust authority in the government or university, so they are much less likely to bow to authority in the union."

Union activists who experienced the antiwar movement in the 1960s also bring their very different attitudes toward war and peace to the labor movement. Their parents' generation, shaped by World War II and the Cold War, were generally hostile to the message of the peace movement. But, as two observers of labor's foreign policy have found, "As Vietnam veterans and other antiwar contemporaries rise through labor's ranks, the State Department has more and more trouble defining the issues and disguising the true costs of intervention."[3] This generational change is evident in unions around the country. For example, in the early 1990s the executive board of one building trade union in Washington was equally divided between older men in their fifties and younger leaders in their late thirties or forties, including one woman. The older generation was openly resistant to working with coalitions, a sentiment captured by one member when he said, "I don't trust peace groups, I don't work with the enemy." The other half of the board favored coalitions and included members who were vocally active in the peace movement.

The younger generation of union members, as with the country as a whole, is also far more attuned to the environment than its elders. These changes are evident even within unions dependent on construction and natural resource extraction, unions that traditionally opposed environmental regulations because they threatened their jobs. The president of a union of pulp and paper workers described how people's attitudes about environmental groups have changed as a result of the media attention about the issue: "How can anybody disagree that you shouldn't spill that shit all over the water? You can't disagree with that, when you see people picking up dead animals and dead birds and everything else. God damn it, they're getting killed because of somebody's stupidity. People are just getting into it more because there's this constant barrage of education out there." Building and metal trades union members in Seattle indicate that many are sympathetic with the environmental movement, although they balance their sympathy with concern for their jobs. As one rank and filer put it,

We need to work together. Union people are more concerned about the environment than the nonunion guys. People care in the union. [There are] lots of good people in the unions, and we need to stick together. Things are getting worse for unions in the economy. We aren't doing as well as the older guys. But we need to take care of the environment too, of the ozone and all. But like the spotted owl or the oil pipeline up in Alaska where I'm from, the environmental people want too much or aren't reasonable. The caribou can go over the pipeline. Animals can live under it too. But I agree we need to take care of the environment too.

It is important not to overplay this generational shift. As another proponent of change warns, the shift alone is not powerful enough to change union politics. There are plenty of conservative young people coming up in the ranks of labor, and not all that many young and outspoken labor leaders. Individuals from every generation support coalitions, and a minority in the labor movement has always supported the peace and environmental movements. There are also many younger union members who express the ideas of their parents' generation. Yet the above examples illustrate a significant trend.

Finally, the union movement is changing because its social makeup is changing. Racial discrimination in the unions kept nonwhites from advancing into better-paid skilled jobs and from participating in union leadership. The building and metal trades were traditionally passed down from father to son, which kept them white. In Washington State, as in many parts of the country, the courts ordered the trades to include women and minorities. Under close supervision, unions began to do so. As a result trade union membership is more diverse now than ever in the past. In addition to the slow opening of the trades, unions have grown in the public and service sectors, which employ many women and people of color. Women made up over 60 percent of new union members by the mid-1990s, and almost one out of every four union members was black or Hispanic by 1997.

In 1996 a crisis within the labor movement produced the first challenge to the leadership of the AFL-CIO since the unions merged in 1955. John Sweeney led a slate that defeated the old guard leadership of Lane Kirkland and his handpicked successor Tom Donahue by promising aggressive change through increased funding for organizing, positive public relations, and grassroots political mobilization. As former president of the Service Employees International Union (SEIU), Sweeney is a major shift from the AFL craft union leadership that dominated the AFL-CIO since its founding. The SEIU reflects the changing composition of the labor movement; it represents both public and private service sector workers, who are half female and 30 percent African American and Latino. Sweeney brought younger union activists to the AFL-CIO staff with experience with civil rights, antiwar, and community organizing.

Organizing is a renewed priority for the labor movement, and union activists are increasingly turning to coalitions with nonlabor organizations to advance their goals. The AFL-CIO created an Organizing Department and committed to raising $20 million for organizing new members. Sweeney set a goal of unions spending one-third of their budgets on organizing, up from under 10 percent. In its Union Cities campaign, the AFL-CIO is mobilizing regional labor councils to increase organizing among member unions and build capacity to mobilize 1 percent of union membership for public actions. New priority is being placed on community coalitions to build political power at the local level.

With a more aggressive and issue-focused political strategy, the AFL-CIO is better poised to be an ally with issue-specific movements. Labor shifted $35 million into political campaigns in 1996 in a high-profile effort to regain Congress for the Democrats. But the unions recognized that blind support for Democrats—the lesser of two evils in the face of staunchly antiunion Republicans—has enabled the Democratic party to take labor's endorsements for granted. So in 1997 the AFL-CIO reoriented its political action resources to emphasize mobilizing its own people around specific issues rather than concentrating on candidates. As Sweeney said, "We must stop giving money to political parties who won't give unions the respect we deserve. . . . It is time for us to begin spending our money on our own media and grass-roots lobbying around the issues that matter."[4] This new orientation will free unions to negotiate alliances with other movements on issues rather than serve as appendages to candidates' electoral campaigns.

The organized labor movement has recognized the necessity of coalition building and made this central to its strategy to reinvigorate its own ranks. Political and economic attacks have provided the impetus for change. The sympathies of younger union members and the greater diversity of union membership will facilitate this shift in union practice.

The Environmental Movement's Shift toward Social Issues

The diverse social and political roots of the environmental movement date from the nineteenth century, when people from different classes and races grappled with pollution and environmental destruction. Elites sought the preservation of pristine wilderness areas as cultural monuments or recreational preserves. Business interests quickly recognized the economic benefits of tourism and joined the push for park development. Settlers trying to make a living from the land advanced rational and fair management of resources against monopolies and overdevelopment. Workers on the front lines of industrial production sought protection from the poisons and hazards destroying their health and lives. Communities fought the open sewers, polluted air, garbage, and home and factory waste that plagued urban life. And Native Americans, finally, fought to preserve their cultures and ways of life outside the urban-industrial machine of Western society with its endless appetite for land and resources.

From these diverse origins, three streams of environmental organizing have developed that address issues in the workplace, the community, and nature. Workplace struggles against black lung disease, asbestosis, radiation exposure, toxic chemical poisoning, and many other hazards pit workers exposed during the production process against employers seeking to profit from their work. Attention to safety and health issues has grown among unions, led by the Oil, Chemical and Atomic Workers Union and by public health and consumer advocates. A second stream of community-based struggles mobilizes residents against health threats from industry, waste disposal sites, or development. Race and class are often factors in these struggles, because communities of color and low-income communities have less political power to resist the location of toxins or to choose other places to live. The environmental justice movement of the past decade has contributed important energy to this organizing against toxins. Third, traditional or mainstream environmental organizations concentrate on the sphere of nature, preserving undeveloped environments and conserving natural resources. This segment of the movement is largely middle-class, often with professional staffs or drawing volunteers who are professionals. These groups are extremely diverse, from large multinational organizations such as Greenpeace to localized efforts to protect a particular river or stand of trees, from direct action organizations like Earth First! to legislative groups like the League of Conservation Voters.

Environmental activism over the past thirty years has dramatically shifted consciousness throughout society. In 1970 the first Earth Day was envisioned as a teach-in to mobilize a broad environmental constituency. Twenty years later, Earth Day was sponsored by major corporations and advertised on grocery bags. Public concern about the environment has shifted dramatically, particularly in the 1980s when belief that the government should spend more for protecting the environment jumped from 48 to 71 percent of the population.[5] People are more aware of environmental hazards as a result of far-reaching educational campaigns. Furthermore, regulations requiring notification of hazards and appropriate safety precautions have raised the level of awareness and concern among workers.

In Washington and many other states, mainstream environmentalists have become part of the decision-making process about an agenda that the movement itself has defined. The Washington Environmental Council (WEC), for instance, is consulted by the state government on a wide variety of environmental issues. The governor appoints WEC representatives to commissions on such diverse topics as water resources, wetlands, old growth, park boundaries, wildlife, water quality, and transportation. As one environmental activist working for the Audubon Society said about the national organization, "We're in power. Environmentalists have played the game and are inside the beltway and got legislation passed."

Public support has translated into membership and growth for environmental organizations when attacks on the environment are visible. During the Reagan years the enemy was obvious, with Secretary of Interior James Watt seeking to sell off public lands, with the Environmental Protection Agency (EPA) and the Occupational Safety and Health Agency having their budgets slashed, and with corporate officials staffing key agencies. As a result membership in environmental organizations soared in the 1980s, with 40 percent of the population making contributions in 1990, up from 15 percent in 1987.[6] In 1994, when Newt Gingrich led the Republican takeover of Congress, funds again poured into the national environmental organizations.

Faced with popular support for the environment, politicians and polluters have both pursued their own green credentials—deflecting energy and attention from the movement. Both George Bush, who called himself an "environmental president," and Bill Clinton, who invited environmentalists into his administration, have combined environment-friendly public pronouncements with favors to timber companies, auto manufacturers, ranching and mining interests, and developers. Having claimed the environmental mantle, the Clinton administration has proceeded to ignore its environmental supporters, assuming that they have nowhere else to go given the staunchly anti-environmental policies of Republicans. Using a similar strategy of greenwashing, major corporations are making significant contributions to the large environmental organizations and joining their boards to both shore up personal environmental credentials and shape their policies. This "kinder, gentler" strategy does less to mobilize public alarm, and has contributed to the decline of national environmental organizations.

Simultaneously, grassroots environmentalists have increasingly lost faith in the political compromises and top-down approach of the national organizations. All too often the nationals have been willing to make deals with government or corporations that violate fundamental principles for many environmentalists. National environmental support for policies such as selling pollution credits, the North American Free Trade Agreement, and Clinton's negotiated settlement over old-growth timber, while not endorsed by all the national organizations, have discredited the big organizations in they eyes of many. Compromises with corporate polluters reached despite the protest of grassroots environmentalists—from the campaign against McDonalds packaging to concessions for oil companies in Ecuador—have also undermined faith in the nationals. They lost further credibility as grassroots activists have become increasingly frustrated with the failures of regulations fought for over the past thirty years to protect ecosystems and environments. This growing skepticism has led to a crisis for the nationals. Membership fell off dramatically in the early 1990s, with the Wilderness Society declining 30 percent, Sierra Club by 21 percent, and Greenpeace plummeting by 68 percent.[7] Organizations were forced to lay off staff and close offices, while some took on large debts.

When the Republicans took control of Congress in 1994, the anti-environmental backlash seemed poised to dismantle the entire edifice of environmental regulations, limited as it was. Support for this agenda came from "wise use" advocates—a corporate-funded initiative bent on destroying the environmental movement. Drawing on economic insecurities in the country, the wise-use agenda is to protect private property and expand access to government resources for private profit. The result has been court rulings and legislation that limit government's ability to restrict development or mandate environmental regulations without paying compensation—severely increasing the costs of protection.

Anti-environmental backlash is forcing the movement to address social issues more seriously. Environmentalists confront businessmen, workers, landowners, and politicians who are angry about the economic consequences of regulations that hinder development, of grassroots campaigns that limit industrial and waste disposal siting, and of protection of endangered species that blocks resource use. The perception that environmental laws are a threat to the legitimate needs of working people to make a living has stymied preservation efforts and forced a greater consideration of community issues. Some see the spotted owl issue as a turning point for the environmental movement by forcing it to address the social and economic impacts of protection. As one environmental leader said about the conflict over old-growth timber, "If we were to do this again, we would look at social issues up front."

The environmental justice movement has also brought human considerations back into the environmental movement. In 1990 this new wave of organizing based in low-income communities and communities of color sharply criticized the mainstream and especially the national environmental organizations for divorcing social justice issues from their agenda. In a letter to the national organizations they said, "Your organizations continue to support and promote policies which emphasize the clean-up and preservation of the environment on the backs of working people in general and people of color in particular."[8] Sustained criticism like this has forced mainstream environmentalists to consider the social and economic implications of their programs. The Clinton administration embraced environmental justice issues and has developed new policies to encourage economic redevelopment of polluted sites and inclusion of social considerations in the development of all levels of environmental policies. Several national environmental organizations have also developed programs to work more closely with low-income, community, and grassroots organizations with varying levels of success.

The internationalization of environmental politics is also forcing middle-class environmentalists to address the human dimension of their policies. Particularly at the Earth Summit in 1992, environmentalists from wealthy nations had to confront the implications of poverty experienced by their Third World counterparts. As a Philippine environmentalist observed, "A year or two ago these same groups answered with a blank stare when you asked them their position on economic issues. They are now coming to the realization that their work is not just management of conservation projects but rather the facilitation of real political action."[9]

Conservative and pragmatic pressure to include cost-benefit analysis in environmental policy making has forced environmentalists to be more aware of economic consequences of their policies as well. The Reagan and Bush administrations embraced cost-benefit analysis, bringing economic policy questions into environmental debates. Conservative environmental organizations such as the Environmental Defense Fund and the National Wildlife Federation have promoted a "third wave" environmentalism that seeks to work with business through incentives and market-based programs. These pragmatic strategies have introduced economic issues into environmental policy in ways unheard of by an earlier generation of environmentalists.

These trends have shifted the framework for environmentalism. As one Audubon activist summarized the shift,

> There have been changes in the environmental movement's approach. Past battles were around park protection or individual site protection. In this forest campaign, we want better management of the whole forest for multiple species. Past fights were for recreation land and scenic beauty; now we're talking about ecological diversity and species. It's more comprehensive, including social impacts and ecosystems, than the past park conservation movement. Environmentalists are talking more about social issues overall at present.

Political betrayals, contractions, successes with their consequent backlashes, international trade agreements, criticisms from grassroots and especially environmental justice activists—these trends are pushing the environmental movement toward greater attention to social and economic issues. In many corners a sense of crisis and introspection is moving activists in the environmental movement to consider new strategies, new alliances. There is a growing understanding that the spheres of nature, work, and community cannot be separated—in the words of the environmental justice movement, the environment is where we "live, work, and play." This is the complex context in which environmentalists of various stripes are currently negotiating coalitions across race and class lines.

THE PEACE MOVEMENT'S SHIFT TOWARD SOCIAL ISSUES

Since World War II there have been two main tracks within the peace movement. The dominant one has been opposition to nuclear weapons. From early efforts to ban the bomb to the Nuclear Weapons Freeze Campaign of the 1980s, this effort has mobilized many people in the mainstream including highly respected scientists, doctors, teachers, and other professionals. The other strand in the peace movement derives from opposition to foreign intervention. This sentiment is strongest during periods of large-scale troop commitment as during Korea and Vietnam, but it has included opposition to U.S. policies in Central America, South Africa, and elsewhere. Whereas the nuclear focus has revolved around East-West, U.S.-Soviet relations and questions the strategy of using nuclear weapons to maintain peace through a balance of terror, the second addresses the U.S. relationship with less developed nations and questions its goals. The first seeks to prevent nuclear war, the second seeks social justice through protecting the rights of other peoples to self-determination.

The peace movement's attention has alternated between disarming nuclear weapons and preventing Third World interventions. The Vietnam War brought a large influx of new recruits who came to believe that the goals of U.S. foreign policy are corrupt. Events between 1967 and 1972 convinced this generation of activists that the war overseas was the same war they were fighting here at home. Violence against the civil rights movement, the shootings at Kent State, military conscription, Watergate, and other events demonstrated the hypocrisies and injustices of the U.S. political system. The result was a generation marked by distrust of government, authority, and establishment notions of progress. As the Vietnam War ended and the mobilization of the 1960s and early 1970s faded, many protesters turned their energy to other issues. The peace movement experienced a lull as the country tried to recover from the experience of Vietnam.

The next major wave of peace activism began in 1980 with the election of Ronald Reagan and his talk of a winnable nuclear war. This prompted an enormous reaction culminating in the massive June 12, 1982, rally in New York, which drew almost a million people. These activists sought an end to the arms race and an acceptance of coexistence with the Soviet Union. The freeze became a major national issue, and Reagan stifled his inflammatory rhetoric. This response on the part of Americans, combined with Gorbachev's policies of reconciliation with the West, brought Reagan back to the arms-control bargaining table. As the Soviet Union began to disarm and quickly disintegrated, the first real disarmament treaties of the nuclear age were signed. In that environment the antinuclear weapons movement faded.

Reagan similarly energized broad opposition to his support of murderous right-wing regimes in Central America. In 1984 the peace movement successfully outlawed armaments to the Contras in their bid to overthrow the democratically elected Sandanista government in Nicaragua. Reagan's efforts to circumvent this law by selling arms to Iran caused the greatest scandal of his presidency and contributed to Bush's defeat in 1992. Effective national organizations such as Witness for Peace, the Pledge of Resistance, Sanctuary, and the Committee in Solidarity with the People of El Salvador organized and coordinated hundreds of thousands of grassroots activists during the 1980s.

Since the mid-1980s, there has been a distinct trend in the peace movement away from antinuclear weapons protests and toward social justice, anti-interventionist work and coalitions. As an article in a National Jobs with Peace newsletter observed in 1989, "In the U.S. Peace Movement, a fundamental change is taking root. The human and economic impact of the arms race—rather than solely the prevention of nuclear war—is becoming the focus for peace organizing. As we move into the '90's, the climate for peace work stands to evolve dramatically."[10] One participant in this transition noted,

I think that post '84 was extremely sobering for the peace movement. I mean up until that time with the headiness of the crescendo of the freeze, the '82 march in New York, moving into the elections in '84, Mondale preaching about the freeze all the time and then realizing that we got our buts kicked. And then the war in Central America continued to escalate, South Africa went on their merry apartheid way, all of the elements of the peace agenda just crumbled. And we realized, I think, that we weren't in this alone, that we were in the margins and that we needed to look to strategies that made connections.

As the freeze movement declined, many local organizations sought to define a new role for themselves. Better relations with the Soviet Union and anticipation of a "peace dividend" encouraged activists to focus on their long-held goal of redirecting federal spending priorities. Thus on the nuclear side as well as the anti-interventionist side, peace organizations began to make the link more and more to issues of social and economic justice. As a conversion organizer from Washington State Sane/Freeze observed, "The peace movement has taken up a new weapon in its war on military spending. The weapon is job security. Instead of talking about how the billions that go into defense could be better spent, peace activists in the Puget Sound area are asking: 'How will the economy react when the spending stops?' It's a new angle for the peace movement. We are really beginning to talk about the economics."

The end of the Cold War brought considerable confusion and decline to the peace movement. Simultaneously the Contra war in Central America was winding down, and Reagan's belligerent policies were replaced with President Bush's less ideological, quieter approach to foreign policy. The public sense of imminent crisis ended, and membership in peace organizations fell dramatically. Change happened more rapidly than the movements were prepared for, and organizations struggled to redefine their missions and strategies. Many local organizations closed their doors. Others continued to focus on the international arms trade, an issue brought to the forefront with the Gulf War against a country previously armed by the United States. The Gulf War highlighted the role of U.S. intervention to support economic interests in oil, yet this issue did not survive once the war ended.

Some of the most vital initiatives in the 1990s focused on conversion and reorienting the military budget. Greater attention to economic issues within the peace movement paralleled a dramatic change in public opinion as well, a change attributable in some part to the peace movement. The public began to redefine security in economic rather than military terms. A poll commissioned by Americans Talk Security in 1988 found that 62 percent of the population believed that "economic power is more important than military power in determining a nation's influence." At that time almost half of the population accepted that military spending harms the economy. A similar poll by the World Policy Institute found that 73 percent of the public agreed with the statement that "the greatest threat to American security is the economic challenge posed by Japan, and that we should therefore shift military spending to domestic investment to make America more economically competitive."

The peace movement in the 1990s is more pragmatic and aware of the complex implications of peace for people's lives. Organizations are more concerned with social justice and with the relationships between peace and other social issues. As one conversion activist described this transition,

> I think there was a time when the peace movement was perceived as being these yuppies who didn't care [about jobs]. I think, personally, that we've moved beyond that, and one of the indicators I see of that is the way the peace movement conducted itself with respect to the Persian Gulf War. We learned a lot in the '70s. One thing we learned is that as a peace movement, it was very self-defeating to spit on soldiers coming back from Vietnam and to call them murderers. It clearly wasn't about them. And so when you saw the peace movement protesting the Persian Gulf War, it was scrupulous in the way in which people said and said and said and continued to say, This is not about the individuals. We support our troops, we support our soldiers. This is not about them, this is about our policy.

Greater awareness of social and economic issues mixed with a reexamination of the peace movement's role and mission mean that the movement is increasingly open to coalitions. As one peace activist said of the changes she saw,

I think the peace movement has matured to the point where it realizes that if it continues to be just a group of campus radicals or nice church ladies who really are unconnected to the real world—by that I'm using the world as labor—they are not going to make significant inroads into the general consciousness of the public. I think the lesson has been that only to the extent that we do stay plugged in to all aspects of society, will we make those inroads and be persuasive and have credibility.

The labor, peace, and environmental movements are all in the midst of fundamental transitions, rethinking old assumptions and strategies. In seeking a way forward, each movement confronts divisions that have defined its past. For the labor movement, the globalization of capitalism once again raises the question of whether it needs to seek to transform the wage labor system. Environmentalists must reconcile their own internal divisions between the spheres of nature, work, and community. The peace movement must redefine its role in a world in which the United States is the global policeman—that is, where the arms race and intervention meet.

Changes within the three movements may be linked. When the labor movement in this country ceased to be class conscious after the Left was purged in the 1950s, it also ceased to ally itself with the peace movement. A new alliance between labor and peace activists may also require rediscovering the need to transform the wage labor system. Similarly, as environmentalists learn to reconcile their diverse spheres of workplace, neighborhood, and preservationist organizing, they will need to integrate human and economic needs with environmental protection. This may well form the basis for a closer collaboration with the labor movement. Confronting the internationalization of both labor and environmental issues will necessarily raise questions about foreign and military policy, questions that the peace movement addresses.

Movement activists are increasingly clear that they cannot accomplish their goals alone. They face similar political dilemmas, with a Democratic party as the lesser of two evils that seeks to win votes from popular movements but continues to undermine their causes. They also face common corporate enemies in many instances; often the same companies that are opposing environmental protections and exporting armaments are fighting unions and exploiting their workers. But politics is not always this simple. Some green companies are antiunion and vice versa, just as some weapons producers have good labor practices.

The major crises that each movement faces are inherent in the emerging free trade regime. Global corporate mobility has shifted the balance of power away from workers and unions. National sovereignty over environmental regulations is being ceded to international trade tribunals. Decades of industrial policy to build up the weapons sector has made armaments one of the exports in which the United States has a clear competitive advantage in an open global marketplace.

In the face of these challenges, each movement is undergoing an internal transition that favors coalition organizing. Energy and resources are shifting to the grass roots as organizers feel increasingly disillusioned with insider politics as practiced in Washington, D.C. The younger generation in each movement is less likely to perceive issues or movements in isolation, and more likely to recognize the importance of economic, social, and political forces. The way ahead is uncertain, although the need to rethink old assumptions and strategies is clear.

▲

Coalitions in Practice

The legacy of conflict and cooperation along with the development of new opportunities provide the context for coalition organizing at present. Part IV turns to the practical lessons that can be drawn from the case studies. If working- and middle-class coalitions are to be more successful in the future, past practices must be analyzed critically. The following chapters examine the strengths and weaknesses of different coalition organizing practices.

▲

CHAPTER SEVEN

Coalition Organizing

In the mid-1980s, when Gorbachev was backing away from the Cold War and Reagan's massive peacetime military boom was passing its peak, the prospect of a "peace dividend" was in the air, and thousands of defense industry workers and armed servicemen would soon be on the streets. Peace activists who had spent a generation calling for military cuts and opposing the deployment of weapons systems were as surprised as anyone that this day had finally come. In communities around the country something new seemed possible, and activists were looking for ways to seize the moment to convert their local military economies into jobs that would meet the needs of people.

Dozens of conversion projects emerged in defense-dependent communities such as Seattle and Tacoma, Boston, Philadelphia, St. Louis, San Diego, Los Angeles, and Dallas–Fort Worth. Sane, which merged with the Nuclear Weapons Freeze Campaign in 1987, continued its national advocacy for conversion, as did many of its state and local affiliates. Jobs with Peace (JwP) emerged as a national network of local efforts in 1981. In the beginning of 1990, the AFL-CIO leadership joined its more active unions in calling for conversion legislation. The executive council of the Industrial Union Department of the AFL-CIO urged its affiliates to work with other organizations and local government to carry out local conversion planning.

While peace protesters and defense workers had opposed each other across plant gates and in Congress on numerous occasions, now many activists believed they were natural allies in advocating for conversion. How to take advantage of these opportunities wasn't exactly clear. But

Maine, Minnesota, and Washington State developed some of the most successful labor and peace coalitions in the country according to national observers.

This chapter examines lessons about coalition organizing drawn from these three cases. The first part identifies the combinations of conditions, strategies, and accomplishments that converge in a successful coalition. The second part looks at the common practices that contribute to the success of coalitions in any circumstances.

COALITION STRATEGIES AND CIRCUMSTANCES

Successful organizing requires the right marriage of strategy with circumstances. The development and outcomes of coalitions depend upon both the external context for organizing and the internal decisions about how to realize opportunities and overcome limitations. Coalitions in Maine, Minnesota, and Washington followed unique trajectories because of both external and internal factors: the political and economic conditions in each community, the personalities of key organizers and leaders, and the strategic decisions made as the organizing developed.

Military cuts impacted communities differently depending on local political and economic conditions. Some communities were more dependent on military jobs, and some faced industries whose production was harder to shift to civilian alternatives. Large multinational firms posed different challenges than small local companies. The degree to which workers, companies, government, and the wider public embraced or fought change varied. Equally significant, however, were differences in the preparedness of unions, the peace community, and economic development agencies to respond to changing conditions. Conversion organizers in each location, therefore, faced distinct challenges.

The strategies each coalition pursued reflected the assumptions of organizers and leaders about how to influence defense firms to convert. Organizers began with different beliefs particularly about the level of conflict needed to make change. Some assumed that powerful corporations would have to be forced to reinvest in civilian jobs, while others favored a cooperative approach that included all the stakeholders in promoting economic development and growth. Maine's emphasis on collaboration and Minnesota's use of conflict provided the poles of a national debate about strategy.

Washington State

Organizers confronted an enormous challenge in a state where prosperity was identified with Pentagon dollars. From Boeing's sprawling airfields outside Seattle to the camouflaged vehicles traveling to military bases around the Puget Sound to the nuclear reservation at Hanford in the east, Washington was the third most militarily dependent state in the country at the end of the Cold War.[1] People still speak about the "Boeing bust" that accompanied the end of the Vietnam War. Between 1969 and 1972, Boeing reduced employment by 60,000, and 140,000 people in the region lost jobs. Unemployment in the state reached 14 percent. Reagan's military buildup fueled a boom in Washington in the early 1980s when Pentagon contracts more than doubled, again led by Boeing. Now the cuts were coming again—Boeing laid off 5,000 people in 1990 and announced another 2,500 cut in 1991. Closing the nuclear reactor that produced plutonium at Hanford also cost 2,500 jobs.

Washington State Sane/Freeze (WSSF)[2] launched its conversion project in 1987 to pressure defense firms to plan for civilian production "should peace break out." An alliance with labor was among the primary goals of the campaign. This was an exciting time for the organization, which had recently played a decisive role in helping the Democratic Party keep control of the state senate. WSSF assisted Rick Bender, a candidate with strong labor backing, to retain his senate seat by a slim 346 votes. This electoral organizing won Sane the cooperation of the Democratic leadership. The organization was growing rapidly too. With twenty-six thousand members in 1992, it was one of the largest local peace organizations in the country. A new director hired in 1987 chose to focus on conversion just as the military budget began to decline.

WSSF negotiated between compromising and conflicting strategies because of a mix of orientations among its leaders. The Economic Diversification Committee debated whether to target Boeing as "a culprit in the continuance of the arms race" or to build a legislative campaign for government assistance based on an emerging consensus about the need to shift government spending to social priorities. The new director, David Fleischman, advocated the former approach. He came to WSSF with the intention of introducing traditional community organizing techniques into the peace organization. He had learned from his previous organizing experiences in Florida that "you have to challenge power to get power." He sent organizers and leaders from WSSF to be trained in techniques of direct action organizing. Leaders in the conversion project were divided over this approach, however, and some argued strongly for a more collaborative strategy. One person claimed, "Sane is not a moralistic organization like others that have done civil disobedience at Boeing's gates. Sane was set up as a practical organization. A lot of the people are electorally oriented."

Conditions in Washington resolved this debate in favor of a collaborative, legislative approach for several reasons. The union at Boeing was not receptive to a coalition that would challenge corporate conversion policy. The Boeing campaign gathered little enthusiasm or results against a company with wide public support as a cornerstone of the regional economy, especially as commercial aircraft production replaced military contracts. Thus the peace group had to seek labor allies from the larger union movement. The Washington State Labor Council had some sympathetic members, but it had to negotiate between diverse member interests from unions differently impacted by military reductions. Shipbuilding, which went into crisis with defense cuts, accounted for only 2.5 percent of the manufacturing economy and was dwarfed by aerospace employment, which had a strong civilian market. These sectors had different interests than the unions at Hanford, whose heavy dependence on federal government support through the Department of Energy makes them far more conservative about nuclear weapons and power issues. Any statewide labor initiative had to deal with these many divisions, making a collaborative and legislative strategy much more palatable than confrontation.

WSSF carefully and effectively began to build trust and credibility within the labor movement. Its goal was to pass legislation that would assist industries and communities reliant on defense contracts to develop new civilian jobs. To accomplish this it first sought to educate politicians and the wider public about the magnitude of the region's dependence on military spending and to develop allies particularly in the labor movement. WSSF used its educational forums as opportunities to involve labor representatives in voicing their support and to articulate its own concern for the well-being of workers in the region. This educational campaign provided a reasonable first step that many people could endorse even if they didn't share WSSF's larger agenda. But it also brought forward opposition.

Sane introduced a bill in the state legislature to study the impacts of military spending on the state economy. The purpose was to convince people that overdependence on military spending poses risks for the state. The Washington State Labor Council (WSLC), which is the statewide AFL-CIO organization, would not support that bill. U.S. Representative Norm Dicks sought to derail the effort, and the state representative from Hanford accused Sane of putting the state "under siege" by trying to cut military spending that supports the economy. But the state Democratic leadership, feeling indebted to Sane for its electoral help, refused to pass aid to Hanford without also passing Sane's study. As a result, the legislature appropriated $40,000 in 1988 to determine the state's reliance on defense industry. It concluded in 1989 that forty thousand jobs were at risk in the state over the next three years due to cuts in military spending.

WSSF worked with the Church Council of Greater Seattle to sponsor a public conference, "Creating Economic Security in a Non-Military Economy," which was endorsed by several local unions. Out of this conference came a call for King County to study the impacts of military spending on its economy. This call was endorsed by representatives from the Seattle Building Trades and Puget Sound Metal Trades. A year later the county designated $25,000 to conduct such a study, which was announced at a press conference that again included labor participation. The press conference gave Sane representatives a chance to stand with the King County Labor Council, the city government, and churches to say that they are concerned about the well-being of working people in the region.

The peace organization devoted itself to building trust within the labor community by contributing to union issues. They supported Boeing workers on strike, took part in their pickets, and refused to cross the picket line to attend a meeting they had arranged with the CEO about Boeing's South Africa policies. Sane's lobbyist in Olympia actively worked for labor-sponsored legislation on such issues as plant closure notification and job training.

Despite these efforts, labor leaders were resistant to an alliance with WSSF. Union allies encouraged WSSF to refrain from advocating for additional military cuts but to discuss how to prepare for cuts already slated. In this spirit they worked behind the scenes to establish the Economic Development and Job Retention Committee in the WSLC. The committee was divided over WSSF's participation, with conservative unions from Hanford blocking any formal relationship.

In 1989 Sane introduced state legislation to establish an economic diversification program to assist industries and communities reliant on defense contracts. Sane's original version of the bill would have taxed gross income from the sale and production of military goods to fund diversification efforts. The WSLC would not lend its support to this bill, and it became clear that this approach wouldn't succeed. So the revised bill in 1990 emphasized providing information to firms and communities about shifts in military spending and encouraging diversification efforts. In February 1990, in the wake of the collapse of the Berlin Wall and with national attention focused on the peace dividend, the state House passed Sane's bill with a two-to-one margin and the Senate approved it unanimously. Washington became the first state to legislate a program to diversify the military economy. The bill allocated $200,000 to document the effects of shifts in defense spending on companies and communities, to educate the public about defense cuts, and to assist firms, communities, and labor with diversification efforts. In the press conference labor's representative said, "Labor applauds the efforts of the legislature and of Sane/Freeze to address an issue whose real consequences will be felt most directly by working men and women in the defense industry."

WSSF had to fight to be included on the advisory board for the Community Diversification Program formed to carry out the new legislative mandate. When the state's Department of Community Development (DCD) established its advisory board, it invited representatives from labor, the business community, and government, but not WSSF. Decision makers at the DCD were nervous about including an overtly political organization on the board because it could alienate others who might participate in the program. Sane/Freeze persisted and was finally invited to the initial meeting and was told it would be allowed to join the board. However at that meeting, the DCD still did not announce the peace group's membership openly. A debate about Sane's participation ensued until the convenor finally explained that Sane had already been invited to become a board member.

Many of the people on the advisory board did not support Sane's agenda. However, the committee shared a common purpose of diversifying the state's economy, given that cuts in military spending were already happening. It did not oppose the efforts of others in the state seeking to retain military contracts, but did accept that securing such contracts was not its role.

The state's diversification program devoted its first year to researching the impact of defense reductions on firms, labor, and communities and to developing policy options to respond to these changes. The result was a report to the legislature, "Diversification: Strategies for Military-Dependent Communities, Firms and Workers in Washington State." The state then provided money and assistance to several small companies seeking to make the transition from military to civilian production.

WSSF had two goals for its work with the state's diversification advisory board. It wanted to convince the state that it has some role to play in helping communities adjust to military cuts instead of focusing its energies on trying to retain military contracts. And it wanted to put pressure on Boeing through the state legislature to plan for diversification. Sane/Freeze's representative to the advisory group was impressed because "everyone on the committee seems to accept the basic premises, one, that military cuts are going to occur and, two, that diversification planning is the right thing to do."

Maine

Bath Iron Works (BIW)—the largest private employer in "Vacationland"—is a uniquely Maine major military contractor. As the state's largest private employer, BIW was 95 percent dependent on Navy production by 1990 as a result of Reagan's policies to end subsidies for commercial shipbuilding and to pour money into the Navy. BIW was owned by a New York city investment banking firm (until the company was sold to General Dynamics in 1995) that interfered little in its operations. Its chief operating officer, Duane "Buzz" Fitzgerald, was a longtime proponent of disarmament and cochair of Bath Area Citizens for Nuclear Arms Control. He had frequently spoken about the need for economic conversion as the "process which will allow sufficient numbers of our fellow citizens to support the reduction and ultimate abolition of nuclear arms." But reorienting BIW's production would not be easy. No American shipbuilders were able to compete with the government subsidies and productivity of foreign competition at the time. Also, commercial ships had little need for the 75–80 percent of BIW's workforce involved in complex outfitting for Navy ships.

With rapidly improving relations with the Soviet Union, the Peace Economy Project (PEP)[3] was established in 1989 by the Maine Peace Campaign (MPC), which had grown out of the nuclear freeze movement and was the largest peace organization in the state. The PEP's goals were to "reduce military spending by 50% by 1995, shift national resources to deficit reduction and economic, environmental and social problems, and shift from a military to a civilian-based peace economy through a process of economic adjustment and conversion according to which military-dependent workers, industries and communities are protected."[4] This represented a new emphasis within the MPC, which had previously focused its energies on stopping and protesting weapons systems.

Although Maine as a whole was not highly vulnerable to defense cutbacks—it was only the eighteenth most defense-dependent state in the country—conversion organizing was a particular challenge in three regions. Loring Air Force Base in the far north of Maine supported 17 percent of the jobs in Aroostook County. The base was slated to be closed by 1994. York County, on the southern border with New Hampshire, depended on the Portsmouth Naval Shipyard, which was laying off workers, and on the recently closed Pease Air Force Base. In the Bath-Brunswick region of the coast, 46 percent of all jobs derived from defense contracts at BIW and the Brunswick Naval Air Station.

Workers at BIW were extremely skeptical about the peace movement, which had been protesting launches of Aegis cruisers for years. Leaders of the International Association of Machinists (IAM) Local 6, which represents skilled workers at the shipyard, have their own relationships with Navy personnel as they vie for new contracts. With thousands of jobs at risk because of reduced military contracts, the union also feared a repeat of the three-month protracted strike of 1985 as contract negotiations approached. The union shrank from 8,400 members in 1982 to 5,700 in 1995 due to declining military contracts. Furthermore, the union was at war internally over the decision of its parent organization, the International Union of Marine Shipbuilding Workers of America, to join the IAM in 1988. A second bitter decertification vote in 1991, between advocates of an independent union and those who wanted to remain with the machinists, failed by a close margin.

In Maine, socioeconomic conditions, culture, personality, and the configuration of the coalition converged to shape a cooperative strategy. In a small state with one major military employer, who is also the state's largest private industrial employer, state and local governments felt compelled to assist Bath Iron Works. BIW's managers, many of whom were from Maine, were also invested in ensuring the viability of the company's local plants. These factors combined to form a strong common interest within the community, union, company, and government to plan for BIW's long-term commercial redevelopment.

The political culture in Maine contributed to a collaborative approach to organizing as well. Maine is a small state where decision makers are relatively accessible, where, as one peace activist remarked, "you can run into political leaders, even the governor, at the airport and call them by their first name and get a hug and a kiss." Smallness encourages civility and collaboration because even adversaries know they will face each other again. Many people attribute BIW's willingness to participate, at least nominally, in conversion planning to this cultural norm of community responsibility. This, indeed, is evident in Buzz Fitzgerald's pronouncement: "I have a duty to be candid, forthright; and to say that we can protect 11,600 jobs, or that we will succeed in doing so, would be misleading. But I am not misleading people when I say that that is our commitment. We think about it every day."[5] In this spirit, the union and BIW signed a contract in 1994 that included a commitment not to lay off workers.

Susie Schweppe, who organized the PEP, is also by nature a consensus builder. Schweppe is a woman with enormous energy, enthusiasm, and personal appeal. She was galvanized to take some action against the threat of nuclear war by her young son's fears and questions. The PEP grew out of her frustration that the peace community was always negative, always opposing policies, instead of raising positive possibilities for change. While recognizing that protests could help educate people, she believed that real change required cooperating even with "the enemy" around practical alternatives. In 1985 she worked with the state United Church of Christ to found the Maine Peace Mission to provide a regular congressional dialogue between peace activists and Maine's elected representatives on arms control and disarmament issues. The organization sent weekly delegations to Washington—more than three hundred people over several years—to meet with officials. These missions reflected Schweppe's personal philosophy about cooperative strategies for change. As she explained,

> I've always believed that the most productive way to do anything is in co-operation instead of confrontation, and the Peace Mission really proved that was true. We changed a lot of minds and votes. At the same time, we were asking to be listened to and considered; therefore we had to listen and do the same. It's the same strategy we use in the Peace Economy Project. We can't go in [like] gang busters and say "we have all the right answers, and you will do x, y, z." It doesn't work. People hunker down in their corners and go off and nothing happens. In the Peace Mission, I think people really did begin to see the value in a cooperative approach.

Maine's PEP pursued three strategies to promote consensus on conversion. First, it held forums with industry and grassroots groups to develop diversification strategies. In July 1990 the PEP sponsored a first meeting between local business, defense industry management, and labor to discuss conversion legislation then being debated in Congress. This led to the formation of the Bath-Brunswick Conversion Task Force to promote regional economic development strategies. At the state level, the PEP used the gubernatorial election in 1990 to convince Governor McKernan to create the state Task Force on Defense Realignment and the Maine Economy. Participants in this group included representatives from state government, business, labor, and academia. The task force produced and distributed a report in 1991 including recommendations for ways to mitigate the dislocation caused by cuts in military spending.

The PEP's second strategy was to conduct baseline research about the impact of military dependence on the economy. As an educational tool, the project first sponsored community impact studies in seven towns. These studies showed that more tax dollars leave these towns for military purposes than return to meet local needs. They concluded that Maine taxpayers contribute more to the Pentagon than to the total cost of running all town and city governments in the state. The PEP also worked with the State Planning Office to document the statewide impacts of military spending. Having documented the local need for a change in federal budget priorities, it sponsored research to forecast the economic, environmental, and social gains from redirecting federal spending to civilian uses. It hired Employment Research Associates from Lansing, Michigan, to study the consequences of an annual 7 percent cut of the defense budget for four years. The final study, "A Shift in Federal Spending: What the Peace Dividend Can Mean to Maine," predicted a net gain of three thousand jobs in Maine in addition to improved education, health care services, transportation, and pollution control.

Third, the PEP sought to educate candidates and advocate for national legislation to shift military spending to social needs. In order to influence national policymakers, the PEP developed a local initiative calling for the federal government to "Reinvest in Hometown America." The initiative proposed that the federal government cut military spending "proportionate to [the] reduced military threat" and reinvest in environmental, economic, and social needs. Faced with more demands for services and the loss of federal funds over the past decade, eighty-three towns and cities—including the state's three largest cities, Portland, Bangor, and Augusta—approved the initiative. In March 1992 the initiative was approved by the state legislature. The PEP cosponsored a public forum, "Rebuilding America," in April to announce its success. Congressman Andrews and staff from other congressional offices attended the forum. PEP staffers proclaimed: "United by the common call for a peace dividend, leadership from all aspects of Maine life—mayors, legislators, business and labor leaders, environmentalists, teachers, clergy, veterans, doctors, advocates for women, senior citizens, children, the unemployed and the homeless—took to the podium under the banner, 'Cut Military Spending—Rebuild America.'"

Minnesota

Representative Karen Clark, an outspoken progressive state legislator, catalyzed conversion organizing in Minnesota in 1984 by introducing state legislation. Some unions, such as the Teamsters at Honeywell, vocally opposed the legislation as "un-American and communist." The bill was defeated in committee in a close vote. But from that effort the organizers developed a conversion campaign which affiliated with national Jobs with Peace (JwP).

Conversion organizing in Minnesota is largely a challenge for high-technology firms located in the urban center of the state. Four corporations received over 80 percent of Minnesota's defense contracts: Honeywell Corporation, Unisys, FMC, and Control Data. Over 95 percent of the state's defense contracts come to the Minneapolis–St. Paul metropolitan area, where the big contractors are concentrated. The defense sector in the state is concentrated in a few industries as well, particularly computers, transportation equipment, communications equipment, and nonelectrical machinery.

Between 1987 and 1989, military procurement dollars to Minnesota declined 29 percent and cost the state 29,500 jobs. Of the 85,000 remaining defense jobs, 27,000 were at risk over the next five years. All the big corporations laid off thousands of employees, but Unisys was the hardest hit, cutting about 5,000 workers between 1986 and 1991. Unisys is a multinational computer manufacturing company that carries out most of its military contracting work in St. Paul but has over seventy other facilities around the globe.

Building an alliance with labor was a significant goal for Minnesota JwP from its founding. The state AFL-CIO passed a statement of support in 1984, but unions in defense firms initially rejected appeals to work for conversion. The Teamsters at Honeywell were hostile to the peace community, partly in response to the Honeywell Project, a peace organization that conducted sit-ins, blockades, vigils, and civil disobedience at the plant throughout the 1980s.[6] When JwP tried to meet with the union they were "practically thrown out of the office." Meetings with the United Auto Workers at FMC did not proceed much better. But with thousands of production workers from the International Brotherhood of Electrical Workers (IBEW) Local 2047 being laid off at Unisys, union leaders were looking for some way to save jobs. As one worker described the situation, "I was working at the shop and saw people go out the door who I had worked with for fifteen years. We raised our kids together, we became grandmas together. So it was very personal. And you know, you're going to fight for your family."

Here as elsewhere, local conditions, personalities, and the configuration of the coalition shaped strategies. Unlike BIW, Unisys in Minnesota is a large, multinational corporation where decisions are made by outsiders without any clear commitment to the local workforce. While Unisys is a significant employer in St. Paul, it is only one of numerous similar companies. The company was particularly concerned with protecting its prerogative to make investment decisions itself, and was threatened by any effort by the union or community to influence these decisions. Unisys management had no inclination to allow others to participate in its decision making process. The alliance between labor and the peace community was threatening to management, who consistently refused even to speak with the community groups. This raised the level of confrontation over time, which coalition partners came to see as necessary to force change. As one labor leader explained, "I believe that had we been more confrontational and polarized, we would have been more effective. The fight is to be treated as an equal. You do these things so the company can't ignore you. Start with as much confrontation as you can and then come to the table and work out cooperation as an equal. We need to be more confrontational, not less."

Mel Duncan, organizer of Minnesota JwP, also assumed from the beginning that conflict would be necessary to achieve conversion. Duncan is an outspoken and energetic man who exudes an intense commitment to social justice. Earlier work with mentally handicapped people led him to a three-year organizing drive to win better wages and rights in the workplace. With roots in the peace and labor movements and human rights organizing, he brought a broad vision of unity to move progressives "out of the margins." In this spirit Mel Duncan described his approach to conversion organizing through confronting power inequalities:

> I'm talking about a basic shift of power. I think that at this point we cannot let go [of the fact] that we're not just talking about shifting product lines. To me it would not be a success for us to convert a plant away from making weapons to making electric tooth brushes. There's got to be an environmental component and a community component and a workers' component. What we're talking about is challenging the way in which production decisions are made. That means that there [needs to be] an element in the decision making that involves the workers. We talk about community responsibility, so we add that on to the profit, bottom line criteria. And we need to continue to present that challenge and to organize.

JwP and IBEW followed three strategies to force Unisys to negotiate with them rather than lay off workers. First, an extensive educational campaign within the union built support among its cautious leadership. The union worked effectively to build agreement within its ranks to publicly press Unisys to listen to its workforce. Conversion supporters in the union printed a newsletter with articles about local and national developments; they held events and organized demonstrations. At every union meeting they would report on their efforts. These steps had some success within the union over time. The executive board became unanimously supportive of the effort. A union conversion activist described these changes: "It took a long time to educate them. When you're talking about someone who's been in a stable job for twenty to twenty-five years, or thirty years, as our executive board members had, it's pretty hard to think of something new. Things had gone well for all these years, and they hadn't had to deal with major changes."

JwP's second major strategy was to develop a committee to identify alternative products with existing markets that could be produced at the plant. In 1989 the union established its Alternative Use Committee, modeled after union organizing at Lucas Aerospace in England in the mid-1970s, to identify profitable commercial products that would use the skills of the existing workforce. Organizers saw this as a way to build ownership in the project within the union as well as to develop new product ideas that could save jobs at the plant. With money and technical assistance from the state and city of St. Paul, ideas from workers on the shop floor were matched with industry studies of markets. Then in 1990 the Alternative Use Committee published a report, "Economic Conversion Opportunities at Unisys in Minnesota," listing thirteen products that could be made at the St. Paul plant and would likely meet an existing demand. These included products for transportation control and management, environmental information systems, and adaptive technologies for the disabled.

When the company refused to discuss these ideas, JwP developed a third strategy to build political pressure against Unisys through pickets, support from politicians, public education, and stockholder resolutions. Unisys management continued to refuse to meet with the Alternative Use Committee despite appeals from the governor and mayor. Activists kept up the pressure with demonstrations and public support. One bitterly cold morning in January when 151 workers were laid off, JwP met the end of the night shift in a demonstration of support that included Governor Perpich, Mayor Scheibel of St. Paul, Minnesota AFL-CIO president Dan Gustafson, and U.S. Senate candidate Paul Wellstone.

Due to public pressure, Unisys management finally agreed to meet with the Alternative Use Committee for the first time in October 1990 and then twice in 1991. The company would not allow nonemployees to be included in these discussions. Unisys explained that it needed to maintain confidentiality, implying that it would be sharing product information at the meetings. The company even asked the union representatives to sign a confidentiality agreement ahead of time. Union leadership agreed to this arrangement because it recognized that the company was hostile to involving its peace and religious allies. At these meetings, management claimed they were already diversifying and ran through a list of products they were developing. But they would not discuss their employees' ideas, which they claimed did not make sense. The union wanted to know how much of the potential new work would be done in Minnesota, but the company would not say. Nevertheless, in 1990 Unisys announced that it would be building a facility to produce one of the products suggested in the alternative use committee's report, a satellite-based remote sensing system. However, the new facility would be in Salt Lake City instead of Minnesota.

Activists continued to build other forms of political pressure for conversion planning. In September 1990 the conversion effort began a petition drive at the plant gate calling on the company to convert. In 1991 JwP promoted a piece of legislation that would have established incentives for companies to create alternative use committees that include management, labor, and community members. These would have priority access to state development and training programs. The bill received union support from the AFL-CIO, IBEW, UAW, AFSCME, and the United Electrical Workers but was actively opposed by Unisys and the other defense contractors.

In 1992 the Alternative Use Committee decided to take its program to the stockholders. It cosponsored a stockholder resolution with the United Methodist Church Board of Pensions and Local 2047 members. These three groups also asked managers of the state pension fund for Minnesota state employees and the State Board of Investments to support their resolutions. The resolution directed management to explore economic conversion options and to use the model of labor, management, and community committees to develop new products. The St. Paul plant would be used as a pilot project. Although the resolution failed, it did spur Unisys management to have their product development staff meet with the Alternative Use Committee. Activists also feel that it contributed to changes in Unisys policy toward civilian products.

One of the major accomplishments of the conversion organizing in

Minnesota was the development of a statewide progressive electoral coalition, the Minnesota Alliance for Progressive Action (MAPA). The group was started in 1988 by Mel Duncan to influence state policies. The alliance eventually included organizations focused on peace, labor, environment, homelessness, and gay and lesbian rights. MAPA has been decisive in the passage of fairer tax laws, anti-hate-crime legislation, and in better funding for low-income housing and for family and children's programs.

COALITION ORGANIZING TECHNIQUES

Coalition organizing requires some common techniques despite the diverse contexts in which these are applied. The remainder of this chapter focuses on the practices of building trust, developing relationships, negotiating areas of agreement and disagreement, and overcoming internal tensions that are inherent in any coalition-building process. Lessons about these techniques are drawn from a critical study of particular coalitions.

Testing Trust: Lessons from Washington

Why should assembly workers at risk of losing their jobs in a defense plant trust a peace activist with a professional job and big ideas about government priorities to care about their fate? The first task in building a coalition is establishing that trust. As a Maine labor activist explained, "You have to build up credibility around the issues that are of immediate importance to the members before you have any platform or ability to talk with people about what they would perceive as 'other issues,' political issues that don't directly relate to their own situation. It's a question of what kind of credibility you have to cash in on." Thus the first stages of coalition building test the integrity of the other side with regard to the movement's primary issues.

Many of the initial tests of trust are symbolic—each side is looking for indications of shared values and understandings that feed confidence. Each group has its own litmus tests that provide shorthand measures of friends and foes. Organized labor looks for the union label on printed material, an American-made car, and other visible indications of purchasing union-made goods. Unions expect respect for picket lines and boycotts, and search for other signs of support for labor actions as well. On a more personal level, environmental and peace activists, particularly women, often find that they must prove that they are tough enough to be accepted by largely male craft unions. One woman activist described, "They test to see if you'll be one of the guys, if you can take it. They respect you if you can."

Peace and environmental organizations also have their litmus tests for allies. Signs of peace movement support include opposition to U.S. military intervention and support for redirecting federal budget priorities from military to civilian purposes. Most peace activists assume that their colleagues support the environmental movement as well. Visible signs include the use of recycled products and conservation of resources in everyday practices. Fuel-efficient cars are more highly regarded than ones made by U.S. unions, and riding a bicycle is an even greater sign of personal commitment. Many look for an appreciation of nature and the outdoors as indicators of allies as well. Respect for gender equality is also expected in these middle-class movements, most visibly in the use of language ("woman" instead of "girl," etc.) and in participation in organizational leadership.

The first meetings among potential coalition partners are critical for building trust. The greater the cultural differences between groups, and the longer their history of conflict, the more negative stereotypes and prejudices each side is likely to have of the other. Participants must be reassured during their first encounters that these stereotypes are either false or do not represent barriers to cooperation. This can be a delicate and sensitive conversation, as each side admits to negative perceptions of the other. However, willingness to state these impressions is a sign of progress toward building trust. If either side is too quick to take offense, participants will lose this opportunity for dialogue, and the coalition will not develop.

WSSF lost such an opportunity in its coalition-building efforts and ended up reinforcing barriers rather than building trust. Its experience offers an instructive example of the importance of these delicate early negotiations.

In the hope of building greater support within the labor community, WSSF approached the Economic Development and Job Retention Committee in the Washington State Labor Council with a proposal to cosponsor a conference on diversifying the defense sector. While the committee agreed, the council refused to approve the conference until WSSF was removed as a cosponsor. One labor leader explained: "When the guys in the Tri-Cities [Hanford] heard that Sane/Freeze is going to be a part of this conference, they went absolutely ape. They just really got pissed. . . .

[They] don't like anybody who's the least bit critical of nuclear. Some of them are environmentalists, [but] they think nuclear power is okay. Among all the environmental choices, and there are no easy ones, probably nuclear power is better than most." Once WSSF was removed as a sponsor, the conference went on with wide union participation.

At the conference union leaders friendly to WSSF agreed to recognize members of the organization from the audience so they could make a statement. The WSSF member who spoke emphasized their common goals, saying, "I know we don't agree on everything, but we have a lot of common ground on these particular issues. And if we put our voices together, they'll be that much stronger." But members in the audience wanted to know Sane's position on nuclear power, the primary concern of the unions at Hanford. While this is a subject on which Sane did not have an official position, a Sane representative answered that most members would probably be concerned about the environmental implications of any energy program, and would probably have questions about nuclear power. This attempted honesty played directly into union fears, which could have been easily avoided by reporting that WSSF didn't work on nuclear power issues. During the break, an angry leader from the labor council warned Sane participants against talking too openly about issues that could divide the people at the conference. He described the event as "a raging forest fire." He recalled having finally had to say, "Look guys, we know you have a strong point of view. We've got to work together on this issue, but we've got to talk about this issue and this issue only. We're not going to talk about nuclear power; we're not going to get into any of these divisive elements. A coalition is people working together on a narrow set of issues. That means we respect the fact that we differ on a wide range of other issues. You don't come in and try to convert people, because it would ruin the coalition."

Sane activists were bewildered by the reaction they received, and they responded to the hostility from segments of labor with a sense of frustration. Concluding that direct cooperation with the unions wouldn't be productive, they decided instead to concentrate on working with labor through state agencies, which the unions viewed as more legitimate. But when the peace organization withdrew from direct coalition-building efforts with labor, it reinforced a sense of difference in the minds of its labor detractors. Sitting on a state committee with few representatives from labor didn't provide any real opportunities to build greater trust. This move essentially blocked the development of WSSF's relationship with the unions.

Subtleties of Relationship Building: Lessons from Maine

Relationship building provides the foundation for cooperation. Potential coalition partners gain familiarity with each other as they begin to build trust during their initial meetings. Development of the coalition depends upon deepening communication and understanding over time so that allies are not just accomplishing tasks together but also strengthening their relationships. As Charles O'Leary, president of the Maine AFL-CIO, explained, "If you want to build coalitions, you have to spend a lot more time than people usually do getting to know the other side. The important thing about coalitions is knowing the people you're coalescing with." Since the complexity of issues that coalitions can address increases with the depth of relationships, seizing an opportunity to deepen a relationship is just as important as working at the task at hand. As a key labor ally in Washington State Sane/Freeze's conversion campaign said, "I think what you will find is that as you take an issue, labor and [the] environmental community and the church council and peace community, and they work with an issue and they get to know each other and they start communicating, and they pick another issue. Through that process they develop a relationship. And through that process, that relationship, if it's managed correctly and if all parties are committed, will continue to grow."

If a coalition succeeds in building relationships across cultural differences, these differences frequently become a source of humor that unifies rather than divides the group. Once people can laugh about their differences, they are united by a shared understanding instead of divided by incompatibility. Stereotypes often become objects of humor, such as unions having a lot of money, peace activists being hippies or having long hair, environmentalists being vegetarians, workers being carnivores or liking to hunt and fish, and liberals insisting on consensus. One environmentalist working in a coalition with labor said,

> Now we know each other's phone numbers, some of each other's likes and dislikes. We now know a little bit how to take each other. In the beginning you don't know what they mean when they say [things] so you react, you're all kind of rough and raw and overreacting and testing and make them jump fences. Things are a lot less sweaty than they used to be in our meetings. People don't get as nervous with each other. Nice things happen in the coalition. When you deal with people over time, you be-

come human to each other. And when you become human to each other, the range of behaviors that you'll accept from each other becomes much greater. We have this thing where we're "the enviro crazies, the labor thugs, the churchies." We kid about it.

To build the relationship, each side must adopt some of the other members' issues as its own. Coalition partners cannot allow themselves to be divided by separate settlements, which is a tactic commonly adopted by adversaries trying to blunt a coalition. As one coalition builder emphasized, "Coalition partners can't be bought off and must stick together." If coalition members allow themselves to be split by making deals with the opposition, they ruin the possibility for future coalitions. Nothing builds trust more than refusing to abandon an ally in the face of an offer for one-sided gain.

Familiarity enables each side to understand and take into account the organizational limitations and pressures experienced by coalition partners. When organizations join in coalitions, they bring with them their unique demands and abilities to act. For example, one union official explained why he could not take positions too far outside the realm of acceptable norms within his organization:

One thing that's keeping me from more involvement with some of the peace groups is the fact that I hold an elected position [in the union]. I have to have the credibility of my members to get elected. I have to draw a line on how far I go with my involvement with some of these [peace] groups to be able to do the job I was elected to do. Other people have more freedom to get involved with some of these on their own because they don't have the influence in the plant that I have. Several of our members have belonged to peace groups in the past.

The experience of the Peace Economy Project in Maine demonstrates the subtlety of relationship building. Judged by public appearance, labor's participation in the PEP was solid. Unions along with management from three major defense employers took part in an initial forum on national conversion legislation. The International Association of Machinists Local 6 from Bath Iron Works assigned an official representative to the PEP steering committee, which also included a representative of BIW management. Local 6 took part in a regional forum about the economic future of Bath-Brunswick, which was addressed by IAM president George Kourpias. When the PEP released its study, "A Shift in Federal Spending: What the Peace Dividend Can Mean to Maine," Local 6 representative Jim Mackie said at the press conference,

> Conversion is the true issue that we in the Machinists Union see as the path to recovery. . . . We must begin producing goods which the consumers can buy. SDI and the B-2 Stealth bomber are not items which we could put under the Christmas tree for our families. . . . Cuts are going to happen—they are happening now. They will not go away by not talking about them. We must embrace studies such as the Peace Economy Project's study and force our legislative representatives, both in Washington and Maine, to assure that DOD [Department of Defense] savings are reinvested back in training and retooling.

But in practice union participants remained skeptical about the coalition and were often privately critical of its activities. Local 6 was leery about working with the peace organization from the beginning. Union staff feared that if their members thought they were supporting disarmament, they would lose their jobs. Indeed, while advocating for conversion, both BIW and the IAM continued to pursue military dollars. From the start the union made it clear that they would leave if they heard that the PEP was doing things the union didn't like.

Union representatives found PEP meetings frustrating and incongruent with their experiences. In the face of additional layoffs, a bitter decertification vote, and pending contract negotiations, one Local 6 activist lamented, "People outside don't understand it's a war going on. They want us to sit down and eat cheese and drink herb tea. We just went through a war. I was telling members they were assholes for trying to decertify the union, and to go from there to a nice meeting with the Peace Economy Project is hard."

Furthermore, union members questioned the effectiveness of the tactics being used, which did not meet their expectations about how to organize. A union leader said, "You can only think about the issue so many ways, and then you need to kick ass about it. We need to run with it. I expect people to fight, not talk nice. If you talk to the governor once and that doesn't work, then do a press conference. Don't wait to talk to him again." Union members felt that conversion "is a great idea, [but] it's pie in the sky." They didn't see conversion as a way of preserving their own jobs. Even the most ardent peace activist in the union felt that worker concern about jobs was not being addressed: "The town meeting initiative or the study that the Peace Economy Project commissioned don't really talk about converting the facility; they talk about taking the money out and putting it into hospitals and schools. Until we deal with facility-based conversion issues and make that a basis of the whole thing, you're basically not going to have a coalition. You're not going to have the self-interest to do so."

Yet labor participants did not discuss their frustrations with other PEP members, who therefore were oblivious to their criticisms and frustrations. Instead, union members chose to limit their participation, although they still remained interested enough in the project to stay minimally involved and to wait to see what would develop. As a result, PEP leaders perceived labor's support to be far greater than it was. They believed wrongly that the unions agreed with them about military budget cuts and the organization's agenda. One key leader said, "They really see the benefits to them, if nothing else the economic benefits, the job benefits, of shifting national priorities. . . . Labor is in tune with the real people who are suffering under the current policies. I think they can see beyond their very own jobs, at least certainly more than business. That's been our experience in Maine, and it may be very unique."

So relationships cannot be taken at face value. They can become frozen in many ways: if partners do not feel that their needs or pressures are understood, if they do not feel listened to and respected, if they do not feel that their interests are being addressed, or if they don't find coalition strategies appropriate. These subtleties can only be understood through honest dialogue when each side feels comfortable expressing itself openly. Without this, coalition partners can always exercise their easiest option—not showing up.

Agreeing to Disagree: Lessons from Minnesota

Agree to disagree—that is the starting point for cooperation. Groups who do not like and trust each other may still find, if they are brought together, that they have reasons to cooperate around a narrow set of issues. As a union activist at Unisys said, "We kept the ground rules strictly 'You talk about what you have in common and what your goal is, and if you do that, you don't get into a lot of discussions about your political differences.' "

This attitude was critical for the coalition in Minnesota between the International Brotherhood of Electrical Workers and Jobs with Peace. However, differences remained that could have undermined the coalition if sides had made different strategic moves. JwP initially had to overcome enormous hostility to build a coalition with labor in Minnesota. The general feeling among defense workers about the peace movement was captured by a member of the United Auto Workers at the Navy contractor FMC when he greeted the JwP delegation, including state representative Karen Clark, saying, "So this is the Karen Clark that wants to take my job away." Unisys workers had also learned to fear peace activists who protested at their plant. Peace activists were shocked to learn that the workers perceived them as potentially violent and threatening. They had a rare opportunity to learn how workers perceived them in May 1989, shortly after the Unisys conversion effort began, when the company announced another layoff. IBEW called a picket at the plant in support of conversion, possibly the first such picket in this country. On the picket line were women involved with Women Against Military Madness (WAMM), who had been part of a peace encampment at Unisys in 1984. Some of the union and WAMM members had an opportunity to share impressions from that encampment five years earlier. Union members told peace activists: "We were actually scared to get our cars in and out of the parking lot sometimes when [you] leafleted [at Unisys]." Unisys workers saw peace activists as dangerous people, although WAMM members had come to educate not intimidate the Unisys workers. These were the attitudes that the peace organization faced in the labor community when it began its conversion organizing.

Not long after JwP was organized, conditions were becoming critical for IBEW Local 2047, which represents production workers at Unisys. The union shrank consistently from 4,000 members in 1985 to just 990 in 1992, due to both the merger of Sperry and Borroughs to form Unisys in 1986 and from loss of military contracts. When the company announced layoffs of another 450 people in 1985, some leaders from IBEW were not satisfied with Unisys's reassurances that business would soon be profitable. Instead they agreed to meet with the state AFL-CIO, JwP, and government advocates of conversion to try to develop a strategy to save jobs. From the beginning the union was cautious about working on conversion. Many union members had a "wait and see" attitude about the project, and the union was reluctant to devote resources to it. The executive board did not endorse the idea initially and was divided about participating in this new initiative. Union leadership was particularly careful to gauge member interest and support when involving coalition members from outside the union.

Caution was appropriate since the union and JwP had different but, as it turned out, complementary agendas. The union was clear that it would never oppose weapons systems that provide jobs for members. But as the military budget declined, workers came to believe that the company should not build its future on trying to get more defense contracts. Unisys's St. Paul facility, they argued, could be a model for the company in its efforts to diversify. By contrast, Minnesota JwP advocated for reductions in the military budget. In 1985 it began to organize explicitly for military cuts through a budget priorities campaign. It worked with service sector unions to try to build a broader alliance that included other peace and justice groups as well as unions. This fundamental difference would have precluded the coalition except at this particular time when the military budget was declining.

But community activists and union members also had different goals for conversion. JwP, while committed to trying to save jobs, defined conversion in broader political terms. The Working Group on Economic Dislocation, a member of the coalition that worked closely with the AFL-CIO, shared JwP's emphasis on labor participation in the decision-making process. Like the peace organization, it saw its role as trying to prod unions to think strategically about their situations and to challenge business decisions about closing facilities. They believed,

> Conversion is about bringing the unions into business planning. The only conversion projects we think are worthwhile are where there's a real role for labor to have a voice in it, where there's a shift in power in the process. Otherwise we're not interested. What are the workers going to get out of it? And so it wasn't enough for us if Unisys said, "Yeah, we'll work on conversion." No, they've got to involve the union and they've got to involve this Alternative Use Committee as a representative of the community because there's a community stake in it. Unisys never bought that at all.

This approach to conversion was significantly different from the union's view about the purpose of its efforts, which were much more narrowly focused on saving jobs. As one union activist said, "We're not asking Unisys for us to tell them what to make, and we're not asking them to invest in something that's not profitable by any means. All we're saying is 'Look at us. We have intelligence, we have ideas, we're a highly skilled workforce. Use it, use it to make more money for the company. Because if you make more money, we get a job.' That's what it boils down to in a nutshell. [We don't even care to be] part of the process—just take the ideas. Accept them, and let us help."

These different goals could have split the coalition, except that JwP accepted that the union had to make its own decisions about how to proceed. There was a debate in both JwP and the union about how confrontational to be with Unisys management. In this discussion, JwP served as advisors to the union. Mel Duncan recounted: "JwP did have a lot of latitude, quite frankly. But it wasn't for Jobs with Peace's board to decide what the union at Unisys should do. We were much more in the supportive role." The union therefore set the pace in terms of strategy, and they were sensitive about not offending the company. Therefore they began very moderately by asking about Unisys's future plans. But the company was not willing to discuss its plans with its workers. Management intransigence about developing new product lines in St. Paul brought together the union and peace positions. IBEW could not hope to preserve jobs without influencing the decisions of Unisys.

As a labor activist put it, "The major hang up on this whole thing was Unisys's absolute refusal to work with the commission or the task force. Their basic line was, 'We don't want the community or union involved in our business plans. We have an R&D department that looks at a whole host of different products. We're very familiar with our business, and we're the ones who will make up our business plans.' They said, 'We don't want your involvement. We don't want the state having any goddamn role whatever in what we do.'"

As this quote illustrates, union members were politicized by management's blatant disregard for their creative efforts and interests. Thus while both labor and the peace organization began by agreeing to work together despite fundamental differences, over time conscious educating and organizing reduced these differences significantly.

Internal Tensions: Lessons from Maine

Coalitions can shift and challenge loyalties as new relationships alter people's focus and understandings. Diversifying the military economy was noncontroversial in Maine—but cutting the defense budget further or opposing existing military production was a different story. The PEP risked its labor and business ties by pushing for greater military cuts, but it risked its peace credentials by being attuned to the concerns of military-dependent allies. It sought to find this balance between its values and commitments both to the peace movement and to labor and other allies.

From the beginning the PEP represented a major shift in emphasis within the Maine Peace Campaign. One member explained that in the past "we were focused on specific weapons systems [such as] killing the MX and Star Wars and Stealth bombers." Now the project began to look "at the larger picture, defining security in terms of global security and in terms of environment and social and economic interests." PEP activists found that many people didn't understand this new direction at first. They found that even after two years "there was a whole educational process within the organization that is still happening and really is just now taking off. . . . I think people are understanding now what it's all about."

To oversee this organizing, the project established a more diverse board than traditionally supported its parent organization, the Maine Peace Campaign. The PEP sought to involve all stakeholders in the community including business, labor, government, religious groups, social service advocates, and peace and disarmament groups. About half of this committee had no prior affiliation with the peace movement. "Before," one recruit recalled, "I would never [have] been caught dead with a peace group. Never. I thought peace people were hippies and extreme. I've never been one to take a position on [peace issues]. But the defense budgets are being cut, [and] the role of peace groups from my perception is changing. Now there is a very positive role for peace groups to play. This [Peace Economy] Project that we're working on is so fantastic because we have built such an unusual coalition of people."

For those from the peace movement as well, this diversity was new. One board member from the Physicians for Social Responsibility (PSR) commented: "The PSR meetings were attended just by like-minded, like-thinking, politically similar doctors. We were all the same age, had the same thoughts. On the PEP steering committee, . . . there are some real oddities for the peace movement: a couple businessmen, a fellow who's fairly high up from Bath Iron Works, labor."

Maintaining trust with this diverse community required the PEP to modify and at times challenge accepted peace movement behavior. Within the Maine Peace Campaign (MPC), disarmament advocates occasionally found themselves at odds with the consensus building of the economic project. These differences were most evident in electoral politics. For example, the PEP blocked the MPC's desire to endorse a vocally pro-peace congressional candidate. Project staff felt that such a step would alienate people it works with outside the peace movement. But they were comfortable with the MPC requesting that national Sane/Freeze give its endorsement instead. In another example, during the Gulf War the PEP decided that it would not take a public position but would try to shift debate back to the military budget and the need for reductions and conversion planning. One PEP activist explained, "Personally it's hard because during the Gulf War I wanted to be out in the streets demonstrating. Parts of me want to lie down in front of busses and things like that. But I don't think that's the most effective way to get the job done. I don't personally do those things."

The PEP is careful to distance itself from peace protests at BIW in particular. The Maine Peace Campaign encourages opposition to the production of military hardware at BIW and other facilities. When BIW launched the Aegis cruiser *Lake Erie* in 1991, the MPC helped organize protests. It wrote to members saying, "As the Quakers say, we have a responsibility to speak truth to power. A few hundred letters from Peace Campaign supporters like yourself can go a long way toward raising public awareness around the Aegis." The union, however, felt that these protests would jeopardize their chances of getting future Navy contracts. One union leader said, "I kiss the Navy's butt in public. The Navy follows everything that happens including labor relations. The peace people don't understand that I need to be seen with the Navy commander on TV at a ship launching saying that we'll build the ships faster than anyone else." He recounted that when he was asked to speak by a peace organization that was also protesting the launching of a cruiser, he told the group he never wanted to hear from them again. The PEP must not be associated with the Maine Peace Campaign protests if it is to work with the unions.

The PEP's efforts to appeal to a wider audience ultimately became quite controversial in the peace movement. As an educational tool, the project first sponsored community impact studies in seven towns. The studies illustrated that more tax dollars leave these towns for military purposes than return to meet local needs. They concluded that Maine taxpayers contribute more to the Pentagon than to the total cost of running all town and city governments in the state. To reach the business community with the message that the country should shift federal spending priorities to domestic needs, the PEP invited the former CIA director William Colby to be the keynote speaker at its press conference presenting the results of its studies. But the peace community remembers Colby as director of the Phoenix program, a brutal campaign that tortured and killed over twenty thousand North Vietnamese civilians suspected of supporting the Vietcong. Colby continued to defend this program, and more recently opposed the peace movement by supporting the Gulf War. One MPC member called Colby "one of the butchers of history" who should not be allowed to speak for peace activists. For her, "People like Colby have no interest in peace as a moral issue. The idea that we can use these people to gain credibility is claptrap. This kind of celebrity endorsement stuff is the exact opposite of grassroots citizen involvement in the peace movement. It is a strategy that doesn't empower citizens and it isn't how we are effective."

To some extent the MPC and the PEP have been able to use their different styles strategically. One MPC activist described how they could play "good cop, bad cop" to influence certain politicians. The PEP would create good working relations with Maine's congressional delegation and would be more conciliatory in style. Then the MPC would threaten wider protests, which would help some people cooperate with the PEP. The two approaches could be used to complement each other. Certainly the division of labor was critical to the success of the PEP, as organizer Susie Schweppe saw: "It's hard to balance your support for all kinds of different strategies, but yet stay separate so that one doesn't undermine the other. We're trying to say that there's room for all of this, there's a need for all of this. You do this, you do that, that and that, we're going to do this. And together we can do it [all]. But there's certain things the project just simply can't do because it would just be suicide."

These tensions precipitated a debate about whether or not the MPC and the PEP should separate. Dividing would allow the MPC to be a strong and vocal advocate and the PEP to pursue cooperation without restricting each other. One proponent of separation believed division would be mutually advantageous. In his words: "I do not want to dilute the effectiveness of the Peace Campaign. And I think if each group were free to follow its own strategies and not undermine the effort of [the other group], together we can make a much bigger difference than if we are forced to compromise some of the things we're doing." As this person saw it, the more conciliatory PEP could play a positive role, even as a separate organization, in shifting public perceptions of the peace movement. He explained, "Ideally what would happen is to change the traditional assumptions about the peace community within the business community and defense contractors and whoever else is out there who has a certain set of ideas about who the peace community is and what they are about. Peace shouldn't be a dirty word, and we should be allowed to speak it. It should have credibility."

Others recognized the positive value of this tension between the PEP and the MPC. A Maine Peace Campaign activist explained,

I feel there's a very constructive tension and a very educational process that goes on by my having to be sensitive to not gratuitously alienating the constituencies that the Peace Economy Project [is] trying to reach out to. And [there's] also a constructive educational process in the Peace Economy Project being careful to be sensitive to the thoughts of the rest of the Peace Campaign on the issues that they're grappling with. I think it's a very good thing. It helps both parts of the organization to keep in mind factors they should be keeping in mind anyway, such as how to work on economic conversion and how to reach out to local business and local officials without losing sight of the peace principles that motivated you to do the economic conversion work. And such as how to do non-intervention and disarmament work while opening instead of closing the eyes of a lot of mainstream constituencies, such as local elected officials. So I think it's an educational and a positive tension that goes on. I think overall it's good for the effectiveness of our work.

The PEP also experienced internal tensions between its goals of changing national spending priorities and planning for local conversion. Overall they saw these goals as mutually reinforcing: changing budget priorities would create the conditions necessary for conversion, yet conversion would be necessary to build the support to change the military budget. But defense firms and workers did not want to see further cuts in the military budget, while some peace activists did not want to devote their energies to revitalizing military firms. The project, however, promoted both openly. Jon Reitman, chair of the PEP steering committee, believed this tension was valuable. As he said, "The cutting edge of the transition of this society right now is how far and how quickly we can make this transition while still reassuring people who work in those defense dependent industries and communities that we haven't forgotten about them."

PEP organizers sought to minimize conflict with its union and defense firm participants over its advocacy for cutting the military budget by linking conversion to calls for cuts. This was often not very effective, however, and labor participants felt that their point of view wasn't taken seriously when it differed from the PEP agenda of advocating for military cuts. For example, the PEP hired Employment Research Associates, a consulting firm from Lansing, Michigan, to study the costs of an annual 7 percent decline in the defense budget for four years. While the study was initially endorsed by the state AFL-CIO and Local 6, both felt that the consultants who interviewed them already had decided that the report would find a net gain of jobs in Maine with defense cuts. They felt their criticisms of this conclusion were not addressed, and they refused to work with the consultants because of their "arrogant attitude." The report did predict a net gain of three thousand jobs from defense cuts in addition to improved education, health care services, transportation, and pollution control. The state AFL-CIO refused to endorse the report's conclusions since, in their minds, it advocated a substantial cut in jobs at BIW. The union representative who convinced the state AFL-CIO to endorse the report felt, "The Peace Economy Project knew what they wanted to find and say. They used labor's credibility to get it out." This feeling among labor played a big role in its tentative participation in the PEP.

Lessons about Coalition Organizing

Coalitions in Maine, Minnesota, and Washington made important contributions to conversion in these states. Washington established the first statewide program to assist communities and firms to shift to civilian production. The program supported innovative diversification initiatives such as manufacturing networks and commercial use of Navy base facilities. Maine developed a statewide office of economic conversion and set up programs to assist communities, businesses, and workers to make the transition to commercial alternatives. They also helped start and nurture broad collaborative organizations including Sustainable Maine and the Maine Transportation Initiative to develop conversion opportunities in the transportation sector. Minnesota's organizing also resulted in statewide conversion programs to assist displaced workers and help companies make the transition to civilian products. Most important, it demonstrated the ability of workers to plan for new product development while building working relationships between unions and other progressive groups in the state.

Organizers in each community also contributed vital experience to the art of interclass coalition building. On the front lines of movement organizing, where every experiment is the best you can do with what you've got, these coalitions made both mistakes and important breakthroughs. They learned lessons about negotiating strategies that drew on the resources of personality, culture, and context. Building trust and relationships and agreeing to disagree are the ingredients that combine to make diverse coalitions possible. But these are evolving processes—most severely tested at first but requiring wise and conscious development over time if the coalition is to deepen and strengthen.

Building trust requires direct, ongoing interaction and honest face-to-face dialogue. Attendance at the same formal meetings isn't enough to allow for meaningful discussion, since people's public statements can hide as much as they reveal about their feelings. Direct communication can be intimidating, especially when potential coalition partners test to see whether the other side respects and supports their primary concerns. But questions about one's trustworthiness can be expected and require careful response. Listening to the other side's feelings provides an opportunity to learn how the coalition can better address the interests and needs of partners, whereas withdrawing from conflict reinforces stereotypes and hinders development of the relationship. It is critical for each side to remain in direct dialogue.

Coalition partners need to agree to disagree about the majority of differences in the interest of cooperating around some mutually beneficial goals. This includes allowing each side the freedom to act on the issues that impact it directly. Working on issues together enables coalition partners to develop deeper relationships. At the same time stronger relationships enable coalitions to take on more complex and politically challenging issues. The complexity of issues addressed evolves gradually with the depth of the relationship.

Successful strategies work within the level of conflict that members and allies accept. Yet, comfort levels evolve and change as the campaign develops, provided the opportunity for change is present. IBEW grew more willing to confront Unisys as it became clearer that the company was blatantly unwilling to dialogue. Political leaders in Minnesota followed a similar trajectory. Washington State Sane/Freeze, on the other side, had to become less confrontational in order to build on its alliance with labor and the state Democratic leadership to pass its legislation. The PEP remained cooperative throughout despite the frustration of labor allies. But given the PEP's broader agenda of building an alliance with all stakeholders, labor's influence on the coalition was limited and so strategies didn't evolve.

Appropriate strategies between peace and labor, that is, between middle- and working-class organizations, depend upon the strategies pursued by management. Where management is hostile, as at Unisys, this presents an opportunity for a coalition against the common enemy. When management is cooperative, as it ultimately was at BIW with both its workforce and the peace organization, there is both the opportunity and the need for collaboration. When labor closes ranks with management, as it did at Boeing, then alternative strategies that work indirectly through other institutions are necessary, as WSSF learned.

Coalition organizing across class lines is ultimately the challenge of making outsiders and strangers into insiders and political allies. Issues matter fundamentally—but the process is a *social process* of integrating groups that ordinarily don't sit at the same tables. Labor and peace organizations are communities unto themselves, comfortable because people with like ideas or like situations come together. Coalitions change these familiar settings. They bring other people to the table who have different interests, customs, and ideas. Those people may even be hostile. They may have beliefs and behaviors that violate each other's fundamental principles. As organizations learn to work with new coalition partners, they may move away from customary practices, which can raise conflicts within their own movements. At best this is a constructive dialogue that raises new questions and provides thoughtful caution for those venturing into new territory. Nevertheless, this process can cause real anger and soul searching within the movement.

Those who venture into these uncharted waters do well to think of themselves as foreigners learning another culture among people who assume they may be hostile. If the other side spoke another tongue or inhabited a far-off place, then the task would be more obvious. But they don't—they use the same words and refer to the same events, but with meanings that are obscure. Coalition builders need to unpack the prejudices and stereotypes, find those common cultural reference points, become familiar with each other's goals, interests, and limitations, and take action together.

▲

CHAPTER EIGHT

Learning in Coalitions

Funny thing about coalitions—as you build coalitions you need to diversify your understandings, to broaden your views to take in what the others see. You start out saying you'll just look at the narrow issues you agree on and ignore the ones you disagree on, and then you end up broadening your views to include their issues and understandings. That's the value of coalitions, that they get people to broaden their understandings.

—A labor leader in Seattle

We're learning to help each other, and that's a big step. There are still, in parts of the country, labor guys who hate enviros or think they're the suburban shit of the earth. There are still plenty of enviros who don't understand labor issues, who probably think these are overpaid, beer-bellied autoworkers who are forcing us to buy inferior products. The whole shebang. A little change happened, a little movement happened [in the coalition]. I think we found that we can help each other, that we have information and ways to get into the structure that are different from each other's.

—An environmentalist in Seattle

It was the summer of 1990 when Bob Dilger, executive secretary of the Washington State Building and Construction Trades, led a delegation to meet with the Washington Environmental Council (WEC) to talk about mending their fifteen-year-old rift. The WEC is the major legislative voice for the environmental community in Washington and an umbrella organization of over ninety local and statewide environmental groups. The Building Trades represents 124 skilled trade union locals such as electricians, plumbers, and laborers from nine regional councils in Washington and Oregon. When the WEC was formed in 1967, the Washington State Labor Council (WSLC) joined as a founding member. Dilger was the same man who led the entire Washington State Labor Council out of the WEC in the mid-1970s because construction workers saw environmentalists opposing job-creating projects such as nuclear power plants, highway construction, the Alaska oil pipeline, and construction at the Hanford nuclear reservation. The Building Trades convinced the Labor Council to join its own alternative organization, the Washington Environmental Trades Association, which had the goal of balancing environmental protection and development.

Now in 1990 the Building Trades decided they wanted to make friends with the WEC. The 1980s had been tough for organized labor in the construction trades, as contractors took their cues from the Reagan administration to declare war on their unions. The unions had lost most of the residential market, and nonunion shops were competing for the big jobs as well. These attacks led the unions to look for other allies. As Dilger explained, "[Business] wants labor to work with them on things like the environment, but [they] fight labor on issues that are good for [labor]. From that experience, [the building trades] decided they would develop their own alliances." But more than that, concern about the environment was also growing among trade workers as more facts about hazards became available. Building trades members were making it known that they wanted a clean environment and good-quality buildings as well as stable jobs.

The WEC also wanted closer ties with labor, particularly after its defeats on growth control. Environmentalists opposed the state's growth management legislation enacted in 1990. They countered with a ballot initiative for "balanced growth," which they hoped would replace the 1990 Growth Management Act. But with concerted opposition from the business community, the initiative lost by a wide margin despite strong public support for the goal of growth management. Ted Pankowski, WEC executive director, explained the council's decision to begin to build an alliance with labor in these terms: "Here we were being beat up [by the business community], run over every chance they get. The powers that be thought we did not know how to form alliances. So I thought, 'Hey, they don't know what we can do.' "

So when WEC and Building Trades representatives met, the atmosphere was tense but expectant. Three representatives from each group sat facing each other across the table. To break the ice, someone commented about WEC president Darlene Madenwald's pin, purchased during a recent trip to the Soviet Union. Dilger too had recently visited the Soviet Union. So for forty-five minutes environmentalists and union leaders discussed travels that would have raised political suspicions only a few years earlier. When the discussion finally returned to the purpose at hand, environmentalists and union leaders agreed to disagree about the unresolved issues that divided them, particularly nuclear power. They recognized that they shared an interest in quality-of-life issues that have both environmental and economic dimensions. As a starting point, labor said it would not support construction projects that are not environmentally safe, and they would work with environmentalists to find alternative locations for projects that are environmentally detrimental. On other issues, such as preserving salmon runs, they would work with environmentalists to reduce the damage caused by construction projects. The environmentalists agreed to expand their attention to quality-of-life issues. And, finally, they agreed to meet prior to the legislative session to discuss issues they could work on together.

Here was a promising start to a new coalition between the two state organizations. But how did this surprising reconciliation come about? Now that each side had expressed its agreement to work for a better quality of life, how would they make this concrete without returning to the well-worn conflict between construction jobs and preserving the environment? Environmentalists knew little about the struggles facing labor, and the unions had their hands full without learning the intricacies of environmental issues. Furthermore, while the leadership had made a step toward cooperating, many members certainly did not see this as appropriate or even desirable. Each side had much to learn if this coalition were to prove politically useful.

LEARNING TO BE CITIZENS

Movements can't afford to stand still. If they don't continue to learn and adapt, they lose ground. Legislation can be reversed, court decisions overturned, rights revoked, gains lost. The labor and environmental movements rediscovered this the hard way in the 1980s. They had to learn to counter the assaults against them and to find new strategies to advance their goals.

In movements, people learn by doing, and the lessons of public life don't come easily. Our initial passions, anger, questions, and ideals are matched by numerous misconceptions about how politics works and what it takes to make change. When people join a movement or begin a campaign, they are never clear about what it will take to win. Most ambiguous are the personal changes required to prevail, since confronting powerful groups collectively in public demands skills and attitudes not developed in people's private lives. Organizing is always as much about political education as it is about achieving specific victories. So movements need to generate a lot of heat to realize a little bit of enlightenment for their members.

By the 1980s, however, many labor and environmental organizations had ceased to function as schools for democracy. National environmental organizations and unions were run like businesses, where members paid for services that were carried out by hired professionals. The number of people sending checks to environmental organizations boomed in the 1980s in response to direct mail campaigns and newspaper headlines about the Reagan administration's blatant attacks on environmental laws. But many of these members faded away just as quickly in the 1990s once the government took a "kinder and gentler" approach to the environment. Signing checks and receiving literature did little to engage thousands of new environmental supporters in the process of changing society.

Union members had also grown complacent about the role of the union. Turnout for meetings and real participation in union business were low. Nationwide antiunion sentiment and attacks by employers were disheartening to some who questioned the effectiveness of unions. Unions spent most of their time serving their members' immediate needs and enforcing their contracts, and had little time to develop strategies to effect fundamental changes. Few unions put resources into organizing. While the number of union members was on the decline, those who remained expected decent wages and regular work. So they were not prepared when their union contractors began aggressively to try to destroy them in the 1980s, a strategy that the Business Roundtable had already been promoting for a decade. Employers set up nonunion companies and hiring halls to undermine union work, established nonunion apprenticeship training programs, and attacked legal protections for paying prevailing wages on government contracts. Business unions had done little to involve union members in the real work of protecting their interests against these tactics.

Active engagement in organizing is critical for people to learn how to participate in the decisions that affect them. Movements provide opportunities for this direct learning-by-doing. When people become active in a movement to promote a cause or fulfill a need, they are forced to express their opinions and translate them into actions. Movements teach people to articulate their ideas and present them in public; to engage in dialogue about values, interests, and strategies; and to research problems and develop strategies for change.

Movements teach an alternative way of interpreting problems and events, an interpretation that provides a framework for collective action. People who were isolated discover that others have the same feelings and interests, and that their problems—which they used to think of as personal failings or the result of eccentric values or lifestyles—are shared. Injustice is given a name. Anger is redirected to the institutions or causes that are responsible.

Movements teach about the ways that power works in society, revealing forms of injustice that are often masked by ideology and misrepresentation. Many people take at face value the ideals about democracy and self-governance, equal opportunity, and morality that are espoused by government, business, and civic leaders. By undertaking actions that test these ideals, people learn about how our society falls short. They see that corporations, organized interest groups, and those with wealth and education have greater access to the media, elected officials, and government bureaucrats. Lessons about unjust and arbitrary power are disillusioning, but they can also increase commitments to work for fundamental change. As Lois Gibbs explains from her experience in fighting toxic chemical exposure at Love Canal,

I grew up in a blue-collar community. We were very into democracy. There is something about discovering that democracy isn't democracy as we know it. When you lose faith in your government, it's like finding out your mother was fooling around on your father. I was very upset. It almost broke my heart because I really believed in the system. I still believe in the system, only now I believe that democracy is of the people and by the people, that people have to move it, it ain't gonna move by itself.[1]

Possibly the most powerful lesson of movement participation is self-respect and a sense of self-worth, which counter that most insidious consequence of oppression: the victim's internalized sense of inferiority, unworthiness, and impotence.[2] Even people who feel very competent in their personal lives find themselves feeling powerless to affect public problems. Acting together can be liberating as participants learn to value their contributions and to assert their rights to equal treatment and respect. The more people see the inner workings of powerful groups, the more they recognize that these comprise people just like themselves, without any special claim on the truth. Activists come to understand their condition as a social and political creation, and not due to their own faults or failings. They gain the confidence to express themselves and act in public. Movement organizations provide the context for disempowered people to learn that they can understand the causes of their conditions, make collective decisions, speak persuasively, and represent their views to the media and to public officials. These roles are not reserved for those with special expertise or talent. As one organizer notes, "People become leaders when they discover they do a whole range of things they never believed they were capable of."[3] Effective movement organizations nurture this personal development.

Finally, collective action teaches participants about their abilities to effect change. It dispels illusions about the inevitability of present arrangements and the omnipotence of those in power. Through action, people come to recognize their potential to change themselves and transform society. They learn that they do not need to accept existing social rules, but that they can act to change those rules. As Paulo Freire says, the oppressed "discover themselves as [reality's] re-creators."[4] Movement participation teaches people that they have the power to remake the world in which they live.

All these lessons of movement participation require the active and sustained involvement of members in the organizing process. Passive membership forfeits these transformative dimensions. When unions and environmental organizations become professionally run service providers, they lose their most important role as forums for political education and participation. In so doing they also undermine their own power, which derives from their ability to mobilize people. When members are uninvolved and cannot be mobilized, an organization grows weak. This is what happened to the movements in the 1980s. In the 1990s both the labor and environmental movements went back to basics—with a renewed emphasis on direct participation of members and local rather than national organizing. At the local level organizers have had to reinvigorate their members by convincing them that direct action on their part could accomplish meaningful changes—in other words, that their participation mattered.

Experiments and Resistance to Change

A cadre of young union organizers and business agents from the Seattle building trades began to face the challenges of revitalizing the labor movement in the mid-1980s as they gathered to discuss organizing strategies. Among the leaders were representatives from Latherers Local 1144 and International Brotherhood of Electrical Workers Local 46. They felt that their unions had to take dramatic steps to preserve their organizations and maintain union protections in the construction trades. In their view the unions were partly to blame for their predicament. They had been complacent about losing smaller jobs to nonunion labor while protecting better wages, benefits, and conditions for their shrinking numbers. Unions also needed allies in the broader community to turn around their fortunes, and they saw coalition building as key to their success. They recognized that labor had acquired a negative public image as concerned only about its own welfare and not about the community. They proposed that if unions worked on wider community issues, then maybe community groups would join in supporting union jobs. All this would add to the relevance and effectiveness of the unions, which would help organizers involve and mobilize their members.

These activists found a useful model for coalition building in the organizing of the Pipe Trades Council of Northern California, which consists of the United Association of Plumbers and Pipefitters (UA) Districts 16 and 51. Their "Job and Community Protection Program" seeks to "force construction companies to pay their employees a living wage, including health and other benefits, and to meet their responsibilities to the community and the environment." The union hired environmental lawyers and building inspectors to help them identify environmental violations at nonunion construction sites. Their efforts forced companies to reduce pollution from proposed industrial sites and to comply with existing codes. The union increased its share of construction work by crippling noncooperative companies and aggressively promoting union contractors. Where the unions had lost almost all of the residential market, now a majority of that work is being done with union plumbers.

In Seattle IBEW Local 46 took the lead in applying these new organizing tactics. In 1987, with the support of the Latherers, it entered its first environmental fight over a change in Seattle's electrical code that would allow the use of polyvinyl chloride (PVC) pipe instead of metal to encase wire. The fumes from burning PVC are deadly, a hazard facing workers as well as the public. But PVC conduits are cheaper and require less labor with less skill to install. The union developed a show of metal and plastic tubing to demonstrate the dangers of PVC. It traveled to community groups, environmental organizations, and others asking for support. Many community organizations were surprised; they had never had a union approach them before. IBEW won WEC board support for its campaign in May 1988. While the union lost the issue, it built some initial ties with environmental and community organizations.

Local 46 then sought support from environmental groups to halt nonunion construction that would harm the environment. The union found that environmentalists were amazed and repulsed at first by the idea of unions using environmental laws to intervene in nonunion construction jobs. In the view of one environmentalist, "It's an unholy alliance in a way." But after they overcame their original repugnance, they began to see that "they could use labor as a tool, and be used as a tool."

Beginning in 1988, IBEW and the Latherers challenged plans by Daishowa Paper Manufacturing Company for the largest industrial expansion in the history of the Olympic Peninsula. The Japanese corporation purchased a paper mill in 1988 in Port Angeles and proposed to invest $560 million to triple production. But union research indicated that the construction would be done with nonunion labor and would create housing and traffic problems in town, potentially harming the local tourist industry. To gain community support, the union developed a plan to contribute money to mitigate housing pressures. They would work long days during the week in order not to compete with weekend tourists, and they would provide their own housing trailers during the peak summer season. Their ultimate means of influencing Daishowa, however, came from the unlikely source of the Australian Labor Party government. IBEW organizers discovered that Daishowa was in the midst of a major controversy over environmental damage from its eucalyptus tree cutting in Australia. Through a labor contact, they communicated with the Central Labor Council of Western Australia and ultimately with the national Labor government. The Australian government informed Daishowa that any agreement over their eucalyptus operations would require a settlement of the company's labor dispute in Washington. The result was a union agreement.

In 1990 the election for business manager in Local 46 was something of a referendum on the new, more aggressive style of organizing in the union. Hank Maguire, one of the key architects of the new organizing strategies, ran on a platform of open communication and debate, increased participation in the union, and public outreach for support. His defeat reflected in part the opposition of the national union to Maguire's more activist organizing, and in part a split among members over this shift away from old-style business unionism. Another organizer, Jim Freese, was elected union president and, because of his popularity, remained the head of organizing. Some organizing continued at the local, but the new administration limited its scope in favor of serving members.

IBEW's organizing, however, had already inspired others in the building trades to follow its lead and continue the coalitions it had begun. Rick Bender, executive secretary of the Seattle Building and Construction Trades Council, recognized that the entire building trades could benefit from the kinds of techniques being used by IBEW, the Latherers, and the Northern California Pipe Trades. So he sponsored a conference titled "Rebound: Tactics for 1988 and Beyond." As Rick Bender hoped, that conference led to the founding of an ongoing organization, Rebound, within the Seattle Building Trades. Its purpose is to enforce prevailing wage, safety, and other laws and to "eliminate unfair and illegal competition in the construction industry." To do this it monitors prevailing wage and other wage/hour violations and implements corporate campaigns directed at owners, contractors, and projects that undercut community economic and environmental standards.

It took Rick Bender about six months to obtain a sufficient base to support the organization. By 1991 around half of the building trade unions had joined Rebound. Some unions, such as the Carpenters, refused to join because of opposition from their contractor's organization, the Associated General Contractors. Keeping with earlier practices, the Carpenters agreed not to work with environmental groups, and instead they set up their own parallel organization, the Northwest Fair Contractors Association, to work strictly on prevailing wage issues.

Uses and Abuses of Power

Learning how to take part in public life is necessary for empowering citizens—but it is no guarantee that the cause will be right or just. Grassroots mobilizations can be misguided, exclusive, or downright reactionary. As movements and organizations build power, they gain the ability to exclude, oppress, exacerbate inequalities, shift balances of power, destroy, or withhold help, as well as to advance their positive goals. The history of organizing is rife with examples of intended and unintended abuses. The father of contemporary community organizing, Saul Alinsky, was horrified when his original Back of the Yards Neighborhood Council in Chicago organized effectively to exclude blacks from the neighborhood. As the timber controversy demonstrates, well-intentioned movements can participate in environmental degradation or the destruction of jobs and communities. The techniques of organizing can be harnessed by reactionary as well as progressive movements, as the New Right has demonstrated. The environmental justice movement has been highly critical of middle-class mainstream environmental organizations for contributing to discrimination against people of color.

Issue organizing must confront the danger of parochialism. Movements often emerge from immediate experiences of problems with limited understandings of their causes or the requirements for change. Movements attract self-selected segments of society who share beliefs, experiences, and assumptions and exclude people with divergent perspectives. In general participants are drawn from fairly narrow class, race, or geographic backgrounds. Community organizations and single-issue movements can reinforce the exclusion of outsiders or the protection of local privileges. They can blame outside groups rather than understand more fundamental social causes.

Movements and social change organizations also run the risk of becoming dictatorial as they pursue their own interests or goals. In their enthusiasm to assert their own just cause, activists can become callous about the legitimate interests of others. Organizing can be reduced to a means for competing for resources that leaves intact the political economic system governed by power competition. As Harry Boyte observed in his thoughtful study of community organizing and grassroots democracy,

> Citizen activism has frequently gained voice for marginal, poorer, minority, or relatively powerless communities historically left out of most decision making. . . . But like conventional politics, much of grass-roots activism has spoken a thin, sometimes cynical language of narrow interests and protests detached from any enlarged social and political vision. This kind of activism also neglects the ways in which citizen politics is an art, requiring such abilities a good judgment, skillful use of power, critical thinking, imagination, and rhetoric.[5]

Organizing must also confront the danger of political expediency, which can determine agendas in the name of practical politics. While movements bring new interests and issues to the political process, external pressures encourage them to replicate the political form of the system in which they function. Every aspect of the political process reinforces single-issue advocacy and a narrow agenda. Complex issues require expertise, which encourages organizations to specialize. When movements seek to influence legislation, they find that interconnected issues are disassociated through specialized committees and reduced to discrete legislative goals within a highly contested process of compromise. Furthermore, support for any one issue may well be divided by associating other issues. Movements are therefore rewarded for maintaining a narrow agenda that avoids differences among supporters. Funders also favor narrow, focused projects with limited goals. These and many other forces drive movement organizations into the mold of single-issue advocacy groups.[6]

This tendency for narrow, single-issue politics has been dramatically highlighted within the environmental movement during the 1990s by the rise of environmental justice organizing. The environmental justice movement has criticized the middle-class environmental movement for its failure to address a range of urban and social justice issues and its exclusion of people of color and low-income groups from its ranks. Centralization of the mainstream organizations in Washington, D.C., and their focus on politics "inside the beltway" made the environmental movement unresponsive to community needs and left it uninformed about the social dimensions of many environmental issues.

Interclass and intermovement coalitions have the potential to overcome the problems of parochialism, lack of vision, and expediency that plague single-issue, socially homogenous movements and organizations. Collaboration with diverse groups provides an avenue for public learning based on a broader, more complex dialogue with people from other classes, races, political perspectives, and social backgrounds. Participants are forced to address issues outside their narrow experiences. They must negotiate and compromise with diverse interests, modeling practices that are essential in a complex, diverse democracy. And they need to balance short-term political gains with the interests and needs of other impacted groups, which requires more complex and fundamental changes than working within the existing political system.

STRENGTH IN UNITY

As interest in working with environmentalists grew in the building trades, so did the desire to mend relations with the Washington Environmental Council. But there were risks as well as potential benefits of building this alliance. Neither side could be sure that its own members would perceive a closer alliance as appropriate, and both sides risked internal dissent. Each side also faced the risk that an alliance would alienate politicians, business interests, and public supporters who were opposed to the other movement. The unions were particularly nervous about working with an organization that had opposed development projects, and they did not want to be perceived as initiating contact. They therefore asked the WEC to write a letter requesting a meeting with them. This provided the excuse for proposing a meeting to the executive board of the state building trades, which led to the initial discussion between the leaders of both organizations.

Not long after the legislative session began in 1991, the building trades called on the WEC to assist in a battle to defend the prevailing wage. State law requires governments to hire construction workers at wages that are typical for each region, which the state determines by regular wage surveys. In the past, union wages set the standard in their communities. Maintaining a union wage scale with public construction projects was critical to the building trades, and they asked the WEC to testify against a bill to exempt school construction projects from paying prevailing wages. The WEC executive committee discussed the matter and agreed that the prevailing wage does relate to its mission of protecting the environment. So WEC's president testified at a hearing before the state Senate Commerce and Labor Committee and explained the organization's position in these terms:

Now what in the world is the president of the Washington Environmental Council sitting up here with labor for? I know you're all asking that question. I just want to talk to you for a minute about a couple of things that are dear to my heart. One is linkages. The environmental community is always looking for linkages . . . with other peoples of this state [to] come together on a common cause, a common issue. And this is one that's brought me here today, and it's a quality of life issue. I've fought for the quality of the environment, but I also care about the quality of wages paid to workers. . . . We . . . at the Washington Environmental Council have limited resources, . . . but we do pay our workers well because we care about the quality of work that they give us. So this is why I'm here today with these gentlemen and why I support the workers in this room, because I dearly care that they care enough to stay in the community, that they're paid enough, and that they care enough that they do the job right.

Environmental support helped defeat the bill to exempt school construction from paying prevailing wage.

Growth management offered a second opportunity for cooperation, despite the building trades' historic opposition to limits on construction. In the 1991 legislative session, growth management advocates proposed amendments to strengthen the 1990 law. The Association of Washington Business (AWB) introduced its own bill on growth management to try to derail amendments supported by environmentalists and the governor. Business leaders called a meeting with the building and metal trades and wanted them to support their bill, but labor leaders refused to be divided from their environmental allies. They responded that growth management affects the quality of life, which Washington needs to preserve to attract business to the area. Thus, they argued, growth management is important for labor. Furthermore, the building trades were already angry that the AWB had opposed growth management in the previous session of the legislature as well. Thus they approached the WEC for information to use in their testimony in favor of greater protection.

At hearings for the growth management bill, the WEC and the building trades leadership testified together. They both argued that the AWB had no right to introduce its last minute growth management bill. Labor and environmentalists favored amendments strengthening the Growth Management Act, which were eventually passed.

These events sparked a debate in the local mainstream press about whether environmentalists should support labor. As a sign of greater acceptance of environmental over labor concerns, the media did not question whether the labor movement should support environmentalists. An editorial in the *Seattle Post Intelligencer* described the alliance as an attempt by the WEC to regain political clout after the defeat of its growth management initiative. Another attacked the WEC's position as an idealistic blunder by the new, young, inexperienced leadership of the environmental movement. Yet another argued that environmentalists were only showing their real radical, socialist colors.

The labor leader Otto Herman, director of Rebound, responded in a letter to the editor that Senate Republicans were antagonized by the WEC's alliance with labor because they were afraid of cooperation between progressive groups. He defended the prevailing wage and praised the WEC for supporting labor's efforts. He concluded, "We cannot make a choice between economic prosperity and jobs and protecting our environment. We need leaders with the vision, guts and determination to deliver on both counts. Nothing less is acceptable."

In response to the misperceptions in the press, the Washington Environmental Council, Washington State Labor Council, and the Washington Building Trades called a joint press conference on March 25, 1991, about their "current legislative agenda and other matters of mutual interest." According to Bob Dilger, the press conference was to set the record straight that labor and environmental groups would continue to work together. WEC president Darlene Madenwald explained to the press,

We share with organized labor deep concerns over the proposed rollback in the prevailing wage structure for public works projects. . . . Everyone in our local economy benefits [from the prevailing wage]. . . . Moreover, WEC's executive committee saw the rollback as another example of exemptions often given to special interests, just as these interests have consistently sought exemptions from environmental laws. . . . I am grateful for labor's support on such a fundamental quality-of-life issue as growth management and look forward to working with them further during my term in office. . . . If some are critical of our alliances simply because they don't agree with our shared positions, I wonder who it is that is really "radical" or "naive."

As a result of this alliance between labor and environmentalists, both fared better in the legislative session than anticipated. The IBEW lobbyist and environmental supporter Ron Judd gave this assessment of labor's success with the 1991 legislature: "The antilabor bills of the Senate Committee on Labor and Commerce . . . died in the Senate [during this legislative session]. As far as I know, this has not happened since the Republicans took control of the Senate. Why did they back off? . . . Many think it is the result of the help we received from the environmental and church communities, who did an excellent job of lobbying and testifying on our behalf." Environmental legislation also fared relatively well in 1991 on such issues as growth management, air pollution control, energy conservation, and oil spill prevention. The WEC's David Bricklin agreed that "the people who were gleeful for the last two years that their divide-and-conquer tactics were working, were upset when we woke up and realized we were shooting ourselves in the foot every day."

Coalitions as Democratic Schools for Community

If movements are schools for democracy, then coalitions are schools for building community. Through building new, diverse alliances, unions and environmentalists did more than advance their specific political goals. They developed trust, confidence, and relationships that provided a foundation for further organizing. Participants who initially were strangers came to know individuals from the other movement; they learned to speak frankly and appreciate the other's point of view. This led both sides to redefine their interests as shared rather than opposed.

Building trust, the first step in any collaboration, is particularly critical when participants differ by class, race, gender, or experience. These social differences produce movements with distinct approaches to social change, political outlooks, and goals. Individuals from different social backgrounds bring distinct motivations to political participation as well. These differences contribute to misunderstandings, as each side interprets the actions of others according to its own framework. This is well illustrated by the different views that working-class union members and middle-class environmentalists have of the environment. For the union, jobs are part of the environment, which is a markedly different view from that of environmentalists, who define the environment in terms of nonhuman nature.

In the early stages of cooperation, each side tests the other to discover whether it really supports its goals and shares its interests. This is particularly true for movements with a history of conflict. Environmentalists in the above case had to convince union members that they were committed both to preserving quality jobs in the community and to the existence of unions, while labor activists had to convince environmentalists that they cared about the quality of the environment and not just saving jobs. As one labor activist said in organizing a conversion coalition, "Unions need to have it demonstrated to them that economic conversion [or environmental protection] is not just a code word for union busting." This is an ongoing process, as more members of each side test their skepticism and distrust of the other.

Trust develops from cooperation, which begins small and builds with experience. In the above case, these incremental steps in trust building between the Washington Building Trades and the Washington Environmental Council began first by exchanging letters, then by meeting and a conversation, then by discussing a common legislative agenda, later by testifying for each other's bills, and then organizing a joint press event. Ultimately each side gains confidence and trust as it sees the other act for its goals. As one labor activist working in an environmental coalition stated, "As people opposed to working with environmentalists see them go to bat for labor, their attitudes change. Some still hate the environmentalists, but not as bad as [they] used to." Thus trust builds slowly through experiences of cooperation and support.

Second, and related to the process of trust building, individuals from each side begin to build relationships with coalition partners. While movements develop their memberships through existing social networks, coalitions between different classes and races are hindered because people often live, work, and socialize in separate social networks. Often environmentalists will have few if any contacts with union members and vice versa. One consequence of this lack of social interaction is that perceptions are often governed by media images and popular myths about construction workers or environmentalists. Beyond these stereotypes, people do not know what to expect from each other. As individuals become more familiar through cooperation, they become more predictable as well. Coalition participants become individuals with personalities rather than just members of a social and political group. This process of relationship building is essential to ongoing cooperation and communication. As one of the labor leaders from the Washington coalition said, "I developed a better appreciation of environmental groups from working with them. When you get to know people, you can understand them better. I learned more about their goals and that they are broader than just the environment. They seem to care about other things too." Another leader reflected a similar sentiment when he said, "One of the benefits of the process is that people find out more about each other, that the 'enemy' is a human being. There are basically good people on both sides."

As collaborators learn more about their partners, each comes to recognize that the other movement is not monolithic, that it cannot be understood as a whole. Support or opposition from one environmental or labor group does not mean that others will follow. Each movement has its own conflicts and political divisions. Coalition partners learn to stop attributing all the "sins" of the other movement to each organization in that movement, particularly their allies.

Third, each side in a coalition learns to appreciate the other's perspectives as valuable. Better understanding is an inevitable result of communication and interaction, even though participants may not have entered the coalition desiring it. As Nate Ford, former secretary-treasurer of the Puget Sound Metal Trades, put it,

There might be a realization when people are about to go [into the coalition] that, "Hey, [if] we want them to listen to us, we're probably going to have to listen to them." But I don't think it's very often realized that we may have to agree on some things or we may have to be willing to understand other points of view than our own. But it is one of the things that I think people really gain out of [coalitions], and maybe without even understanding it. It could be evolutional, where they don't understand. Or it could be lightning striking, where they suddenly understand.

As each side comes to understand the other's perspective better, it also comes to appreciate its unique contribution and the potential for greater cooperation. In the Washington case, each side developed a greater appreciation for the other as the coalition developed. While earlier building trades leaders dismissed environmentalists as extreme outsiders, leaders today accept them as allies and reject choosing between jobs and the environment. Environmentalists also learned to recognize that their issues benefit from good-quality work, which depends on good wages. Each side not only came to trust the other but also to understand and recognize the merit of the other's goals and contributions.

Fourth, not only do successful coalition partners learn to appreciate each other's perspectives, but they also come to rethink their own views in a more comprehensive and inclusive way. All organizing requires the construction of an alternative view of reality to motivate action, and this is no less true for coalitions. One of the fundamental challenges for coalition organizers is to reconceptualize their goals as shared—articulating a new definition of issues that incorporates the goals of each movement.

Environmentalists and union activists expand their perspectives in characteristic ways when they build coalitions. Environmentalists learn to think about the economic implications of their goals through collaborating with labor unions. This is significant for labor, since middle-class activists are frequently oblivious to the economic consequences of issues they promote. Even sympathetic environmentalists often lack an understanding of the specific problems and needs confronting union members. To address issues such as resource conservation or pollution prevention with labor, however, the environmental movement must learn to think about the organization of production, economic development, and economic policy. These are generally issues that middle-class activists know little about. For instance, Ted Pankowski of the Washington Environmental Council described how their growing relationship with labor changed their thinking:

> Our association with labor has made us sensitive that there is a broader community out there, and our messaging and our positioning had better have broad-based appeal or it's just not going to work. Labor provides that good kind of sounding board. The environmental community can be very strident. I've heard some so-called environmental leaders say, "Why should we give a damn about jobs and economics, that's not our bag?" And so that alliance helps us steer our own membership's thinking along ways that are more inclusive than they might be otherwise.

On the other side, labor develops a broader understanding of the relationships between the economy and the environment through collaborating with environmentalists. The labor movement has generally focused narrowly on immediate economic and workplace issues. But cooperation with community organizations requires unions to consider the quality of life outside work as well. This includes lessons about such things as the relationships between health and safety issues at work and in the community, the environmental implications of production processes and materials, and the social value of their products. It becomes necessary to consider not just jobs for their own sake but also the kinds of economic development that are socially and environmentally desirable.

Coalition participants eventually redefine their issues in language that is more inclusive of their partners' concerns over time. Interests that were previously seen as separate or divided are redefined as common. This shift in perspective enables coalition participants to explain the coalition to their own constituencies. It provides a framework for interpreting the relationships between issues and movements over time. In the Washington case, both unions and environmentalists began to speak about their common concern in terms of the quality of life for the whole community versus the special interests of companies seeking private profits. While at first unions approached environmental regulations as a means to save jobs, they eventually began to speak about "a clean environment and good-quality buildings," as the head of the Washington Building Trades said. Environmentalists saw similar links between issues—as did the president of the Washington Environmental Council, for example, when she argued in public, "I've fought for the quality of the environment, but I also care about the quality of wages paid to workers."

As a result of the broader perspectives that emerge through the coalition process, coalitions are able to address broader issues as they evolve. Coalitions often begin by agreeing to work on a narrow set of goals and to avoid the many other issues about which participants disagree. But as one union activist said, "When you're spending a lot of time with these people, you can't help learning some of their other issues." In the early stages of cooperation between IBEW and the WEC in the Washington case, participants agreed to ignore their many disagreements about building limits in Seattle, nuclear power, and other matters. Rather they focused first on a limited initiative about Seattle's electrical code and the use of PVC pipe. As the coalition evolved, it became more possible to include other issues and understandings. That the building trades eventually testified in favor of stronger growth management demonstrated the extent to which they had expanded their perception of their interests.

A final example draws together various types of learning and illustrates the kinds of personal transformations that are possible from coalitions. The following story comes from a labor activist in a defense plant in Minnesota who learned to work with the peace community. He described his personal history in this way:

> We had some members of peace groups in our local union, which we considered to be a little odd because they were making defense weapons for a living at the same time that they were out protesting defense. So we shunned them a little bit. One of them about six or eight years ago asked our negotiating committee, which I was a part of, to meet with some [visiting] people from England who had worked on conversion projects in England. I was totally against it, told them that I thought economic conversion was a plot to affect the defense worker. In effect, I mocked them severely at the time.
>
> The union had a cable television program, *Focus on Labor*, at the time years ago, and we did a program on economic conversion. I interviewed [Representative] Karen Clark, who's one of the most commonly known names in economic conversion in the state of Minnesota. At the same time I was opposed to it, but I interviewed her to get her side of it and why she was involved with it. She said she was forming this task force on economic conversion and wanted involvement from unions. If nothing else, it was a good watchdog to see what they were doing. So we had another member of our organization join their task force for a couple of years until he resigned and I took over on the task force. And I referred to myself as the closet hawk on the task force. People would come up and not know who they were talking to, and I would reveal that I'm a defense worker and proud of it. And a lot of the legislation that they were trying to gear up for, I was opposed to, I had problems with.
>
> As time went by and I learned about more of the aspects such as alternative products, diversification—those things were palatable. Not only that but they were advantageous to our local union. Four years ago, when I traveled to London with Karen Clark and the four other members of our task force on a little speaking tour, I met with people over there who were involved with economic conversion. I ended up meeting some of the

people who I had [shunned] several years before, only here now I'm talking about economic conversion, and these are the people that I scoffed several years before. So it was a little odd.

There are people in those [peace] organizations who do realize that we are in economic danger, who are interested in converting us logically and rationally over to something where we can maintain our employment. There are others who just don't want a gun in the house, and I have a gun in the house. I'm not totally in accord with some of their thinking. I still believe if they had their druthers they'd close us down, but not until they found something else for us to do. That I've got to respect. At least some of the people at Jobs with Peace and MAPA are looking at making sure that we don't suffer any injury by getting rid of defense. I believe a good number of them are sincere in wanting to do that.

▲

Bridge Builders: Agents of Reconciliation

When the Peace Economy Project wanted to build an alliance with labor in Maine, organizers went to Tom to set up an initial meeting. The peace activists knew Tom because of his involvement opposing U.S. military policy in Central America. But he was exceptional among their colleagues because he was on the staff of a local union. Early in Tom's life, he had chosen to cross the class line between peace and labor, which made him an ideal person to build bridges.

Tom grew up middle-class and was active in the peace and student movements during college. He met some labor activists while doing support work for striking employees at the university. After school he volunteered for the farm workers for a year. From there he was recruited by the Amalgamated Clothing and Textile Workers Union to work on a national boycott of Farah slacks, along with twenty to twenty-five other student activists. This was a national campaign, and the union needed people with organizing experience. Tom described what it was like to join the union campaign: "It's a little unusual that some college grad with long hair would show up to work in the factory. Fitting in with people who didn't have a college background, who worked in the industry and mills for many years, [was a challenge. But] we were accepted by people at the time, some I'm sure with more skepticism than others, [as] an important component of what the union was trying to accomplish." Tom found the campaigns exciting and a natural extension of earlier student organizing. While he would never have joined the union if he hadn't been recruited, he has stayed with union organizing ever since. He sees the labor movement as a place to advance social change, and he's accepted that this is where he's going to do his work. True to his original values, he remains active in peace issues both within and outside the union.

Ted Pankowski, executive director of the Washington Environmental Council, played a key role in building an alliance with the building trades unions, a role he was well suited for because he understood unions intimately. His father had worked for the United Auto Workers as director of its environmental program. The elder Pankowski was an organizer in the auto industry when the UAW was started in the late 1930s and 1940s. Walter Reuther hired him on his staff when the union was founded, and he worked there until he retired. His son inherited an activist drive to organize for social justice. Since the antiwar and civil rights movements "were saturated" with organizers at the time, he was drawn to the fledgling environmental movement. While living in Washington, D.C., he organized a successful campaign against gentrification of an African-American neighborhood in the Old Town of Alexandria, Virginia, and against a high–rise apartment complex that would block public access to the Potomac River. The Izaak Walton League at the time was interested in building broader coalitions, and they hired Pankowski because of his congressional and labor connections. In that position, he developed what he thinks was the first union-conservation coalition for funding of sewage treatment plants, the Citizens Crusade for Clean Water. Pankowski attributes his success to two factors. "Part of it obviously was the issue. Everybody recognized it as being a worthwhile issue, other than the White House of course. The other part of it boils down to who you trust and is it worthwhile to spend your political coin on this issue as opposed to some other issue. And what I heard consistently out of the AF of L was they not only trusted the issue, but they trusted my credentials." After working with the League, Pankowski had no contact with organized labor for several decades, and not in any continuous way until his coalition work in Washington State.

Ted Pankowski and Tom share an exceptional quality with other activists who were critical to building coalitions between working-class unions and middle-class peace and environmental organizations. Each had crossed the class divide in his personal life in one way or another. They are examples of the rare environmental or peace activists with working-class backgrounds, or of the equally uncommon union activists with experience working with middle-class movements. This gave them an intimate understanding of both working- and middle-class cultures and politics. They learned to be bilingual, capable of translating between different classes and movements. They are bridge builders, people who are comfortable and competent to act within diverse social groups.

BECOMING A BRIDGE BUILDER

Bridge builders gain their interclass experiences from the distinct economic, social, political, and ideological conditions of their generation. Economic opportunities determine class mobility, and the Great Depression, the economic prosperity after World War II, and the deep recessions of the 1970s and 1980s each created their own forms of interclass experience. Social movements, too, shape the experience of interclass politics. The expansion of the labor movement in the 1930s and 1940s touched a whole generation, as did the civil rights and antiwar movements of the 1960s. Ideology and political events also shape the personal decisions of activists as they choose where to place their energies. Finally, dramatic political events shape each generation's beliefs about which causes and strategies are worthy and effective. These historic circumstances impel some members of each generation to learn to work across the class divide.

At least five types of bridge builders, distinguished by generation and class, are actively building interclass coalitions at present. The first consists of a generation of activists who grew up in the working class and experienced the New Left movements of the 1960s and 1970s as college students. Also emerging from the New Left is a second cohort of middle-class activists who joined the labor movement. A third group of middle-aged, upwardly mobile activists grew up in working-class, union families but became middle-class during their own lifetimes. Fourth are middle-class radicals who believe in working with the labor movement for ideological, political, or moral reasons but remain in middle-class occupations. Finally, an older cohort of bridge builders developed their political experiences during the prewar socialist movement and the New Deal. These five types of bridge builders, each of which is described in more detail below, are reshaping the contemporary landscape of coalition politics.

Cross-cultural socialization can be consciously chosen or a personal adaptation to given life circumstances. Many of these people would not recognize their versatility as a skill, but it is one: a person must learn to comprehend the values, attitudes, and worldviews that make the politics of a movement intelligible. This is less evident for those who develop an experiential understanding of both working- and middle-class societies as an outgrowth of other activities. Others consciously decide to work across the class and movement divide. Although in crossing over they make plenty of errors, over time they too gain some competence as bridge builders.

A New Generation of Union Activists

A new generation of labor activists shaped by the politics of the 1960s is coming of age within the ranks of labor. Union families sent their children to college in unprecedented numbers as part of the post–World War II economic boom. In college these young people joined their middle-class peers in the civil rights, antiwar, and other student movements of the day. After graduating, many working-class progeny eventually returned to the trades and crafts of their parents, bringing their new political and social experiences with them.

Seattle's environmental activists in the building trades fit this pattern. Jim, for example, comes from a union family but developed his political views in the student and civil rights movements. As a child he had learned to read using a labor newspaper, the *Militant*, that he was given by his grandfather, an activist in the railroad union. His other grandfather was also from the working class, a crane machinist. During three years of college at UCLA he opposed the Vietnam War and the draft and became involved in civil rights organizing. He also helped organize a union at the college. In Seattle he worked with a union organization seeking to expand opportunities for people of color in the building trades. They forced the trades to integrate through a court order. His colleagues convinced him that he would be a more effective advocate within the trade union movement, and he soon found a job welding. He got a reputation as a "big-mouth radical" and "pinko" until he learned to tone down his rhetoric. Over time people saw that he cared about the union and would act for its best interests. Eventually he became a shop steward and business agent, and he remains an advocate of coalitions.

A former leader of the Seattle Metal Trades tells a similar story. His father came to Seattle with the Navy and then got a job in the shipyards as a union member. After high school he worked in a steel mill for a couple of years, then was an iron worker driving a crane, and eventually found a job in the shipyards with his father's help. In the early 1960s he was drafted and served in Vietnam. After another stint in the shipyards, he went to college and got a degree in psychology. He worked for a couple years as a counselor for chronic mental patients, but he soon returned to the shipyards because he could earn more money. He became a shop steward, officer, executive board member, then business agent. His family has always been involved with the Democratic Party, a tradition which he has continued. He has long been a civil rights activist in the union and community. In addition he considers himself a peace activist and environmentalist.

Ron Judd also fits this pattern. Judd was raised in southeastern Kentucky, where his family worked on farms and in the coal mines. They were strong labor supporters but also raised him to enjoy the environment. "If I owe them anything," Judd said, "I owe them that." After college Judd came to Washington State to lead mountain-climbing expeditions and to ski. He found a job as an electrician at Todd shipyards, where he became concerned about safety and health problems. During his ten years in the yard, he became chief shop steward. In 1986 Todd asked Judd to become its labor relations manager, and the union offered him a job as business representative. The union paid less and involved longer hours, but he decided to stay with the union. He then was appointed to represent IBEW on the Seattle Building Trades Council, the Joint Crafts Council, and the Metal Trades Council before he was elected secretary-treasurer of the Seattle Building Trades in 1991. Judd describes himself as "a very strong environmentalist."

Many other young union leaders were similarly shaped by the movements of the 1960s during their college years. Some participated in the Vietnam War or describe the powerful experience of participating in a mass antiwar movement; others were influenced by the civil rights or environmental movements. One union activist describes himself as "a hippie type" in those days. Another remembers, "When I was young I followed Martin Luther King."

This new generation of leaders is far more willing to work with middle-class organizations than their parents' generation. Like the country as a whole, they have a very different sense about war, the peace movement, and the environment than the generation formed by World War II. And with the labor movement in decline during the antiunion 1980s, these activists see the need to change union politics. Yet they have had to wait until their forties to attain leadership positions and begin to apply the political lessons they learned in their youths. One labor organizer laments how "people get their values set in their twenties, but it isn't until twenty more years have gone by that they have the knowledge and clout to carry them out." This new generation is now changing the face of the labor movement by building broad coalitions with other movements.

New Left Activists Who Joined Labor

Unlike the working-class participants in the movements of the 1960s who returned to their parents' trades, this second cohort of activists with middle-class backgrounds abandoned the occupations of their parents. Many of them entered blue-collar jobs because they were convinced that working-class support would be necessary to change society. Others were recruited by the labor movement seeking new organizing talent and energy. Still others found jobs where they turned their organizing skills to workplace issues. Without the social background to function in working-class society, many of these middle-class activists found the transition fraught with difficulties. Those who remained in the labor movement spent decades learning a trade, becoming accepted, and slowly influencing union politics. For instance, here is how Eric Mann describes the community-labor coalition that successfully challenged General Motor's plans to shut down its Van Nuys plant in Los Angles: "To begin with, the campaign evolved out of politically conscious activism. Mark Masaoka, Mike Gomez, myself and several other workers at the plant had come out of the anti-war and civil rights movements of the 1960s and many had gone into the plants with the express goal of organizing a new union movement from the bottom up."[1]

Another New Left activist in the Washington building trades came from a middle-class family with no union background. He went to law school at the University of Washington but was expelled for his antiwar organizing. At that time he decided that the movement needed to build working-class support if it was to successfully oppose the Vietnam War. He therefore decided to get a factory job with the idea of developing antiwar sentiment in the union. He described himself as "wet behind the ears" and said he didn't know anything about these people who were struggling to survive. While he failed to build any antiwar support there, he did develop a commitment to working-class politics. He decided to join the union and was a pipefitter for many years. Now he works with his elders in the union to contribute his ideas to building the labor movement. Eventually he finished his law degree and began a private practice assisting working people. He remains active in anti-intervention organizing and the peace movement as well as labor.

These activists never abandoned the New Left politics of their younger years, and indeed see union organizing as a direct outgrowth of that earlier political work. They often remain affiliated with peace, environmental, or civil rights organizations, although, having made the transition into the labor movement, they frequently seek to work through union organizations. Since their transition from middle-class to working-class organizations was conscious and abrupt, they are also often acutely aware of the cultural differences they bridge. As one activist from a middle-class background said of his peace organizing within his union,

> I don't see us working that closely or that immediately with peace organizations, but, in our own way, in our own membership, working on the same issue. We're going to get a lot more mileage out of this if we try to work primarily within our own constituencies. The gaps are social; there's a whole different culture between [labor and] the traditional peace movement constituency, which is largely white, middle- or upper-middle class and university based. . . . Our experience has been that it's more effective to try to work on similar issues or the same issues with the same focus, but tailoring what we're doing within our own constituency in a way that's going to make it more real to them, and not try to jam a square peg into a round hole.

MIDDLE-CLASS BELIEVERS IN LABOR

Another cohort of middle-class activists believe in working with the labor movement but have not made the personal change of obtaining a working-class job. These people remain middle-class by occupation but have chosen to devote their political activities to working with the labor movement. Because this conscious effort must reach across the social divide, it is often accompanied by cultural misunderstandings at first. Many of these people work in community organizing for a time, where they are trained in working-class organizing and gain experience in working-class communities. When they bring this know-how to their work with peace and environmental organizations, they often provide a cultural bridge between the education-based approach to social change of middle-class movements and the interest-based organizing of the labor movement.

David Fleishman, formerly executive director of Washington State Sane/Freeze, grew up in a middle-class suburb of Hartford, Connecticut. At one time his father owned a restaurant across the street from Pratt and Whitney, which built weapons for the Vietnam War. Fleishman "saw the civil rights movement and Ralph Nader doing their things" while he was growing up, and he had a sense that something was wrong. He joined the canvass for Connecticut Citizen Action, where he knocked on doors in working-class neighborhoods. At that time statewide community organizing was new, and there was a sense that they could really make a difference. After eight or nine years as a community organizer, he was hired by Puget Sound Sane, which later merged with the Washington Freeze Campaign. He took the job because he wanted to apply techniques of "power organizing to working with middle-class people who have some power to start with."

Another middle-class activist with a background in community organizing works with the Washington State Department of Community Development Defense Diversification Program. There he builds bridges between the peace movement and the economic development community. This economic focus brings him into contact with labor leaders as well as business and government. He grew up in a middle-class family in Philadelphia and worked with Fair Share doing community organizing for a number of years after college. He has also always been a strong peace and environmental advocate, serving on the board of WSSF. Yet he believes that community organizers need to bring their values and skills to economic development. Although grassroots organizing introduced him to working-class culture, coming from an upper-middle-income family made it possible for him to move in economic development circles. With his first "suit and tie" job with an economic development agency he realized that he can wear jeans one day and a tie the next and it doesn't change him. Moving back and forth can be very effective. He was recruited to work for the state because of his ability to move between activists, developers, and CEOs. He finds that there is a real need for people who can function in both worlds.

Many middle-class activists in the previous cases consciously chose to work with the labor movement. One environmental activist in Seattle is typical of those who include labor in their broader sense of a progressive movement. His father is an airline pilot, and he has no labor history in his family. Yet he generally assumes he'll be for labor unless some specific reason comes up not to be. In his words, "I want to see labor as a good guy." He's not sure why, except that he sees big business as the enemy, "and the enemy of my enemy is my friend." He was also trained in community organizing with the Public Interest Research Group, which contributed to his appreciation of working-class concerns even now that he works on environmental issues.

UPWARDLY MOBILE BRIDGE BUILDERS

A somewhat older generation of bridge builders grew up in working-class families but moved socially in the growth years of the 1960s and 1970s. These people, now in their fifties and sixties, attended college prior to the rise of the New Left and attained middle-class status. Nevertheless they remember their working-class childhoods and the union politics of their parents. Because their personal transition into the middle class was gradual, they are often not conscious of the social barriers they have crossed. As middle-class activists in the environmental or peace movements, they are sympathetic to the issues of the labor movement and the experience of working-class life. Perceiving less of a break between the New and Old Left, they tend to have a pragmatic view of cooperation between these two political worlds.

WEC president Darlene Madenwald, like its executive director Ted Pankowski, came from a working-class background. She grew up in a farm community in the Midwest but moved up socially by becoming a nurse and then marrying a doctor. Her environmental activism dates from the mid-1980s when she joined a campaign to fight air pollution from a Texaco coke-processing plant near her home in Anacortes. She had never been active in working-class political issues, but when the opportunity to work with the labor movement arose, she was sympathetic. She said that when she spoke before a state senate committee on the prevailing wage, she was reminded of her working-class father. She saw a "sea of her fathers" as she spoke.

OLD RADICALS/LIBERALS

A final cohort of bridge builders developed strong political convictions during the Great Depression and the New Deal. Some of these "old radicals" were politicized during the great union organizing drives of the 1930s and 1940s. In the socialist tradition, the union movement at the time opposed war as contrary to the interests of working people. This socialist perspective can be found as well among older activists within the labor movement. Others less involved with labor's struggles at the time learned from the New Deal that government intervention was needed to overcome poverty and correct the excesses of business. These people emerged during the Great Society programs of the 1960s with a positive sense of the role of labor, government, and community organizations in solving social problems. Many of these seasoned activists remain willing to work in coalitions across class lines.

Toby Lapakko, from the Minnesota AFL-CIO, calls herself an "old radical." In the 1940s she worked in the packinghouses six days a week, ten hours a day. She joined an early CIO organizing drive by the packinghouse workers and later became part of the national staff of the union. Her husband worked with the building trades and was able to find work only three months of the year. She continued to work for unions until finding her present position with Minnesota's state labor organization. She has been sympathetic to the peace movement and she and her husband opposed the Vietnam War early on, seeing it as an evil war. She supported conversion organizing in Minnesota and encouraged unions to work with the peace movement. Yet she also advised peace activists to allow labor to take the lead. Over time, she said, she has learned the need to work within existing institutions and not to alienate others with provocative language.

Some of these old radicals succeeded in passing their political views on to their children. One activist from the Machinists union in Maine grew up with protests and politics. He remembers how his father, in the hotel union, took him to "Ban the Bomb" rallies as a kid. As a young man he was a union activist with the merchant marines for many years before settling down and finding his present job with Bath Iron Works. Having inherited his father's understanding of the connections between peace and labor issues, he was always active in the union and also sympathetic with the peace movement. During the Persian Gulf War he was critical of the patriotism he saw around him, symbolized by yellow ribbons. He has experienced "conflicts in terms of getting people to understand some of the connections and to work in their own interests. The yellow ribbon disease of the recent war and the usual propaganda roundup [were] a major disruption to a lot of [conversion work]."

Charles O'Leary, head of Maine's state AFL-CIO, is representative of a generation of New Deal liberals who see the connection between labor's agenda, peace, and reducing military spending. He considers himself "a child of the 1960s" who thinks you need to talk about troubles here in this country like poverty, drugs, and racism. Inspired by Kennedy's claim that government could and should work for change, he worked with community action programs during their heyday. He also supports the peace movement and said he has "marched with every Buddhist in America." He is willing to work in coalitions with peace and environmental organizations, although he has grown cynical about the lack of support labor has received from these organizations on its issues.

Joan Thomas, former president and board member of the Washington Environmental Council, also comes out of the New Deal and good government tradition. Thomas grew up during the Depression in Detroit and has always been sympathetic to the needs of working people. She became president of the Washington State League of Women Voters and promoted government reforms particularly in the area of tax policy.

When she left the presidency of the League she joined the WEC and became its third president. She continued to advocate for tax reform and was appointed to the state Board of Tax Appeals. For her, good government, public welfare, and environmental advocacy go hand in hand.

ROLES OF BRIDGE BUILDERS

Each type of bridge builders plays important roles initiating, developing, and maintaining coalitions among diverse movements. Four roles are vital to the formation of interclass, intermovement coalitions: initiating contacts, communicating inside member groups, dialoguing across movements, and defining a common purpose in public. Without the unique cross-cultural experiences and skills of bridge builders, these roles are often not filled, which weakens the coalition or hinders its formation in the first place.

Bridge builders can play direct or indirect roles in coalitions. In the labor-environmental alliance in Washington State, bridge builders from each side of the coalition were directly involved in organizing the coalition. In contrast with this direct role, some bridge builders worked behind the scenes to bring people together and begin dialogue. They helped other organizers to assemble diverse constituencies but were not themselves doing this work. This was the pattern in the conversion coalitions in Maine and Washington, which were primarily organized by people without significant interclass ties but who relied on other bridge builders to help them.

So the first role of bridge builders is to provide the initial contacts between organizations and arrange the first meetings. This is often the most important role played by indirect bridge builders, who draw on the trust and relationships they have in different movements to bring diverse groups to the table. For example, a peace activist and labor union staff member in Washington was approached by Washington State Sane/Freeze to help them develop their initial contacts with labor. In Minnesota a peace sympathizer in the state AFL-CIO convened the first meeting between the union and Jobs with Peace.

The second important role of bridge builders is to explain the issues and actions of the other movement to members of their own organization. Bridge builders are critical to interclass coalitions because they are the people who can teach each movement about the other. People do not often alter their perceptions because of the ideas of those whom they consider outsiders, even if they are working together in coalition. They are much more likely to listen to and learn from insiders, members of their own organization. Furthermore, insiders know how to express concerns in ways that speak to the life experiences and worldview of peers. The union member who cares about the environment, for example, is far more effective explaining that concern to his friends than someone from an environmental organization. Even if his comembers disagree, they are more willing to accept that difference without rejecting the individual who expresses it. That difference becomes part of the relationship and can be raised in other circumstances in the future. A difference with a friend always remains a potential source of learning, while a difference with a stranger is readily dismissed. As William Gamson observed in the context of his experience as an organizer during the Vietnam War, "Opposition from 'movement' people, however vaguely defined, was a problem and their objections had to be taken seriously; opposition from others . . . was inevitable and could be written off."[2]

One union activist described his role—explaining the peace movement to labor colleagues—in the following terms:

> From my own experience, I feel like a lot of times I'm trying to bridge the gap between [peace groups and] a lot of union folks who for a variety of reasons would be rather suspicious or distrustful of people who have never shown any interest in them or their struggles for economic survival, who arrive on their doorstep and want their help, their bodies, their person power, their organizational abilities, and so on. People are skeptical about that. You clearly need someone or some people who are in some kind of position to try to make these coalitions happen. They don't happen organically. People don't just decide one day that they all have self-interests in the same place. [This effort would fail] without a person like myself who's been trying to bridge that gap and point out the commonality of interest and overcome the cynicism of union members. It's not going to happen on the basis of the Central American support committee coming into the factory and preaching to the workers about the importance of solidarity with the revolutionary struggles. That doesn't do it.

Bridge builders play a third important role by facilitating communication between coalition partners. Different movements have distinct ways of interpreting politics and social change, and they express their concerns using different languages. Movement ideologies become barriers to communication between classes and organizations. Bridge builders are able to translate or interpret the concerns of another movement into the language and framework of their peers. They then work within their own movements and organizations to persuade comembers as only insiders can.

In the absence of people who are sensitive to the concerns and perceptions of the other movement, well-intentioned participants can inadvertently alienate others. This occurred in the meeting between Washington State Sane/Freeze and the Washington State Labor Council on diversifying the defense sector. When a Sane/Freeze member stated publicly that most of its members oppose nuclear power even though the organization has no position on the subject, she reinforced her outsider status. This statement on such a sensitive issue infuriated leaders in the labor council, who reprimanded members of the peace organization for their divisive statements. Just as bridge builders are needed to explain movements to their own colleagues, they play an invaluable role ensuring that movements communicate well when they do come together. This is particularly critical at the beginning stages of the coalition, before trust is developed among participants and a clear agenda established. Over time other coalition participants gain some of the skills and develop some of the relationships of bridge builders, and they can serve this role of facilitating communication as well.

The fourth critical role for bridge builders is to define and defend a common purpose or framework for the coalition in public. Statements before organizational gatherings, to the press, in public hearings, and during protests establish how the public and other movement members interpret the work of the coalition. In the absence of a clearly articulated alternative, movement issues are often expressed as separate and even opposed. This was the case in each of the coalitions examined in this study, in which environmental protection and peace had previously been seen as opposed to union jobs. For these coalitions to succeed, leaders needed to propose an alternative perspective explaining how jobs and peace or jobs and a clean environment are in the shared interests of both movements. Bridge builders have the credibility and understandings to challenge public perceptions and put forward this alternative perspective. To succeed, their ideas need to be adopted by key leaders in each organization as the new rationale for their work.

Bridge builders in the labor and environmental coalition in Washington were particularly effective at defining a common purpose in public. In a joint press statement the leaders of the Washington Environmental Council and the Building and Construction Trades explained that attacks on prevailing wage and environmental laws are both examples of exemptions given to special interests at the public expense. This press statement was made in defense of labor and environmental legislative cooperation that successfully stopped anti-environmental and antilabor bills. In this statement both sides rejected arguments put forward in the press and by political and business opponents that claimed that environmental protection and labor issues are unrelated and that environmentalists would only hurt their cause by tying it to worker rights. It was the bridge builders on both sides of the coalition who countered these attacks and provided the evidence and ideas to support the alternative view.

The strengths and weaknesses of coalitions can be evaluated in terms of their effectiveness at carrying out the four bridging roles. The labor and environmental coalition in Washington was particularly effective because its many bridge builders on both sides were able to carry out all of the important bridging functions. There were tense moments, particularly the first meeting between the unions and environmentalists after decades of public conflict and opposition. However, leaders from both movements were savvy enough about the other side to agree quickly which issues would be off-limits; they established a rationale for cooperation and began to build trust. Each side went back to its board and members and promoted the coalition strongly in terms that they could understand. Bridge builders from both sides spoke informally to each other to work out details that could have raised conflict. When both sides spoke publicly they endorsed the coalition and the rationale for cooperation. As the organizations built more trust, they were able to increase the complexity of their joint efforts.

The Minnesota coalition shared some of these strengths, but it was hampered by the absence of direct bridge builders in the union. Indirect bridge builders were effective at arranging meetings, encouraging participation, and providing support, but were not involved in direct organizing within the union. Without active bridge builders, avenues for communicating about the peace agenda were limited. The peace organization, however, was able to appreciate labor's agenda, drawing on the understandings of its organizer–bridge builder. Cooperation in this lopsided situation was only possible because the peace organization put aside its broader agenda and agreed to address the jobs impacts of defense cuts without raising issues of peace or further military cuts with the union, although it did continue to pursue these goals outside the coalition. The result was a functioning but one-sided alliance based on labor's terms.

The peace and labor coalitions in Maine and Washington, similarly, suffered from the lack of direct bridge builders. In these coalitions cooperation took place largely behind the scenes around specific tasks. Very little education occurred within these organizations about the perspectives of the other side. And in meetings between the groups there were few opportunities to reconcile different perspectives. As a result many differences went unaddressed. Cooperation remained infrequent and limited to a few people. When a public rationale for cooperation was put forward, it generally reflected the thinking of one group rather than a consensus of both. Actions by the unions and peace groups remained largely separate. Over time the peace organization in Maine did try to develop a rationale that would incorporate labor's interests. But its alternative frameworks of a peace economy and later a sustainable economy did not adequately express labor's concern about jobs, and the union never embraced this language.

DIFFICULTIES AND RISKS FOR BRIDGE BUILDERS

The act of bridging classes and movements is fraught with difficulties and personal as well as political risks. Although bridge builders begin with the trust of their colleagues, the more they venture outside their organizations, the more they too become objects of suspicion. There is a delicate balance between serving as a conduit for social and political learning and undermining the trust that comes from being an "insider," being accepted by one's peers. In this delicate process, bridge builders commonly confront charges of having "sold out" as they challenge both predominant ideas and relationships.

John, who works at a defense plant, described how his loyalty was questioned as he became more convinced of the value of conversion. He was initially very vocal about his suspicions of the peace movement and its conversion efforts. Yet his views changed over time as he participated in programs sponsored by Jobs with Peace. As he built relationships with peace activists, his union comrades let him know he was stepping outside of their comfort zone. He found that

A lot of my people now look at me as a little questionable, possibly a little pinko, because I will deal with these [peace] people. I went down to various peace groups and actually spoke. I told them I'm not ashamed to be a military contractor, but I wouldn't be ashamed to build refrigerators either. [But] now I'm in a little bit of a stinker. Now I've got my people who aren't sure they can trust me on some of these things. They trust me to do the normal parts of my job, but this here's a little odd. I've got management who's totally convinced I'm there to undermine them, and all I'm trying to do is get more work in there. And my family life suffers.

John's willingness to associate with the peace movement posed a challenge to his union. It raised questions both about who should be included in their circle of allies and about what ideas are acceptable by the organization. All groups, from families to communities to organizations and movements, divide insiders from outsiders. Insiders are expected to share some common beliefs and ideas that unite them and distinguish them from outsiders. These unifying beliefs justify the group's separateness and give value and meaning to belonging to the group.

Yet bridge builders pose a challenge to the group because they hold different understandings of issues than their peers as a result of their unique experiences. For instance, one conversion activist compared her understandings with others in the peace movements in these terms:

> We're working on things like economic diversification where we're dealing with the effects of military spending on workers. Many people in the peace movement feel like these workers should never have been doing this job. [They say,] "They should have known that it was wrong and they shouldn't have done it, and we don't owe them anything." I know—I was at a town meeting about the peace dividend back before the [Gulf] war and there were labor people on the panel as well. Someone from the audience got up and said, "You guys don't deserve a penny." The people that work on our committee, the diversification committee, have gotten past that or see it in a different light. They think that that's not really a fair way to talk about the workers.

When bridge builders act on their different ideas and challenge the rules and beliefs of their own organizations, they are inevitably pressured by their colleagues to conform. To venture into relationships with "foreigners" and to take seriously their ideas threatens to betray the existing norms of the group and unconsciously brings its order into question. To break through the boundaries of ideas and relationships can raise fears of betrayal and disloyalty and ultimately will lead to testing the bridge builder's position within the group. Group members intuitively fear that the group will lose its identity if it goes outside its established boundaries. Charges of "selling out" are as much about maintaining the integrity of the social group as they are about being true to specific ideas.

Jane, a lobbyist for a peace organization, found that her loyalties and politics were questioned as she learned more about the political process and adjusted her beliefs. She described how "some people say that their lobbyists sell out in public interest groups. But I think that you have to compromise to get somewhere in the system. You can stay pure, but then you do not get involved in the hard decisions about how much wetlands will be used or not. These decisions are always being made all the time." But lessons about the need to compromise did not fit with the beliefs of her own organization. Instead of accepting these lessons, some people in the organization questioned Jane's integrity as a member.

People who step outside acceptable norms in their organizations feel pressure to conform. For example, members of the building trades experience pressure from employers and coworkers to oppose environmental protection measures. As one sympathetic union business manager said, "Employers don't want to hear about environmentalists. I called OSHA [the Occupational Safety and Health Administration] on an employer once, but if that employer knew I talked to EPA [the Environmental Protection Agency] or OSHA they wouldn't hire me. Management singles out workers who care about the environment, and I caution people to be careful. If you care about fish or the environment you're considered a leftist. I keep my concerns to myself at work. I care about the environment personally and report things anonymously. You get labeled if you talk out."

But it's not only the employers who pressure workers to conform; other workers create a culture of conformity on the job site as well. As one activist explained, "In the trades you have to conform to a certain image of being tough, talking tough, being competitive. There's a lot of pressure on the work site. People who are different politically or personally, women, minorities, can't express themselves and don't say too much. What people say and appear to be at work is not who they are. People's different personalities come forth at different times."

Environmental and peace groups also generate pressure among their members to conform to established norms of behavior. The Peace Economy Project was strongly criticized by members of the Maine Peace Campaign as it began to shift its tactics and priorities to work with labor and other new allies (see Chapter 7). The New York State Citizens' Environmental Coalition (CEC) experienced similar pressures as it focused on building a collaboration between labor and environmentalists to control toxins in the community. By working with unions, CEC made job issues an important priority in its environmental work. Other environmental organizations in New York pushed CEC from their lobbying organization because it had strayed too far from their agenda. Members of CEC experienced similar pressures. For example, one staff member of a Committee for Occupational Safety and Health (COSH) group received intense criticism from her organization as she built a closer working relationship with labor unions. The organization felt that her work drained resources from the organization's primary mission. As a result she reduced her paid staff hours so that she could continue her coalition work half-time.

The choice to challenge norms of behavior is difficult for bridge builders as well, and many struggle with their own fears of compromising themselves. One middle-class activist said of working with coalitions, "Sometimes I do worry about incremental changes in myself. I worry about it; I don't think about it much. I do feel pressure sometimes, especially from my hipster friends in Seattle. They never gave it to me explicitly, because I'm always able to describe what I do in progressive terms, which is the way I see it."

So bridge building is a risky and challenging process, with the biggest danger that coalition builders become isolated within their own organizations. To succeed, bridge builders must incorporate other colleagues in their efforts, which requires convincing others of the merits of their views. This can be the source of great tension for bridge builders. If they fail to translate personal learning into learning by the group, then the coalition will not develop. But communicating with coworkers is complicated by the bridge builder's unique experiences, which are difficult to recreate for others. Darlene Madenwald explained this difficulty:

> It is hard to translate [my experiences building relationships back to other WEC members], so I have a lot of work cut out for me on my side because I have to bring people along with me. . . . For instance, I've met with the Wheat Growers on my own. . . . The Wheat Growers Association took me on their bus last year, just me. So you see that's one person bridging the gap. But this year our whole board's been invited. . . . There's a lag time between when I make the bridges, and then I bring the board along. That's my plan. I'm not going to get very far out by myself without bringing on the board. So what if one person does it? If there isn't a whole bunch of people then it's lost effort.

Jane, the peace lobbyist, also expressed her difficulty communicating what she learned from direct experience to her colleagues. "I wasn't good at translating the lessons I learned by lobbying to other people," she admitted. "I had lots of chances to sit with people who were writing about economic development. I learned a lot and tried to talk to people at Sane about it, but didn't communicate that."

But many coalition builders avoid the challenge of directly confronting other movement activists with ideas that challenge basic assumptions. Instead of facing the difficult task of educating peers, it is common for bridge builders to segregate their coalition activities in order to minimize conflicts and safeguard their own positions. Coalition work is frequently limited to a few individual leaders, while the membership remains ignorant of these activities. It is always easier to work with a few responsible and interested individuals than to face a broader society of people with their established patterns of behavior and beliefs.

All of the coalition cases in this study suffered from this tendency to work with a few accessible leaders. Washington State Sane/Freeze abandoned its attempts to reach a broader labor audience when it met with hostility. It has since worked within the limited forum of the state's Department of Community Development, where only one peace representative and two from labor meet face to face. In Maine only a handful of members of the Maine Peace Campaign took part in the Peace Economy Project, and only three members of the Machinists union took part in its meetings. Even in Minnesota the ongoing work of the project remained the work of a very small number of activists. In Maine, BIW's representative to the PEP observed, "The vast majority of the managers at BIW have never been exposed to any of this [conversion] thinking. And the vast majority of the liberals, for lack of a better category to throw them in, the liberal folks on the Peace Economy side, have not been exposed to BIW folks, or at least taken the time to understand the business."

Coalitions in which only a few participants meet face to face minimize the level of social learning, which presents risks in the long run. If individual leaders fail to achieve the internal organizing necessary to build a broad base of support for the coalition, they inevitably face a more difficult task as the coalition develops over time. This can lead to individual isolation and, ultimately, a challenge to that person's position in the organization.

Bridge builders who are "fluent" in both working- and middle-class cultures are critical to the development of coalitions. These are people who can interpret the goals and actions of other movements for their colleagues in a way that facilitates understanding. Bridge builders are shaped by unique generational and class conditions, and the cases contain five distinct types: young working-class activists who experienced the movements of the 1960s; young middle-class activists who joined labor; middle-class activists who support labor; middle-aged, upwardly mobile working-class activists; and "old radicals."

Bridge builders inhabit a unique world where they must integrate starkly different experiences. As they enter coalitions, they are influenced and changed by the process in ways they cannot anticipate. They place themselves in positions where they will learn and change, even while playing their roles in their own, unchanged organizations. In doing so, bridge builders risk the easy comfort of remaining within their own classes and movements. This inevitably raises controversy, because the mechanisms that maintain class divisions are well ingrained. It is common to try to minimize these tensions by removing coalition work from the organization's view.

The potential for broad support and learning depends, however, upon engaging other organizational members in the debates that coalitions raise. When bridge builders take this necessary step, they can expect to confront social pressures because they are breaking ranks with their social groups and their established ideas. Forced to bring others along at the risk of alienating them, bridge builders become conduits for learning and agents of social change.

▲

Finding a Common Language

> Drawn to public life by personal need, fear, ambition or interest, we are there forced to acknowledge the power of others and appeal to their standards, even as we try to get them to acknowledge our power and standards. We are forced to find or create a common language of purposes and aspirations, not merely to clothe our private outlook in public disguise, but to become aware ourselves of its public meaning.
>
> —Hanna Pitkin

In 1992 Washington State Sane/Freeze's Economic Diversification Committee changed its name to the Peace Economy Campaign. Maine's Peace Economy Project made the opposite transition in the same year and started calling itself the Economic Conversion Project. Although the project kept this name until it closed its doors in 1996, Maine activists increasingly described their goals in terms of sustainability rather than conversion. Minnesota also used the terminology of conversion, diversification, and peace economy strategically at different times throughout this period.

Conversion, diversification, peace economy, or sustainability—these were some of the frameworks activists experimented with to express and communicate their goals. All organizing requires the construction of an alternative view of reality to motivate action. Unlike conventional ideas, which generally justify the status quo and make change seem impossible, movement frameworks identify social problems as injustices that are caused by adversaries and that can be successfully opposed. Thus a critical part of building an organization or movement is winning over people's hearts and minds to this alternative interpretation of their conditions.

Finding the right language is a process of direct and indirect negotiation between leaders or organizers, who articulate a vision, and members, sympathizers, and critics. The right framing of an issue must name the cause that members are fighting for, and it must express their core motivations. But since it must also serve as a rallying cry for potential recruits, it has to appeal to the passions and interests of the wider community. It also needs to draw the battle lines by attributing responsibility for the injustice to some group and distinguishing defenders or victims from oppressors. Naming the issues both gives voice to deeply felt values and interests and serves as a political tool for engaging in the struggle for change.

Coalitions face an added challenge when they seek to reframe the goals of different movements or organizations. Labor unions and peace or environmental groups conceive of their issues in very different terms. They have each already defined their causes worth fighting for, established rallying cries for sympathizers, and drawn battle lines with opponents. In so doing they have also frequently interpreted their interests and values as opposed or unrelated. Coalition builders need to provide an alternative interpretation to unify its members. Movements that in the past have appealed to different communities must now speak to a combined audience, and injustices that were seen as unrelated must be reinterpreted as the result of a common cause.

Activists organizing to redirect the military economy at the end of the Cold War experimented with different ways to frame the issue. Ideas that successfully unite diverse movements do not come ready-made. Organizers discover an effective language in the act of explaining, justifying, and interpreting the coalition to peers, decision makers, and the public. This language is tuned through trial to the multiple and competing demands of organizing.

CLASS CULTURE AND COALITION FRAMES

Environmentalists and peace activists often expand their existing frameworks to connect with the economic needs of working people. For example, Friends of the Earth president Michael Clark wrote about his organization's social goals: "We define 'environment' broadly. We focus upon people and how they interact with their political and economic environments—because we believe that the quality of these environments defines the quality of the broader environment that sustains us all."[1] To achieve a clean environment, in other words, society has to meet people's economic needs, so the interests of working people must be addressed as an extension of the organization's environmental values.

By contrast, building trades activists from Seattle described their environmental concerns in terms of personal interests. In the words of one activist,

> We're exporting our pollution and exporting jobs. . . . But polluting down there will eventually effect us too. It's all connected. You can't protect just your little environment. It's the same with unions—if you just protect yourself, you'll get isolated and eventually lose out too. We're not islands. My generation is a lot of "I've got mine so why care about my neighbor?" I have a problem with that. I see what happens to neighborhoods; it will affect my house value and job. If they lose their jobs, why won't I? If they live in a polluted environment, mine is next. You can't just take care of yourself.

Here the logic moves in the opposite direction from the environmentalists: from the immediate needs of working people to the broader social values of the environment and care about others. Values are seen as an extension of interests.

It is not an accident that middle-class and working-class activists follow different strategies to integrate the interests of working people with the values of peace and environmental protection. To find the language for their issues, people draw on their own cultural resources. True to their class cultures, the working class extends the language of interests, while the middle class applies the language of values.

Middle-Class Frameworks—Interpreting Interests as Values

Bridge builders from middle-class movements have developed a variety of ways to reframe their values to encompass economic interests. The conversion movement commonly uses three frames: conversion, diversification, and peace economy. The peace movement uses two others: one equates national security with economic security and the other relates peace to economic justice. The environmental movement has spawned two major ways to conceptualize a joint agenda with the labor movement: sustainable development and the extension of the term "environment" to social realms. All of these are attempts to reframe established values in terms that encompass working-class interests.

The peace movement, for example, has long promoted the idea that national security derives from economic security as a way to bridge issues of peace and social welfare. For example, the "Reinvest in Hometown America Resolution" promoted by Maine's Peace Economy Project urged the president and Congress to "recognize that the security of our country is dependent on the well-being of our economy, environment and people and to use the opportunity of dramatic improvements in relations between the East and West to reduce military spending proportionate to reduced military threat." This works as a bridge with the labor movement since economic security is one of its fundamental goals as well. Economic security implies both job security and economic well-being. The first requires a contract and union protection, while the second requires a decent income and benefits. Framing the issue in this way provides a way for the peace movement to define the interests of labor and the labor movement in terms of its value of peace.

The peace and environmental movements' approaches to reframing their goals extend traditional movement ideas to encompass economic interests and the needs of working people. They have not generally adopted the language of interests per se, and they remain within the value framework typical of their broader middle-class cultural context. Yet they have taken important steps toward finding more inclusive organizing frameworks that make space for working-class people. Many of these frames appeal directly to concepts already in circulation within the labor movement and working-class communities, such as economic security and social justice.

Working-Class Frameworks—Interpreting Values as Interests

Where coalition activists from the peace and environmental movements seek to broaden their conceptions of values like justice, sustainability, security, peace, or environment to incorporate working-class interests, the labor movement extends its conception of interests to accommodate middle-class values.

Labor activists use two broad approaches to integrate labor's agenda with social values like peace or the environment. The first argues that all groups are motivated by interests; the second, that values reflect the universal application of interests. In the first, peace and environmental protection are perceived as interests just as the rights of workers are. Those with legitimate interests, be they economic or noneconomic, have a moral right to promote them. Mel Duncan, a bridge builder from Minnesota, articulates this connection between interests and values in this way:

In a healthy approach, there is not a divergence between morality on the one hand and bread and butter on the other. To me it is a very moral thing for a single woman to work her ass off to support her kids. I just don't understand why there's a dichotomy. . . . Maybe that's the nexus, where morality and self interest converge. To me—sure it's in my self-interest that this world doesn't blow up. It's also in my self-interest that our community doesn't disintegrate before or after the explosion. . . . I don't trust sheer benevolence. Benevolence has to have a self-interest component or I don't trust it. I mean, we're fighting for our lives, right? And that's real different than fighting for their lives.

Coalition builders from labor find different ways to relate their interests in peace and a clean environment with job issues. Many cite Abraham Maslow's hierarchy of needs and propose that peace and environmental protection become important once more basic needs are met. They argue that the peace and environmental movements should work for a strong economy, since only a strong economy can provide the resources to protect the environment and the conditions for peaceful coexistence. Others propose that the working class has an immediate interest in peace and protecting the environment. In this view, corporations and elites that fight unions are the same ones that pollute the environment. Working people are the greatest victims of war, and they suffer the consequences of an economy devoted to military rather than social needs. Working- and middle-class movements are united against a common enemy. Therefore labor should join with the environmental and peace movements to further the interests of working people.

Where a common enemy clearly emerges, the task of reframing interests in common is relatively straightforward. Yet often there is no glaring villain. The situation is particularly difficult when cooperation requires compromise and even short-term losses for some members of the coalition. For instance, growth controls in Washington State potentially meant fewer construction jobs, which could have an immediate effect on union members despite the long-term advantages for the community. Peace organizations working with labor, as in Maine, found that they had to restrain some of their more virulent criticisms of military contractors to work with labor. Workers were being asked to consider risky job changes in the face of large-scale layoffs. In this and many other cases, both sides need to compromise for any cooperation to be possible. This requires a more subtle definition of shared interests than the simple claim of a common enemy.

An alternative and more complex framing of the relationship between interests and values recognizes that interests may diverge in any particular moment, but that in the long run the interests of working- and middle-class movements are shared. In this view, morals are interests applied universally to the community as a whole. Interests cannot be defined through an individual's experience, but require a broader identification with the interests of the group. As one labor activist explained, "Morality is just self-interest by another name. It's self-interest applied to everyone, what's good for everyone's interests."

Evolving Frameworks

Peace and labor coalitions in different communities experimented with different ways to frame their shared goals that spoke to both their memberships. These organizing frames evolved as movements found old ones less useful and experimented with new ones. At different times, different metaphors may be most appropriate to the level of trust and understanding that has developed between organizations. When coalitions first form, they may need to use terms that reflect the narrow, single-issue agenda that brings them together. As they evolve, coalitions are able to broaden their common goals. The old language becomes inadequate, and projects may feel the need to alter their names and the descriptions of what they do. Thus these reinterpretations of issues and interests are a living, changing part of the process of coalition growth and development.

The frameworks of conversion, diversification, and peace economy were each useful in particular contexts, but they had serious limitations as well. Conversion differs from other frameworks because it entered movement language through both the peace and labor movements. Before the United States entered World War II, Walter Reuther proposed that idle commercial plants be converted to military production, and then, after the war, he developed a detailed reconversion proposal. The Machinists union also has made conversion a cornerstone of its policies. Peace organizations such as Sane began to speak in terms of conversion in the 1960s, although the concept was already in circulation. In the labor movement, although the idea of conversion was advanced by a few key leaders, it went largely unheeded among members except in times of job loss due to military cutbacks. It gained wide circulation during the cutbacks of the 1980s and 1990s.

"Conversion" provides a way for peace and labor to identify a common agenda. As one peace activist explained to the labor community,

"We want disarmament and you want jobs, and conversion is about what we have in common." Conversion therefore redraws the lines of allies and enemies. In the absence of a planned redirection of military production, unions which depend on military spending oppose peace activists who want the military budget cut. Conversion provides a counter-framework to the accord between labor, management, and the Pentagon. Whereas the previous divisions were ordered around support for or opposition to military spending, this framework defines a shared interest based on local economic security as opposed to the interests of the military-industrial complex.

But conversion is flawed as a unifying agenda because it is so ambiguous. Conversion to what? How will this conversion be achieved? Conversion implies some level of reduction in military spending and some sort of alternative economic activity, but it fails to define these. Conversion can occur without attention to the social or environmental merits of the resulting production, and without accounting for the quality of the jobs created. As even conversion advocates note, "When companies do successfully convert or diversify, the results may not produce jobs for laid-off defense workers or jobs in existing communities." The problem is that conversion alone does not necessarily meet the goals of either the peace or labor movements. Indeed, many defense workers resist conversion because they do not believe that their jobs will be included in this agenda.

Many organizers have found diversification to be a more effective concept than conversion to initiate labor, peace, and community cooperation. Diversification emphasizes the need for new economic activities either by companies or within the local economy. It deals strictly with the economic side of conversion, and the hope is that more jobs will benefit defense sector workers. This provides a way to frame the issue even in an environment that is hostile to the peace movement's agenda. For example, in Washington State the nation's first conversion bill was passed as "an act relating to promoting economic diversification for defense-dependent industries and communities." The diversification advisory committee that it created included many individuals who personally supported military spending. The committee was therefore only able to function by restricting itself to an economic program.

Diversification as an agenda can unite peace and labor only in the limited historic context of military budget cuts, however. When cuts are happening, the argument goes, communities must plan to maintain their economies. Only in this circumstance will communities dependent on military spending seek to transfer that production to civilian uses as an economic development program. In another time, a more diverse economy might be achieved by increased military production. As one conversion activist admits, "Whereas diversification sells real well, we're not really talking about diversification. We're talking about another boat to step into before ours fills with water. And of course that has to do specifically with what is happening with the budget. If the budget becomes unproblematic later on and military spending is on the upswing again, then that motivation is gone. Diversification—that's not quite the issue."

So diversification does not provide a context for long-term cooperation between the peace and labor movements. It does not necessarily include good-quality union jobs, and frequently the diversification strategies of defense firms take place at the expense of their workers. More limited than the "conversion" framework, diversification abandons even the suggestion that economic development come from transferring production from the defense sector. It implies that participants will not promote further military cuts but discuss only those changes inevitably forced on the community. Diversification fails to create a long-term framework for labor and peace cooperation when pressure to increase the military budget inevitably returns. Thus it remains only a short-term agenda for coalition building.

The danger of short-term expedients is that activists abandon their agendas in the process of accommodating the present situation. This, indeed, seems to have happened with Washington State Sane/Freeze's participation on the state's diversification advisory committee. Their representative to the committee stated,

> I have no desire to talk about peace with people from economic development groups. What's the point? All I care about, especially given the changes in the world, [is that] we can all sit in a room and say that the reduced threat of nuclear war is the greatest thing that's happened to this country in decades and that the amount of resources that have been directed into this military machine can be redirected now to some of these unmet needs. And they don't ever have to agree on whether they ever should have gone into the military before. That doesn't even have to enter into the discussion.

When movement members stop representing their issues, they lose their significance to the coalition. Washington's diversification program is no longer a coalition that incorporates the peace agenda, but an economic development program which will pursue goals that may eventually run counter to the peace movement's purposes.

It was because of these limitations that Washington State Sane/ Freeze's diversification committee decided to change its name to the Peace Economy Campaign in 1992. The Maine project defined peace economy as "an economic system based on civilian enterprise established by the orderly redirection of resources now employed in military activities to socially useful economic endeavors." Diversification had been a valuable starting point in Washington as the organization sought to build its credibility and establish relationships with labor. But the group also eventually found this limiting. The new name became necessary to reintroduce the peace agenda back into the project's work. As a key member of WSSF's campaign explained,

> I would prefer at this point to say peace economy because I think that we've worked on diversification long enough that people do have some sense that we know what we're talking about and that we are talking about economic measures. I think for a while we needed that name to establish our credibility, and now I'd like to see us really talking about peace economy more because in my mind that encompasses more. The peace economy campaign really encompasses changing federal budget priorities as well as diversifying on the local level. I kind of like that bigger name. We're advocating for diversification and conversion; we're also advocating for big cuts. We're going for both. And I really feel like you can't have one without the other. We need the big cuts for other reasons, and with that will come more desire to work for conversion, diversification.

So this project felt the need to reframe its mission based on the work it had accomplished under the previous title.

However, peace economy is a limited agenda for coalition building as well, because it does not explicitly incorporate the agenda of the labor movement for preserving local jobs. Like diversification and conversion, the transfer of budget resources could be accomplished without protecting the rights of workers. Again, during a time of economic hardship, looming budget cuts, and a possible "peace dividend," labor may come to support such a macroeconomic redirection of federal spending. But many potential labor supporters remain skeptical of the relationship of this program to their own.

Thus at the same time that the Washington group was shifting its orientation toward a peace economy to broaden its agenda, the Maine project was shifting away from this conception as too limiting. "Peace economy" largely refers to a macroeconomic shift in budget priorities from military to civilian uses. Maine's organizers wanted to focus more on local initiatives that could create jobs, which was not identified explicitly enough in a peace economy. The Peace Economy Project "changed its name to the Economic Conversion Project of Maine to more accurately reflect who we are. 'Economic Conversion' describes a process to enable military-dependent industries, workers and communities make a transition to civilian pursuits and a participatory economic restructuring process to transform our overall economy into one that is sustainable in the long-term."[2]

Yet Maine's Economic Conversion Project also found the need over time to supersede economic conversion with a more positive statement of its goals. Their later conception of a common agenda became sustainable development. The Project proclaimed this transition, saying,

> We have come a long way since the days of only two years ago when the words "economic conversion" were met with a blank stare and scratch of the head. Today, "economic conversion" has become a household word. . . . Phase #1 of our work is almost complete. We have succeeded in educating the public and policymakers on the need and possibilities of economic conversion. . . . Our goal over the next year is to turn conversion planning into concrete examples of how Maine reduced its defense-dependency and increased business, jobs, profits, and long-term sustainability in the process!

Sustainability is an attempt to answer the question, Conversion to what? by providing an overarching principle for the economy. For a society to be sustainable over time it must promote social harmony and economic security. Sustainability implies that nations will be at peace since the use and destruction of resources during war is unsustainable. Therefore as Maine organizers shifted in their organizing to advance a positive vision of their goals, they again changed the metaphor they used to describe their work.

Activists continue to experiment with the best language to bring together working-class labor unions, middle-class peace activists, and other stakeholders. Coalitions provide a particularly rich opportunity to learn how to speak to these different communities. Participants encounter activists who share their desire for social change but who enter the political arena with very different cultural perspectives, expressing qualitatively different kinds of goals. By working together, groups must develop shared frames that reinterpret the separate goals of each movement in a common language. No single metaphor has emerged as most effective for bringing people together across the class divide. As conditions change and trust develops, frameworks evolve as well. For the time being, many alternative frameworks coexist in the context of new and shifting relationships.

HYBRID ORGANIZING STRATEGIES

Working- and middle-class movements need to come together around more than their ideas if they are to work in coalitions; they also need to agree about the strategies that they will pursue together. Labor organizing teaches the value of mobilizing around people's immediate, perceived needs and interests. By uniting people who share common interests, powerless groups can counter the explicit use of force and manipulation by elites. This approach begins with interests and produces changes in awareness as a consequence of interest-based action. Middle-class organizing, on the other hand, provides important lessons about the role of consciousness in shaping perceptions of interests and therefore behavior. Largely through educational campaigns to alter popular understandings about universal goods, people begin to redefine their interests and to act differently. To reconcile the perceptions of working- and middle-class activists about social change, coalitions must apply the insights of the two approaches to organizing. They must develop hybrid forms of organizing that build on the strengths of both an interest-based and a consciousness-raising approach to social change.

The most sophisticated models of organizing do recognize the roles of both interests and consciousness. Paulo Freire offers a model which both addresses explicitly recognized interests and incorporates a process of consciousness raising and learning about unrecognized interests. In his view, interests are a matter of perception, and through critical dialogue and action both consciousness and concrete interests can be transformed. Freire summarizes how this enables the oppressed to overcome their current limitations:

> It is not the limit-situations in and of themselves which create a climate of hopelessness, but rather how they are perceived by men at a given historical moment: whether they appear as fetters or as insurmountable barriers. As critical perception is embodied in action, a climate of hope and confidence develops which leads men to attempt to overcome the limit-situations. This objective can be achieved only through action upon the

concrete, historical reality in which limit-situations historically are found. As reality is transformed and these situations are superseded, new ones will appear, which in turn will evoke new limit-acts ([acts] directed at negating and overcoming, rather than passively accepting, the "given").

Many community organizers subscribe to a similar model, as exemplified by the philosophy of groups such as ACORN and Citizen Action. They use interest organizing as a process to alter consciousness. One longtime activist summarizes this relationship between building power and altering consciousness: "The process, then, is continual: research-action-reflection-research. The point is not just to build a machine that can win concessions from this complex socioeconomic system. The real challenge is to create an institution that can collectively validate an alternative view of social reality and redefine appropriate behavior and collective action."[3] This approach has the advantage of attending to the multiple levels of power and human action that are guided both by interests and understandings. In this model, social change is an evolving process that moves from interest-based organizing to reflection/consciousness raising and back again in an extended cycle.

From the perspective of value-based organizing, this interest/consciousness-raising model of organizing has three limitations. First, while this approach develops a process for raising the awareness of participants, it does not address the consciousness of the wider public. In this model, the emerging understandings of oppressed people become the basis for more effective political action by building the commitment and effectiveness of the group or organization. As the oppressed gain more sophisticated understandings of their own interests, they are better able to oppose the interests of powerful elites.

Value-based organizing is particularly attuned to the possibility of altering the perceptions of others. Organizing, in this view, strives to influence the awareness of either adversaries or the broader public in order to alter their behavior. These movements claim that certain goals—such as peace or environmental protection—are valuable and advantageous for everybody. If the public reaches a new awareness, its perceptions of interests will change. A new awareness makes it possible to advance the interests of groups in ways that could not have been accomplished within the confines of interest organizing.

The second limitation of the interest/consciousness raising model is that even the most critical reflection and dialogue about one's present condition cannot in itself create the vision of what should be. Perceptions of self-interests are limited by the social structure, which segregates groups and shapes perceptions of interests as divided and opposed. Critics of interest organizing make this point about Saul Alinsky's instrumental approach to organizing: "[Alinsky's] narrowness of focus proved a shortcoming, for it was often easiest for one oppressed group to achieve its objectives at the expense of another. . . . Indeed, Alinsky's approach, for all its militancy and iconoclasm, could finally fit into the traditional interest group form of American politics, in which different powerless groups accept the 'givens' of income distribution and corporate structure and compete for scarce but expanding resources through the use of whatever tactics they can devise."[4]

The labor movement is also frequently criticized for its narrow attention to practical politics and interest organizing. All too often these movements have reproduced existing divisions of race, class, gender, and geography. Reflection about self-interest is not in itself sufficient to transcend the limits of the present society. Lenin captured this limitation of interest-based organizing when he wrote:

> "Every one agrees" that it is necessary to develop the political consciousness of the working class. But the question arises, How is that to be done? . . . . The economic struggle merely brings the workers "up against" questions concerning the attitude of government towards the working class. Consequently, however much we may try to "give to the economic struggle itself a political character" we shall never be able to develop the political consciousness of the workers (to the degree of Social-Democratic consciousness) by confining ourselves to the economic struggle, for the limits of this task are too narrow.[5]

The third difficulty with this model of interest/consciousness raising comes from the question, Who organizes the reflection process that develops critical thinking? Freire observed that dialogue requires an "other," an instigator who asks questions and spurs reflection. Freire assumes the existence of a highly enlightened cadre of revolutionary educators motivated by love, solidarity, and faith in the people. Lenin's solution to this dilemma was a revolutionary vanguard party. Gary Delgado proposes that organizers play the role of researching community problems, identifying values, initiating a dialogue with community members, convening an organizing committee, developing a campaign strategy, building an organization, and initiating the process of self-reflection.[6] These solutions require an enlightened and dedicated cadre of individuals who come from outside to mobilize and engage the group being organized. Obvious difficulties exist with outsiders who bring their own biases to the changes they consider and promote. Furthermore, they too are potentially corruptible and will have interests in advancing their careers or other needs.

Cross-class coalitions can contribute to the process of dialogue in an important way that minimizes the dangers of a powerful, minority cadre. In these coalitions, the dialogue is between two movements and not with some enlightened third party. Movement actors learn important lessons about themselves and the organization of society from other movements. Since movements respond to systematic problems, they offer the potential for dialogue that is particularly revealing about the nature of society.

What is needed is a model of organizing that responds to people's immediate interests but also projects some clear vision of the alternative society that movements are working to create. It must be sophisticated enough to recognize that both the oppressed and oppressors are motivated by their perceived interests and consciousness. Freire teaches us that this organizing approach must involve a process of dialogue and critical reflection based on people's present perceptions of their interests. Reflection on the present can teach people to claim their own ability to create their own lives, but this is not sufficient in and of itself to transform the values that underlie society. We cannot just assume that a newly empowered underclass will build a society based on new principles. We must add to this model a process for introducing new values into interest organizing and reflection that builds on the lessons drawn from intergroup interactions.

The cases of working- and middle-class coalitions described in this study suggest hybrid models of organizing that address the complex relationships between interest organizing and the creation of new values in the process of social change. Theories of social change are rarely discussed explicitly, and these hybrid organizing models remain largely unconscious. Most organizing attention, rather, is devoted to discussion of tactics and goals. Yet implicit in these more concrete details are ideas about how to organize for change. Adaptations in strategy emerge piecemeal as the group seeks to accommodate diverse participants. Therefore hybrid organizing models generally remain unrecognized by the coalition, and organizers frequently continue to espouse their previous ideas about strategy. As a result, conscious models of social change are revised more slowly and more tentatively than the definitions of issues or specific organizing tactics.

Three distinct hybrid approaches to organizing emerged in the conversion cases studied here. The first, from Washington, utilized interest-based organizing techniques to alter consciousness. The second, from Maine, sought to alter perceptions of interests first, as a foundation for interest-based organizing. The Minnesota model was to pursue interest organizing and value-based education simultaneously but independently as mutually reinforcing political processes. As mentioned earlier, none of these are consciously articulated, nor are they fully developed "models" of organizing. Rather, they are practical strategic compromises emerging in each situation.

Washington State

The case of Washington State Sane/Freeze was the most well articulated hybrid model because of the explicit efforts of David Fleishman to apply community organizing within the peace movement. Fleishman developed his approach to coalition organizing from working with an Alinsky-style organization in Florida. He recalled, "Coming out of an Alinsky organization like I did, our goal was to build political power by finding common-denominator issues. Part of the goal of these organizations is to find those common self-interests. We try to see, 'What could we develop that would tie in the broadest range [of people]?' " He joined Sane/Freeze with the idea of applying these same techniques. As he explained, "My theory in coming to WSSF was to see if you could take the low-income tactics and put [them] in a white middle-class organization, with people who have a tiny smidgen of power, with tactics that really challenge power. That was my thinking in coming here." Fleishman said that people really resisted his talk about power when he first joined Sane, that they thought he was crazy. He felt that people did not really understand what he meant. But over time they became more comfortable with community organizing techniques.

Fleishman developed a conversion strategy applying interest-based organizing techniques. Labor's interests were straightforwardly material, in his view: "Labor had a self-interest in keeping jobs." The peace organization, on the other hand, seeks to alter national policy. Since this is a collective and not an individual agenda, it requires altering public beliefs and voting behavior. Fleishman described this in the language of interests as well: "Our (WSSF's) self-interest was in creating the will to cut military spending." Within the interest model of organizing, he believed that the way to serve these dual interests would be to guarantee workers jobs through conversion. That would free workers to support military budget cuts. In Fleishman's words, "You create the will by having workers not so scared shitless that they're going to lose their jobs."

"We [labor and peace organizations] had different self-interests around the same common denominator. We both needed some planning around military budget cuts."

Fleishman's efforts to pursue this community-organizing strategy were modified through the activity of the diversification committee. As director, he joined in promoting an Alinsky-style campaign to confront the power of Boeing directly, based on a shared community-workforce interest in conversion. Others on the diversification committee did not believe that a Boeing campaign would succeed. They became convinced by the work of Sane's lobbyist that a legislative strategy could be more effective. Legislation could also mobilize workers, communities, and peace organizations around their interests in promoting conversion. But here the outcome would not be a more powerful organization that could directly achieve the interests of its members. The results would be broadly educational. The purpose of the legislation and its supporting studies was to convince the state government and public that conversion is a viable economic alternative. This would hopefully limit attempts to resist federal defense budget cuts and convince decision makers to assist defense companies. The program could indirectly create jobs for displaced defense workers, which could again convince them to favor military budget cuts as well.

In sum, what evolved in the Washington case was an organizing strategy that used people's perceived immediate interests as a basis for an educational campaign that would change perceptions of alternatives. Sane/Freeze appealed to unions and the peace community with the argument that conversion planning is necessary to renew jobs that are already slated to be cut from the defense sector. These groups supported the campaign because of their currently perceived interests. But community organizing techniques became a means to educational ends, namely, to alter broad perceptions about economic priorities and interests. The target of this education remained the broad, unspecified public, in keeping with the approach of middle-class organizations. In turn this education was a way to win elections or pass other legislation favored by the peace organization. In the long run, this lobbying would hopefully contribute to the immediate interests of workers whose jobs are threatened and to the peace movement seeking to reduce the military budget.

Maine

Maine followed something of the opposite organizing strategy. Whereas WSSF organized around specific interests of some groups in society as the basis for broad education about values, the Peace Economy Project sought first to alter public perceptions of interests as the basis for further organizing. Here the principal organizer, Susie Schweppe, began with a peace movement background. Her past experience convinced her that cooperation would be more productive than conflict and that dialogue was an effective way to change people's ideas and accomplish political goals. Thus her orientation was to identify a basis for cooperation and to organize from that shared sense of purpose.

Schweppe's strategy with the Peace Economy Project was to build a consensus among the various stakeholders in the community. This meant focusing attention on the benefits of shifting national and local resources to meet social needs. This focus could be seen as challenging the present interests of defense contractors and their unions, and the community could also resist these changes as threatening to the state's economy. Thus the educational task was first to reorient these groups toward the long-term benefits of deep cuts in the defense budget, which meant shifting their sense of self-interest. ("Make them think something you want is in their self-interest," said Schweppe.) The Project initiated a series of studies to document the negative community impacts of military spending and the positive benefits of redirecting those resources. All this was geared toward "educating the public and policymakers on the need and possibilities of economic conversion" and "raising the public comfort level" about economic shifts.

As the Project began to work with management and labor, it had to address the specifics of industrial change and job renewal. Participants in the project from Bath Iron Works and the Machinists union demanded this kind of practical detail, and challenged the Project to be concrete about its proposals. The Project's main response was to facilitate community planning processes. It also worked toward an inventory of worker skills and spurred the creation of a state task force to assist with the economic transition. Once a broad community agreed that they shared an interest in economic diversification, the Project could then organize around this collective interest.

Overall, the Peace Economy Project sought to alter public awareness about interests vis-à-vis military spending, and then to organize to meet this interest. The group devoted significant time to defining a shared vision that all participants could embrace, and to educating the general community about the value of economic conversion. Feeling they succeeded in this educational task, the Project advanced its educational program to include sustainable development. But the kinds of specific economic assistance that they were able to offer was limited. Thus the organization did no more than begin to meet the interests it helped to articulate for nonmilitary economic development. The Project's organizing challenge was to learn to organize effectively in the economic arena.

Minnesota

Jobs with Peace in Minnesota effectively divided its interest-based and educational organizing as two separate, complementary agendas. The organization participated in many of the typical educational efforts of the peace movement, but it also assisted with one of the most extensive interest-based organizing campaigns around conversion. Jobs with Peace's principal organizer, Mel Duncan, had experience with both the peace movement and the organizing of disenfranchised groups. He wanted to bring the lessons of his workplace organizing to peace issues with the idea of shifting decision-making power to workers and communities and away from big corporations. He saw conversion as an issue through which such a change could be accomplished.

Jobs with Peace simultaneously developed an interest-based campaign at Unisys and a broad educational campaign directed at the general public. Duncan's personal approach to organizing is interest based, and the campaign that he helped IBEW organize against Unisys sought to build sufficient power to pressure the corporation to adopt conversion planning. The union made the ultimate strategy decisions in the campaign, which followed the usual adversarial relationship between management and labor. The peace organization limited its role to providing technical assistance, and did not explicitly promote its peace agenda with the union. At the same time, Jobs with Peace developed a separate campaign to educate the public so that it would pressure the state and federal governments to support conversion. They worked through the state Task Force on Economic Conversion to document the benefits of reducing the military budget and the need to plan to reverse job loss in manufacturing. Drawing upon this research, they developed an educational campaign to generate support for this perspective.

Although the research and educational organizing remained separate from the interest-based campaign at Unisys, these efforts complemented each other. The interest campaign provided the demand for change from the company. Political leaders from the mayor to the governor felt compelled to echo this demand. The educational work was designed to make the broader policy case for conversion assistance from the government. It sought to convince the public that changes in federal spending are desirable, and that the community should require and assist conversion efforts such as those proposed by the workers at Unisys. The Unisys organizing proved invaluable in this educational campaign. It dramatically illustrated the need for public action for conversion by demonstrating the lack of cooperation of management with the reasonable and creative efforts of citizens. Management's noncooperation publicly demonstrated the nature of the problem and justified the organization's call for mandatory corporate planning. IBEW's efforts also provided a context for reaching union members with information about conversion that they would not otherwise have seen. On the other hand, the educational work of Jobs with Peace supported the organizing campaign at Unisys by raising the level of awareness and public pressure for response. This dual effort defined the issue in terms of the long-term benefits of military cuts, where the community and corporations have responsibility for replacing jobs lost in the transition.

The effect of Jobs with Peace's dual campaign, if successful, would have been to realize the peace organization's values in a way that would also benefit the immediate interests of workers. The educational campaign would alter public awareness about the value of a peace economy, producing policy changes that would also meet immediate needs. The organizing campaign would create the demand for changes that would also respond to workers' needs. The value of peace and the economic security needs of the community were linked.

Here are three tentative models that link interest-based and education-oriented organizing in a broad process of social change. One strategy uses interest organizing to win changes that become the basis for education about new values. Another strategy first educates people about common values as the basis for concrete organizing around group interests and goals. A third approach organizes complementary interest and educational campaigns, with the former mobilizing oppressed groups and the latter directed at the wider public and policymakers. All three of these approaches learned from middle-class movements to change values, and thus create support for alternatives to the beliefs and understandings that govern people's lives. And they learned from interest-based movements that the present organization of society has failed to meet people's needs, which must be considered in any new organization of society.

The common framework for all these hybrid models is the advancement of new values in a way that meets the specific interests of those most in need in the community. These frameworks emerge as working- and middle-class groups seek to respond to each other, rather than relying on an independent, enlightened organizer. This interaction becomes the source of dialogue and learning. None of these hybrid organizing approaches is fully developed or conscious, but each suggests ways to organize that go beyond isolated interests or abstract values, that is, beyond reproducing class divisions. They advance change that seeks to meet the immediate needs of working people in an economic system that reflects social values, and thus they illustrate political processes that could reintegrate economic and social development.

▲

Prospects for a Working- and Middle-Class Alliance

The social and economic questions raised by struggles over jobs, the environment, and peace are enormous. How can an economy that requires growth and expansion to create jobs also protect the environment? How can a community or country maintain environmental and wage standards while competing in a globally open economy? With the unprecedented wealth we produce every day, how do we make resources available to meet everyone's basic needs and advance values such as peace and the environment? How do we wean the U.S. economy from its dependence on military spending? And how do we limit the power of capitalist interests so that countries can experiment with their own forms of development without war or economic blackmail forcing them back into the global marketplace?

During an earlier generation people could turn to the great visionary movements of their day for answers to these fundamental questions. Socialism, communism, liberalism, and other inspirational belief systems have, however, been largely discredited in our cynical age. The movements of the 1960s, the most recent mass revival of a social vision of participatory democracy, ended in profound disillusionment for many. A new international movement for change ultimately needs to provide an alternative vision for a just society and a sustainable economy.

Advancing a progressive agenda depends upon finding ways to bridge divisions of class, race, nationality, and gender. Past progressive changes have depended upon multiclass coalitions, not single-class movements. These coalitions have been forced to find ways to promote both jobs and social and environmental goals. The social democratic experiments in Scandinavia provide clear examples of working- and middle-class alliances, as did the New Deal coalition in the United States. These coalitions are no less necessary today. As Carl Boggs explains, "The prospect for radical social change in the advanced industrial countries will ultimately depend upon a convergence of labor struggles and popular movements around feminism, ecology, peace and social equality—a convergence that links material and quality-of-life demands with a coherent political strategy."[1]

The experiences of local working- and middle-class coalitions suggest that a national movement and alternative ideology will not emerge from the top down. A progressive majority must first bridge deep divisions between constituencies and issues. Local interclass and intermovement coalitions are learning important lessons about how to develop practical programs for building a new society. But instead of a grand new ideology, these coalitions are framing transitional agendas that move toward larger transformations. These experiments in progress point the way to broader national alliances and platforms.

CONFRONTING NECESSITIES

Social, economic, and environmental issues have become inseparable. According to the Oil, Chemical and Atomic Workers (OCAW), whose members work in some of the most polluting and toxic industries in the country, "Nature has become a central issue for our economy, and economics has become a central issue for virtually every regulation to protect nature and public health. . . . The collision between nature, community and the economy signals a new era of environment/jobs tension and conflict. . . . Labor unions and mainstream environmental organizations (e.g., Sierra Club, Greenpeace, etc.) increasingly are pitted against each other, each side struggling for what it perceives as survival."[2]

This dilemma has many faces. Middle-class advocates for peace and the environment are pitted against working-class people seeking to protect jobs and economic security. The timber wars continue in the forests of the Northwest, claiming the life of another environmentalist when he was crushed by a falling old-growth tree in the Headwaters Forest of California in September 1998. A very similar debate rages over global warming. Coal miners and mining companies have joined together to fight environmentalists' efforts to reduce CO_2 emissions. Numerous other issues—use of public lands, resource use, endangered species, toxic chemical use, and biodiversity—risk pitting working people against environmentalists. Peace and defense sector unions face the same kinds of conflicts in the 1990s as the military budget rises and military firms shift production to the global arms trade.

Working- and middle-class movements are not the only progressive causes in conflict. People face other difficult choices: funding welfare versus balancing the budget; affirmative action versus opportunities for whites; economic prosperity versus government regulations to protect health, the environment, and social welfare; and free trade versus protecting worker health and quality of life. Opponents of social welfare policy present these as necessary choices for a society that has been overindulgent to the poor and minorities and that can no longer afford the luxury of economic prosperity and social policy.

Divided and too often working in isolation, social movements are losing ground on both their issues and their capacity to advocate. Labor membership continues its long decline. Extinction of species, crises in coastal fish populations, global warming, unsafe sweatshop production at home and overseas, and many other environmental problems continue unabated despite decades of environmental regulations. Renewed growth in the military budget and failure to pass a real conversion policy are major setbacks to the peace movement.

Even worse, global corporations have outmaneuvered grassroots movements by instituting a free trading system that supersedes national sovereignty. Society's rules have shifted so far in favor of money and corporate power that local communities have few institutionalized ways to protect their interests. Corporations now have the option of leaving instead of negotiating with workers and communities for decent wages and for adequate environmental protections. The arms sector continues to be an entrenched part of the U.S. economy. Decision making is more and more removed from local communities as large multinational firms assume control of banks and financial institutions, corporate employers, and retailers. These conditions make organizing even more difficult.

POLITICS OF SOCIAL DIFFERENCES

Social movements organize against problems that are inherent in the way society is structured. Workers who have political rights as equal citizens organize against their subservient role as employees in the workplace. Environmentalists and peace activists organize against the destructive consequences of technological development and power. As products of society, movements incorporate society's internal contradictions. Peace and environmental activists promoting broad social values produce unintended economic consequences for working people. Unions advancing the interests of labor produce unintended consequences for peace and the environment. Conflicts within and between these movements inevitably reflect structural contradictions in the society they seek to change. This situation is compounded by corporations and policymakers who use the perception of divergent interests to divide working-class from middle-class movements.

Different degrees of power and vulnerability are also divisive. Middle-class movements tend to have greater access to the bureaucracy because it is staffed by their professional peers. Bureaucratic processes also function through expertise and abstract rules that reflect middle-class values. The middle class tends, therefore, to have greater faith in the ability of these institutions to accomplish its goals. The working class, by contrast, is often the weakest party in conflicts and tends to pay the costs of many political and economic decisions. Its strategies reflect both this vulnerability and the interpretation of politics as a conflict about interests. Peace and environmental movements frequently impact the lives of working-class communities directly through influencing regulations and government spending. The labor movement, by contrast, has little impact on the lives of the middle class even when it influences issues of concern to middle-class movements.

Cultural differences add to the difficulty of working across the class divide and make it more likely that movements will interpret their interests as opposed. Working- and middle-class activists often do not have relationships with each other, not only because they work and live in different places, but also because they build relationships of community and friendship differently. Associations based on profession and activity, typical of the middle class, draw different social circles from the workplace and neighborhood associations found in the working class. Furthermore, the working and middle classes understand and pursue their goals differently. Since members of the working class join organizations to protect their immediate personal interests, they are likely to disagree with middle-class activists seeking to promote universal social values. Finally, classes have different expectations about how to work together for change. The interest-based organizing of the working class uses different strategies and tactics from the education-oriented organizing of the middle class. Each is adapted to the distinct kind of change that a working- or middle-class movement seeks. Movements must overcome these differences if they are to develop a shared strategy for organizing.

Workers, environmentalists, and peace activists have choices about whether to work separately, work together, or ally instead with powerful business or government interests. These choices are very real. It's the question of whether or not to join a union, follow management's lead, or seek out other allies in the community. For middle-class professionals, it's the question of whether to apply one's expertise to enhance corporate profits, to be an advocate within a professional setting, or to seek out alliances with people from other classes.

Each alliance has potential risks and rewards. The incentive to collaborate with those who have power and resources is the tangible reward that other groups cannot provide. But the risks of being the expendable partner in an unequal collaboration are also great, as the labor movement found all too well in the 1980s. After benefiting from the loyal collaboration of unions during the Cold War decades, government and industry unleashed a concerted onslaught that accelerated the decline of union membership and influence. Meanwhile, labor's participation in Cold War foreign policies seriously undermined progressive labor movements in Europe, Latin America, Asia, and Africa. This contributed significantly to the inability of labor to build an effective global response to corporate mobility and paved the way for the dominant position that corporate interests now enjoy. Collaboration, as in the case of old-growth timber, has often been a short-term expedient; the long-term costs of resource depletion and occupational hazards plague workers once corporations move on. These alliances have proven short sighted and destructive to the labor movement overall.

Labor alliances with peace and environmental groups also have their many risks and pitfalls. Given the history of conflict between movements, coalition builders may confront hostility from the groups they would like to work with, as Washington State Sane/Freeze did from labor unions in Hanford. But they also could find themselves attacked and criticized by members of their own movements for compromising too much, as the Peace Economy Project found in Maine. Collaborating with other movements can alienate some members as organizations expand beyond the least common denominator issues that unite their constituencies. These internal controversies can be exploited by opponents to divide and weaken challenging groups. As the building trades–environmental alliance in Washington found, successful coalitions can expect direct and visible attacks in the newspaper and from business and political adversaries who feel threatened by coalitions.

Although each of us must decide which uncertain strategy to pursue to guide our personal fates, the course of history depends upon the direction that large numbers of class members choose particularly through their organizations and movements. Working- or middle-class alliances with wealthy and powerful classes inevitably come at the cost of excluded classes and class-based movements. Change requires a majority that refuses to compromise on the need for jobs, peace, and a healthy environment.

Coalition organizers in Washington, Minnesota, and Maine chose to build coalitions across the class divide that began to shift the political landscape in their communities. Individuals in each of these coalitions took personal and organizational risks to work together. Organizers from the trade unions in Washington took the bold step of sitting down with environmentalists to build relationships and a common agenda. Unions and peace activists in each of the conversion cases also decided to move into uncharted waters. These choices led to victories that otherwise wouldn't have been achieved.

PRACTICAL LESSONS

Class shapes people's choices and how they interpret their situations, but the specific political ideas and beliefs that people follow are not determined by either class position or class culture. Rather, the specific strategies individuals choose, be they competition, class solidarity, collaboration with powerful groups or interclass coalitions, are negotiable. The more ephemeral aspects of people's lives—relationships, personal experience, historical context, political opportunities—contribute to the way people perceive their interests. Social processes can go a long way toward bridging these differences. Careful organizing can shape people's relationships, agendas, and strategies. How people are approached and how they work together has a significant impact on how they perceive their interests and define their loyalties. Under the right conditions, working- and middle-class organizations can bridge these cultural differences and build alliances that can shift the balance of power.

To those who choose the strategy of coalition building, the experiences of conversion and labor-environmental coalitions described here have much to teach. These pioneering coalitions illustrate both successful techniques and pitfalls to be avoided. None of these lessons can be applied mechanically, since each situation is unique. But they do begin to build a vocabulary for developing coalition strategies.

Relationship building and learning are the two master processes of coalition building. Interpretations of events and options are shaped through dialogue, so choices about allies and interests depend fundamentally upon the diversity of people's contacts. Bridge builders who already have relationships with diverse groups are critical to the process of bringing together coalition partners in the first place. Bridge builders provide the opportunity for other participants to gain their own cross-class experiences and develop new relationships as well. But coalitions err when they relegate their communications to formal meetings where people do not express their real feelings and criticisms. Only through direct personal dialogue can partners understand each other's points of view and deepen their relationships.

Conditions favoring coalitions vary from community to community. Opportunities for people to build relationships across class lines are critical for developing coalitions. Bridge builders from different generational groups may be more or less available in a community, depending on such factors as the existence of jobs for upwardly mobile people, the organizational environment (including the presence of unions and other movement organizations), and the opportunities for professional jobs. Other institutions can also provide avenues for people to get to know each other through such activities as political campaigns or community events. For example, the social conditions in Seattle contributed to the formation of a coalition between unions and environmentalists that could not easily develop in the rural timber communities of the Olympic Peninsula. The labor-environmental coalition in Seattle resulted from the effectiveness of bridge builders in key positions of leadership, which did not exist in the timber communities. Moreover, inhabitants of urban Seattle have greater access to integrating institutions like electoral politics, other coalitions, and professional networks. Given that most of this state's environmental organizations have their offices and the bulk of their memberships in Seattle, the opportunities for relationships to develop are far greater there than in the timber communities. These factors made the difference between developing a coalition and moving into open conflict.

Once people do come together, their initial contacts are often uncomfortable as each side tests whether it can trust the other. Participants need to be prepared for harsh questions and criticism, and they need to remain in dialogue to prove that they are sincere about working together. Agreeing to disagree about controversial issues allows coalitions to build trust and relationships. If this trust is to deepen, partners must prove that they are committed to each other's goals as their own.

As people work together on a narrow set of issues, they begin to learn about their different perspectives. Even if the initial reason for coming together is for some limited political gain, coalition participants have the opportunity to understand each other's concerns better through cooperation. This makes it possible to address more complex issues over time.

Coalitions need to develop strategies and tactics that are attuned both to the comfort levels of participating parties and to the tactics of adversaries. Partners need to be particularly careful to work within the accepted level of conflict of their partners—a level that will evolve and change as the coalition develops. Management's response to a coalition will shape the appropriate strategy as well, with hostile responses making more militant replies possible and cooperative behavior requiring more collaborative replies.

Local interclass coalitions are developing important models for organizing that combine pragmatic achievements with a larger vision for change. These hybrid organizing models draw on the best of both working-class interest-based organizing and middle-class education-based organizing. Interest organizing teaches important lessons about building power based on the collective action of people who share the same interests. More sophisticated interest-based organizing approaches encourage activists to develop their own understandings through evaluating and reflecting on their actions. But education-based strategies also teach the importance of addressing the consciousness of other potential allies and adversaries. Working- and middle-class coalitions need to develop strategies that incorporate the strengths of both organizing approaches.

These and other lessons from the coalitions of the early 1990s point the way to more effective organizing. But the leaders and organizers in each case had to rediscover many of the lessons of coalition building themselves. Practical advice about the dilemmas of working across the class divide is hard to come by. Experiences need to be analyzed systematically and communicated widely to improve people's abilities to create more successful coalitions over time.

COALITION DEMOCRACY

Coalition building between movements and community organizations is a vital process to revive our democracy. Movements are schools for democracy where citizens learn what they can never understand from formal civics classes or from armchair infusions of media sound bites. But movements working in isolation are not enough. They require coalitions, democratic schools for community building, to bring people another critical step closer to a democratic society.

Movements alone—without coalitions—can teach people how power actually works in society, as opposed to what idealized versions of democracy and equality claim. They can provide participants with skills and experiences to formulate and articulate their ideas and to work collectively for change, rather than remaining passive observers of electoral spectacles. Movements can bring together people with common struggles and purposes, exposing the lie that these are either personal failings or paranoid fears. Most important, movements can raise people up and teach them to trust and value themselves not as clients, consumers, or victims but as worthy equals. Movements can assist in healing an afflicted democracy.

But these movements have their own limitations as expressions of the society from which they emerge. Movements form to address the specific interests of people in a common situation or with a shared belief or value. But our individualistic society has fractured life and accelerated its pace so much that the interests around which people gather are isolated and disjointed. Work and community concerns are separated as people leave their race- and class-segregated neighborhoods behind for workplaces that are highly specialized by occupation and industry. With cars, home entertainment centers, malls, personal computers, and an ever expanding array of personal technologies, people consume in their own little anonymous worlds. The units of social relationships—families and communities—are dramatically disintegrating. It is no wonder that each movement tends to focus narrowly on some specific issue or problem that a small fraction of the population has as its priority. Although movements draw people together around common interests and goals, members tend to be homogeneous groups who already share experiences and perspectives. This is not a broad enough basis for overcoming the fragmentation in society. The great political challenge is to weave disparate lives into a mutually supportive community, to shift from partisan advocacy for separate interests and issues to a shared commitment to common goals, to bind together our proliferating individualities in a common destiny.

Intermovement coalitions teach what movements alone cannot about life in the broader community. They provide a practical means for people, perhaps already empowered through acting for a common cause, to learn the lessons that come only from confronting differences. Through coalitions people build relationships across class and other lines. To do so they need to reframe their issues as shared. As collaborators learn more about each other and their different perspectives, they shift their worldviews to incorporate these new people and ideas. They can no longer disassociate from the real needs and problems that motivate people they now know personally.

While all intergroup collaboration can help build community, interclass and intermovement coalitions are necessary to build a progressive majority for change. Single-class movements alone lack the numbers and the perspective to transform society. They need allies to build numbers, but, equally important, they need allies to help them learn how to appeal to a majority of people. They need to develop a more comprehensive agenda worthy of majority support, and they need to develop practices and processes that can include diverse people. Interclass coalitions create the opportunity for social learning as a means for developing a more inclusive conception of the common good. Coalitions provide the opportunity to synthesize new conceptions, goals, and techniques for organizing that go beyond reproducing the oppression of others. This process has the potential to produce a more comprehensive movement for change with an agenda worthy of change.

PROSPECTS

Conditions for interclass coalition building are more favorable now than ever since World War II. The generation that came of age in the 1960s and 1970s is now coming into power in many institutions in society. This generation is exceptionally rich in bridge builders both among middle-class activists who support labor and social justice coalitions and working-class activists who gained experience with the student, peace, and civil rights movements. Younger labor leaders are transforming the labor movement with their greater willingness to work in community alliances. Support for working-class organizing can be found among segments of peace and environmental activists from this generation as well.

New coalitions frequently form in times of crisis, when old relationships are breaking down. With the end of the Cold War, the collapse of the post–World War II labor-capital accord, economic instability and insecurity, globalization of production and corporate mobility, and constrained government spending, the present period provides exceptional opportunities for coalition building. As the Peace Economy Project recognized in the context of Maine:

Maine faces an historic watershed of economic change, change that is markedly different from anything we have ever experienced, one that is inseparable from a national and global perspective, and sensitivity to the interdependence of economic, environmental and social well-being. . . . Our current situation provokes us to explore new criteria for economic development, and new partnerships and inclusive decision making processes that balance the needs of our many diverse but inter-related interests within a comprehensive plan for our future.

Environmentalists are also coming to recognize that their abilities to advance their goals depend upon working with communities and labor. This has become evident from the old-growth timber conflict, the free trade issue, and many other resource use and environmental issues that have direct impact on jobs and the economy. The labor movement is also at a crossroads after decades of decline, the flight of American industry, the end of the Cold War, and widespread union-busting activity.

However, the same conditions that encourage cooperation between movements create the potential for conflict. Military spending levels and the fate of workers and military production facilities are highly contested issues. Conflicts over the use of resources will continue to pit environmentalists against communities and labor in resource-dependent economies like that of Washington State. Cooperation in conditions of crisis cannot be taken for granted.

While not inevitable, the number and variety of peace, environmental, labor and other coalitions is on the rise in the United States and Europe. Coalitions around conversion, and between labor and environmental organizations around corporate responsibilities, safety and health, trade, and environmental protection, demonstrate the potential for cooperation. Some of the most effective workplace struggles in recent years have been based on this broader intersection of activists in community, labor, and middle-class social movements. Environmental and labor coalitions are emerging in many communities through such local initiatives as the Pipe Trades Council of Northern California, the building trades–environmental coalition in Washington, and the coalition between paper workers and Greenpeace in Maine. Peace and labor coalitions for military conversion expanded dramatically when the military budget was being cut between 1986 and 1996. The conversion issue faded significantly, however, when the military budget began to rise again and the number of dramatic layoffs declined.

Local coalitions can win local victories, but a national movement is needed when the struggle is against national or multinational companies or the federal government's spending priorities. This is all too often the case, since decision makers are found less and less within the boundaries of our communities. The Unisys campaign in Minnesota shows that even if the local coalition is strong and has wide local political support, large multinational firms may still be beyond reach. Federal action would have been needed to force military corporations built by public dollars to invest in local conversion programs. But the national peace and labor coalition at the time was weak and lost the national debate over conversion policy; military and corporate interests emerged the victor. So national corporations were able to keep big profits while millions of workers lost their jobs. Local initiatives could not prevail in this situation. Local struggles need to find local victories as they build toward a national coalition that makes larger victories possible.

A national working- and middle-class alliance will have to develop on the building blocks of strong local coalitions. Coalition building is a localized process which requires face-to-face relationship building and dialogue. Each coalition in this study reframed interests in new ways that incorporated the goals of participating movements, but different language was useful in different circumstances. Peace and labor coalitions found "conversion," "diversification," "peace economy," and "sustainable economy" all useful frameworks in specific circumstances and specific times. In fact the appropriate framework evolved as coalitions developed and campaigns shifted focus. Even more complex for a national agenda, working- and middle-class partners often used different language to express their coalition agendas to their members. Working-class leaders expanded the language of interests to include environmental or peace values, while middle-class leaders expanded their value frameworks to include the interests of the working class.

These experiences suggest that no single framework will serve as a unifying agenda for an emerging national working- and middle-class coalition. Local frameworks are attuned to the specific chemistry of conditions, organizations, and personalities in each community. Local coalitions have to develop significant sophistication and experience in cooperation before participants from around the country are likely to coalesce around a national agenda. They have much to learn first about how jobs, peace, and the environment overlap in practice.

The way to build a peaceful, environmentally sustainable, and economically just society is through these local experiments. The final form of that society is not clear, but alternatives will emerge from working- and middle-class alliances struggling with their interests and differences in specific situations. Ordinary people working day by day to confront their differences can remake the political landscape and build a progressive majority for change. The outcome of these experiments will determine the course of our history.

Society is a vessel containing a variety of political choices. Most of what we do every day is fight about politics while leaving the shape of the vessel unchanged. Those who benefit from the existing shape of society, those with wealth and power, devote their resources to keeping the vessel intact. But there are systematic ways to move and shift the vessel and thereby change the range of political choices. Interclass coalitions can accomplish this. They force participants to challenge the boundaries of social practices, to create a new social space where peace and economic prosperity coexist, and where economic well-being and environmental sustainability are mutually reinforcing.

▲

Research Methods

FIELDWORK

The fieldwork for this study combined ethnographic research and detailed case studies carried out between January 1991 and May 1992. The ethnographic research took place over a ten-month period with three organizations leading the peace, environmental, and labor movements in Washington State. These organizations, described below, were selected because (1) they are major regional or statewide organizations in the mainstream of their movements, (2) they or their members are involved in ongoing coalition work with organizations from the other movements, and (3) I was able to attain access to meetings and members.

The *Puget Sound Metal Trades Council* is the coordinating council of trade unions working in the Puget Sound shipyards. It incorporates fourteen unions including shipwrights (ship carpenters), pipefitters, painters, electrical workers, sheet metal workers, laborers, boilermakers, and teamsters. A few of these unions are solely or primarily shipyard unions, such as the boilermakers and the shipwrights. Most of the others do a majority of their work in the building and construction trades, and ship workers are a small proportion of their members. These are the old AFL, skilled craft unions which represent their trades in many different firms and industries. The trade councils are the coordinating bodies in their industries. They traditionally negotiate contracts (although individual unions sometimes break from this pattern), address grievances, and develop strategies which are industry wide.

Although most unions are highly secretive about their meetings, the

Puget Sound Metal Trades Council was exceptionally open and generous, allowing me to attend and observe their proceedings. The Council's members and leaders pride themselves in their openness and progressiveness. The Council is made up of relatively young men who, I was told, eased many of the traditional restrictions on outside attendance. Another factor that was critical to their openness was the organizing I had done several years earlier in support of the metal trades unions. I had worked on a campaign in Tacoma, Washington, in 1985–87 to diversify shipyard work and replace disappearing Navy contracts. Through that work I built relationships with union leaders and credibility that was critical to opening doors four years later when I returned to Washington to conduct my research.

Washington State Sane/Freeze (WSSF) was formed in 1989 from the merger of Puget Sound Sane and Washington Freeze. Puget Sound Sane was formed in 1983 as a "citizen's lobby created to reverse the nuclear arms race." Its major focus was national lobbying on such issues as the MX missile, Nicaragua, Hanford, the comprehensive test ban treaty, and U.S.-Soviet arms control negotiations. In 1986 it became involved with statewide electoral work and helped maintain a Democratic majority in the Senate by one vote. In 1987 the organization began to address conversion as an issue.

Through its active door-to-door canvassing, WSSF became the largest peace organization in the state. It had twenty-six thousand members in 1991. Despite its national affiliation, it acts almost entirely as an independent organization, developing its own agenda, raising its own funds, and organizing its own internal processes. Although it is organized statewide, the vast majority of its members live in the Puget Sound area, especially in Seattle.

The *Washington Environmental Council* (WEC) is the primary voice for the environmental movement on statewide issues. It is an umbrella organization for state work by local environmental groups as well as state and local chapters of national organizations. The WEC represents over ninety organizations in addition to individual members. It has an active lobby in the state capital and provides information about state legislative issues. It participates in state regulatory and oversight processes, with members on a dozen of the governor's committees for such issues as water resources, wetlands, wildlife, transportation, and growth management. When the legislative process fails to produce results, the WEC has run several statewide initiatives with significant impact.

I had no difficulty gaining access to meetings, people and records at Washington State Sane/Freeze or the Washington Environmental Council. These groups are quite accustomed to having new people at their meetings. It was also relatively easy for me to be accepted in these groups because I have worked with similar organizations in the past and was familiar with their styles and procedures. Furthermore, many members in these groups had done some graduate work themselves, so they empathized with my experience as a researcher.

Like many peace and environmental organizations, the WEC and WSSF are more familiar with university life than the unions, and they have their offices in the university district of Seattle, far from the largely working-class and historically industrial district of the city where most of the unions have their offices. This does not mean that they are university based, although WSSF does recruit a significant number of students for its canvassing work and activities. But more significantly, they operate in a political culture shared with the university.

In addition to the ethnographic research, I developed five case studies illustrating cooperation and conflict between peace, environmental, and labor organizations. I began by seeking examples of the best practice of labor and peace movement cooperation on conversion. I was directed by activists and national organizations to half a dozen cases. I chose three case studies in Maine, Minnesota and Washington for the following reasons: (1) all had significant histories of accomplishment, (2) all involved blue-collar trade unions and peace organizations that were chapters of national organizations in the forefront of conversion organizing, and (3) each coalition pursued a unique approach to organizing. Together they represented a range of organizing strategies. Minnesota's organizing was conflict oriented, Maine promoted cooperation, and Washington tried to balance both approaches. Washington tried to use labor-style organizing to serve peace movement goals, Maine sought to use peace-style organizing to meet labor movement goals, and Minnesota pursued traditional labor movement and peace movement organizing separately and simultaneously.

As I carried out my research, I discovered far more examples of coalitions between labor and environmental organizations than between labor and peace groups. I also found that unions were almost uniformly more sympathetic to the environmental movement than to the peace movement. I therefore decided to include labor and environmental coalitions in my study as a valuable comparison with the conversion coalitions. Because environmental organizations and the peace movement share a similar social background, this comparison helped me distinguish between conflicts that derive from social background and those that are issue specific. I chose a case of labor and environmental cooperation in Washington State because it included many of the same actors as my ethnographic research and Washington conversion case.

The last case I chose was the conflict between environmentalists and unions over old-growth timber protection in the Pacific Northwest, which was rapidly becoming the most prominent national example of contention between these movements. This example of conflict, which clearly demonstrated the differences between labor and environmentalists, provided an informative contrast with labor-environmental cooperation in other communities in Washington.

The five cases provided an overview of coalitions between blue-collar unions and mainstream peace and environmental organizations in many contexts. They include regional, state, and local examples. There are examples of coalitions initiated by a single organization—labor, peace, or environmental—and by different sides simultaneously. Among the five are examples of diverse strategies ranging from cooperation to conflict, from local to national targets of change, and from interest-based to education-oriented organizing styles. All were active during the same period.

RESEARCH TECHNIQUES

My ethnographic and case study research evolved together. As I developed the case studies through participant observation and over two hundred interviews, I documented different attitudes, organizational environments, and personal histories among peace and labor organizations. As I moved back and forth between ethnography and case studies, my cultural and social observations informed my interpretation of how movements behave, while the cases forced me to understand the groups I was observing as part of a larger system of social relationships.

Ethnographic research for this study included attending meetings, observing the functioning of daily office routines, reviewing minutes and documents from past meetings as well as internal documents, examining newsletters and other publications, and conducting interviews with organization members, staff, and board members. My ethnographic research and analysis was guided by a comparison of labor and peace/environmental movement organizations. I continually sought to understand the differences I observed among participants in terms of an organization's working- or middle-class roots. These differences encompassed individual behavior, ways of communicating with each other, formal organizational practices, relationships with me as an outside researcher, and observations about the physical environment and behavior of members. This comparison between organizations guided my observations and provided a useful check on my own middle-class biases as I sought to treat each class with similar standards of analysis.

I placed considerable emphasis on gathering life histories. All my interviews began with a series of questions about personal background. I asked people about their work history, about the circumstances that brought them to the movement, and about their experiences working for other organizations or issues. I devoted more time gathering the personal histories of individuals who played key roles organizing coalitions. I wanted to know about their backgrounds, their political and organizing histories, and the development of their ideas and beliefs about political involvement.

When I began my research I used a standard format to conduct interviews. It included questions about life history; organizational history; perception of the present organization; attitudes about peace, labor, and environmental organizations; perceptions about coalitions; beliefs about peace, about work and unions, and about the environment; and attitudes about social change. I quickly realized that my interviews were far more productive without a formal script, when I was free to pursue topics as they emerged naturally in discussion. I therefore sought to cover all my topics in the course of an hour-long interview, but without rigidly defining the order or always asking my entire list of questions.

I tape-recorded interviews when possible, and took extensive notes when not. After each interview I wrote down my observations and listed the highlights of our discussion. I interviewed central figures multiple times, and for these individuals I would also make sure I asked unanswered questions from my standard interview format.

My research depended critically upon developing trust with the organizations and activists in my study, and trust played an important part in my interviews. Union members in particular only shared information to the extent that they felt I was a friend of labor. I therefore began my interviews stating that I am a supporter of each movement. Interviewees would share more personal views and experiences as they developed greater trust through the course of the interview. At times I felt that I had to share some of my own opinions if the other person were to feel comfortable sharing more of her or his own perspective. But when I did express my own views, it was only after the other person had spoken on a subject first. I was continually aware of the trade-off between sharing enough to continue to develop trust and possibly influencing what the other person says. Any bias that this might have introduced into individual interviews was, I believe, countered by the large number of interviews, observations, and surveys conducted. The generalizations and case study descriptions included in this research have been confirmed by multiple sources.

My own activist experiences informed my discussions. In this book I have sought not only to convey people's perspectives but also to bring forth implications that are often not articulated. In my interviews I asked people to reflect, to dig deeper into their own understandings, and to be self-conscious about their own actions and beliefs. I would also paraphrase the viewpoints of other individuals or groups and ask for their reactions, enabling them to respond without the other person's inhibiting presence. So my research created an indirect dialogue between organizations in addition to my observations of coalition activities.

SURVEYS

In the course of my fieldwork I found that there were relatively few active participants in the coalitions I was observing, although the actual membership of each organization was quite large. I wanted to understand how the viewpoints of active coalition participants compared with the views of inactive members. I also found that organizations had almost no demographic information about their memberships. Because such information was vital for my class analysis, I decided to conduct a survey of organization members.

The survey was developed in consultation with coalition leaders from each movement, and survey questions were included in my more extensive interviews with activists as well. I conducted my surveys by telephone rather than in writing to ensure a high rate of return. This procedure also enabled me to engage members in a far more meaningful discussion of their answers. Telephone interviews lasted about twenty-five minutes, sufficient time for me to determine the broad perspective of participants as well as their more specific opinions. The entire process was enormously time consuming, even after I limited the size of my sample. But the information I gathered provided a much clearer indication of opinions than a brief survey could have accomplished.

The Maine Peace Campaign, Washington State Sane/Freeze, and Washington Environmental Council willingly gave me random lists of members and access to telephones. Time became the limiting factor, and I was able to conduct 52 surveys with the Maine Peace Campaign, 75 with Washington State Sane/Freeze, and 144 with the Washington Environmental Council.

I made a major effort to include members of several labor unions in my surveys, but with no success. Unions guard their membership lists closely, and although I received permission to distribute a written survey in one case, the union was sufficiently wary to make it nearly impossible to execute. The expense and my inability to follow up on nonrespondents also dissuaded me. The best I was able to achieve was to stand outside union membership meetings and speak with members as they came and went. These brief encounters enabled me to gauge member reactions to the issues that I had discussed in more detail with coalition activists. The members I spoke with were hardly a random sample, because only a small fraction of more active members attend meetings. My findings, however, generally confirmed the perceptions of coalition leaders. In broad terms I found that there was significant sympathy for the environmental movement among the rank-and-file members I spoke with, and a combination of incomprehension of, confusion about, and dislike for the peace movement. The specific responses I found, therefore, helped confirm the conclusions I was drawing from my in-depth interviews.

Pursuing union participation in my survey, however, provided me with additional insights into the decision making of the unions I was observing. I had many discussions with executive board members and union officers about their fears of such a survey. Union leadership feared that information would be used against the union by management, that members might be shown to disagree with union policies, and that a poll might tilt the balance of power in the union among delicately balanced factions. Some "progressive" members feared that the membership might be shown to be more conservative than the leadership, although conservatives feared the opposite. As an outsider I also experienced how difficult it is to win the trust of union leadership, particularly in comparison with the ease of gaining access to information from peace and environmental organizations.

▲

NOTES

Chapter 1: The Progressive Logjam

1. Brad Knickerbocker, "Oregon's Other Threatened Species: The Timber Worker," *Christian Science Monitor*, August 9, 1990, p. 1; Margaret E. Kriz, "Jobs v. Owls," *National Journal*, November 30, 1991, pp. 2913–16; "Saving Spotted Owl and Destroying Families," *USA Today*, May 13, 1992, p. A11; T. Gup, "Owl vs. Man," *Time*, June 25, 1990, pp. 55–56.
2. Timber worker interviewed by author.
3. Lansing Scott, "Ancient Forests' 11th Hour," *Seattle Community Catalyst*, September 1991, p. 13.
4. Ched Myers, "Open Letter to Local IAM 508 Members" (n.d.). Myer is a member of the Pacific Life Community, a nonviolent, direct-action organization in California.
5. Barbara Ehrenreich, *Fear of Falling* (New York: Pantheon, 1989), p. 256.
6. John Stuart Mill, *Considerations on Representative Government* (New York: Henry Holt, 1882), p. 172.
7. This theme has been developed by "neorepublicans" such as Robert Bellah, Richard Madsen, William Sullivan, Ann Swidler, and Steven Tipton (Bellah et al., *Habits of the Heart* [Cambridge: Harper and Row, 1985]) and William Sullivan (*Reconstructing Public Philosophy* [Berkeley: University of California Press, 1986]), who draw from the tradition of Rousseau, Jefferson, and Tocqueville; and by "communitarians" such as Michael Sandel (*Liberalism and the Limits of Justice* [New York: Cambridge University Press, 1982]) and Alasdair MacIntyre (*After Virtue* [Notre Dame: Notre Dame University Press, 1981]), who draw from an earlier tradition of Aristotle.
8. Putnam's much cited article "Bowling Alone: America's Declining Social Capital" (*Journal of Democracy* 6 [January 1995]: 65–78) claims that participation in civic organizations is declining dramatically.
9. Sullivan, *Reconstructing*, p. 158.
10. Charles Derber, William Schwartz, and Yale Magrass, *Power in the Highest De-*

gree: Professionals and the Rise of a New Mandarin Order (New York: Oxford University Press, 1990); Barbara Ehrenreich and John Ehrenreich, "The Professional-Managerial Class," *Radical America* 11 (1977): 7–31; David Nobel, *Forces of Production* (New York: Oxford University Press, 1986).

11. Otto Herman, "Environmentalists Have Natural Link with Labor," letter to the editor, *Seattle Post Intelligencer*, March 31, 1991, p. A5.

Chapter 2: Coalition Democracy and Class Politics

1. According to random phone surveys carried out by the author in 1991–92, the average income of Maine Peace Campaign members in 1992 was $53,500; of Washington Environmental Council members, $67,300; and of Washington State Sane/Freeze members, $52,000. Forestry worker wages are cited in Department of the Interior, Office of the Secretary, *Report of the Secretary of the Interior to the Endangered Species Committee* (Washington, D.C.: Bureau of Land Management, 1992). Construction worker wages are from *Construction Review*, Winter 1994, p. 52.

2. According to the author's survey among members of the Maine Peace Campaign in 1991–92, 82 percent had college degrees; among Washington Environmental Council members, 92 percent; and among Washington State Sane/Freeze members, 86 percent.

3. The Maine Peace Campaign membership was 69 percent professional; the Washington Environmental Council, 62 percent; and Washington State Sane/Freeze, 45 percent, according to the author's survey in 1991–92.

4. The European literature notes the predominance of the new middle class among activists in the peace, environmental, women's, and related movements. See Claus Offe, "New Social Movements: Challenging the Boundaries of Institutional Politics," *Social Research* 52 (1985): 817–68; Hanspeter Kreisi, "New Social Movements and the New Class in the Netherlands," *American Journal of Sociology* 94 (1989): 1078–1116.

    Within the peace movement, studies of the Campaign for Nuclear Disarmament in Britain have found disproportionate support from "welfare and creative professions. "See Frank Parkin, *Middle Class Radicalism* (Cambridge: Cambridge University, 1968); and John Mattasch, "The Sociology of CND," in *The Sociology of War and Peace*, edited by Colin Creighton and Martin Shaw (New York: Sheridan House, 1987), pp. 199–217.

    Profiles of the environmental movement in Europe and the United States show similar trends. See Stephen Cotgrove and Andrew Duff, "Environmentalism, Middle Class Radicalism and Politics," *Sociological Review* 28 (1980): 333–51.

5. Working-class children tend to be disciplined by rewards and punishments that are more stringent than in middle-class families. See Herbert Gans, *The Urban Villagers* (New York: Free Press, 1982); and Lillian Breslow Rubin, *Worlds of Pain: Life in the Working-Class Family* (New York: Basic, 1976).

    Middle-class family life, by contrast, is regulated by the avoidance of conflict and by emotional pressure. See Mary P. Baumgartner, *The Moral Order of the Suburb* (New York: Oxford University Press, 1988); and Urie Bronfenbrenner, "Socialization and Social Class," in *The Impact of Social Class*, edited by Paul Blumberg (New York: Crowell, 1972).

6. My approach charts a path between two opposing views of culture: culture as false consciousness, as outlined by Karl Marx in *The German Ideology*, and culture as the product of creative agents making their own history, as developed by E. P. Thompson and Raymond Williams. Class culture is understood in this book to be both structured, shaped, and limited by class position *and* endowed with significant opportunities for agency, initiative, and innovation in specific situations. It is therefore an intermediary variable which reflects class in unconscious ways but allows opportunities for creativity and innovation. Pierre Bourdieu's theory of practice provides a useful foundation for an approach to class culture that balances structure and agency.

   My approach, however, departs from Bourdieu and Passeron's concept of cultural capital, which refers to skills that provide for social advancement. The framework of cultural capital highlights power differences that are inherent in the class hierarchy. It assumes, however, that institutions reward the same behaviors in all classes equally. Thus it measures classes by a common standard and finds the middle-class better endowed with certain resources. Yet if the conditions of working- and middle-class lives differ significantly, as the above analysis indicates, then the cultural practices that advance members of one class may be maladaptive in another class. Similarly, skills that appear to be virtues for the middle class are likely to provide poor "capital" for working-class life.

7. Organizers are careful to distinguish between self-interest and selfishness. While selfishness focuses on personal gain at the expense of others, self-interest is used to refer to individual needs that exist in relationship to others and to the broader community. Self-interest is about meeting needs that require attention to the needs of others, where the relationship is as important as the gain.

8. Robert Muehlenkamp, "Organizing Never Stops," *Labor Research Review* 10 (1991): 4.

9. International Brotherhood of Electrical Workers, "Tradesman Contact Book" (n.d.) .

10. David Croteau, *Politics and the Class Divide: Working People and the Middle-Class Left* (Philadelphia: Temple University Press, 1995), p. 197.

11. Offe, "New Social Movements," pp. 832–38.

12. T. H. Marshall identifies the first three of these strategies in "The Nature of Class Conflict," in *Class, Status and Power*, edited by Reinhard Bendix and Martin Lipset (New York: Free Press, 1966).

13. *AFL-CIO Manual for Shop Stewards*, AFL-CIO Publication No. 75 (June 1988), p. 5.

14. Ralph Turner, "Sponsored and Contest Mobility and the School System," *American Sociological Review* 25 (1960): 855–67.

15. Charles Chatfield and Peter Van Den Dungen, *Peace Movements and Political Cultures* (Knoxville: University of Tennessee Press, 1988), p. xiv.

16. The case for why economic prosperity with peace or environmental protection requires fundamentally changing the way society is organized is beyond the scope of this book. The need for social transformation is certainly not universally

understood, and as environmental values have become widespread, more and more people invested in the existing organization of society have claimed that ordinary market processes can protect the environment. However, perpetual economic growth and capitalist development are inherently environmentally destructive, and environmental protection implies significant transformation of our most polluting industries. The costs of industrial shifts are generally born by workers and their communities. Furthermore, we in the United States have used war production to sustain economic activity ever since World War II brought us out of the Great Depression. The United States has regularly used foreign military intervention and support of client states to advance economic interests. Thus, achieving peace and environmental protection while protecting the economic interests of vulnerable groups requires fundamental changes in how our society is organized.

17. This interpretation of the Progressive Era is supported by many other authors. Stephen Skowroneck emphasizes this rise of the professional class as part of the reconstruction of the American state in *Building a New American State* (New York: Cambridge University Press, 1982). See also Gabriel Kolko, *The Triumph of Conservatism* (New York: Free Press, 1977).

18. See Mark Dowie, *Losing Ground: American Environmentalism at the Close of the Twentieth Century* (Cambridge: MIT Press 1995), for a description of how large, professional environmental organizations have acted against the interests of poor communities.

19. Karl Marx, "Communist Manifesto," in *Karl Marx: Selected Writings*, edited by David McClellan (1848; New York: Oxford University Press, 1987).

20. Carl Landauer, *European Socialism: A History of Ideas and Movements*, vols. 1–2 (Berkeley: University of California Press, 1959).

21. Adam Przeworski (*Capitalism and Social Democracy* [New York: Cambridge University Press, 1985]) presently counts the European working class as 19–38 percent of the population. Dennis Gilbert and Joseph A. Kahl (*The American Class Structure*, 4th ed. [Belmont, Calif.: Wadsworth, 1993]) estimate the working class at 30 percent of households, while Richard P. Coleman and Lee Rainwater (*Social Standing in American Society* [New York: Basic, 1978]) count 37 percent of the population. Eric Olin Wright (*Classes* [London: Verso, 1985]) is among a minority who claims that the working class does represent over half of the population, 52 percent in the United States and at least 61 percent in Sweden.

Wright and Gilbert and Kahl estimate that the professional-managerial upper middle class consists of about 14 percent of the population, while Barbara Ehrenreich and John Ehrenreich ("The Professional-Managerial Class," *Radical America* 11 [1977]: 731) estimate closer to 20–25 percent. The remainder of the middle class consists of lower managers, semiprofessionals, higher-paid salespeople, and foremen who are less educated but still perform nonstandardized tasks. Somewhere around 20–35 percent of the population fits this category (Gilbert and Kahl), bringing the total middle class to about 35–40 percent of the population.

22. Sidney Tarrow argues that "the Marxists misspecified a crucial factor in the great movements of their time: That they were interclass networks of democratic

workers, literate artisans and middle-class radicals whose power came from the fact that they could challenge authorities from different angles" (*Power in Movement* [New York: Cambridge University Press, 1995], p. 60).

23. Gosta Esping-Andersen and Roger Friedland, "Class Coalitions in the Making of Western European Economies," *Political Power and Social Theory* 3 (1982): 1–52.

24. Steve Fraser and Gary Gerstle, *The Rise and Fall of the New Deal Order, 1930–1980* (Princeton: Princeton University Press, 1989), p. xxi.

CHAPTER 3: BATTLES OVER OLD GROWTH

1. Robert Lee, "Social and Cultural Implications of Implementing 'A Conservation Strategy for the Northern Spotted Owl' " (University of Washington, 1990, mimeographed).

2. Beverly A. Brown, *In Timber Country* (Philadelphia: Temple University Press, 1995).

3. Brian Tokar, *Earth for Sale: Reclaiming Ecology in the Age of Corporate Greenwash* (Boston: South End, 1997), p. 145.

4. John Bellamy Foster, "Capitalism and the Ancient Forest," *Monthly Review* 43 (1991): 1–16.

5. Ross Mickey et al., "Spotted Owls, Old Growth and the Economy of the Northwest" (Portland, Or.: Northwest Forest Resource Council, 1989), p. 37.

6. Michael Anderson and Jeffrey Olson, *Federal Forests and the Economic Base of the Pacific Northwest* (Washington, D.C.: The Wilderness Society, 1991), chap. 5.

7. Jonathan I. Lange, "The Logic of Competing Information Campaigns: Conflict over Old Growth and the Spotted Owl," *Communication Monographs* 60 (1993): 239–56.

8. Report by Greer, Margolis, Burns, and Associates to the AFL-CIO, as cited in "Authorized AFL-CIO Report Seeks Lovelier Image," *Union Democracy Review* 10 (1995): 1.

CHAPTER 4: WHEN CLASSES MEET

1. Jerry Lembcke and William Tattam, *One Union in Wood* (New York: International, 1984), chap. 1.

2. Andrew Prouty, *More Deadly Than War* (New York: Garland, 1985), p. 45.

3. Ibid., p. 169.

4. Mathew Carroll and Robert Lee, "Occupational Community and Identity among Pacific Northwestern Loggers," in *Community and Forestry*, edited by Robert Lee, Donald Field, and William Burch, Jr. (Boulder: Westview, 1990), pp. 144–46.

5. Ibid., p. 147.

6. Statistics are based on the author's random survey of WEC members in 1991–92.

7. Steve Chase, ed., *Defending the Earth: A Dialogue between Murray Bookchin and Dave Foreman* (Boston: South End, 1991), pp. 37–39.

8. Herbert Gans, *The Urban Villagers* (New York: Free Press, 1982).

9. Lembcke and Tattam, *One Union*, p. 153.

10. Robert Lee, cited in Fred Moody, "The Vanquished," *Seattle Weekly*, February 12, 1992, p. 22.

11. Ibid.

CHAPTER 5: HISTORY HANGS IN THE BALANCE

1. "Resolutions Adopted by the American Federation of Labor," 1887, Swarthmore College Peace Collection.

2. For a detailed examination of Gompers change from a peace to war advocate see Simeon Larson, *Labor and Foreign Policy: Gompers, the AFL and the First World War, 1913–1918* (Cranbury, N.J.: Associated University Press, 1976).

3. American Friends Service Committee, "Labor Says No to Peacetime Military Conscription," 1951, Swarthmore College Peace Collection.

4. Ibid.

5. John Luecke, "Labor's Stake in Peace," April 30, 1937, Swarthmore College Peace Collection.

6. This section borrows from the ideas of Ronald Radosh, *Labor and United States Foreign Policy* (New York: Random House, 1969).

7. There is some debate about what to include in military spending. The Office of Management Budget (OMB) defines the defense function as including the Department of Defense, nuclear weapons spending through the Department of Energy, and defense-related activities. Peace organizations generally add to this a portion of interest on the national debt, veterans' benefits, foreign military assistance, and portions of NASA, Coast Guard, and the Maritime Administration. In the 1980s, these added another 30–40 percent to the OMB numbers. I will use the latter approach throughout this study, since it is a better approximation of the total cost of military activity.

8. Figures from Robert W. DeGrasse, *Military Expansion, Economic Decline* (New York: Council on Economic Priorities, 1983). These statistics can be presented very differently depending on whether one wishes to make military spending appear to be a large or small share of the federal budget. If one includes nondiscretionary funds such as social security and unemployment benefits in the federal budget, then total expenditures appear much larger, making military spending appear much smaller. The figures cited here exclude entitlement programs from the budget since these are not allocated in the budget process.

9. *Wall Street Journal*, September 21, 1970, as cited in Philip Foner, *U.S. Labor and the Vietnam War* (New York: International, 1989), pp. 13–14.

10. Caleb Foote, letter, March 23, 1945, cited in Lawrence S. Wittner, *Rebels against War: The American Peace Movement, 1941–1960* (New York: Columbia University Press, 1969), p. 48.

11. Statement of Purpose, cited in "Short History of SANE," National Committee for a SANE Nuclear Policy Papers, Swarthmore College Peace Collection.

12. Milton Katz, *Ban the Bomb: History of SANE, 1957–85* (New York: Greenwood, 1986), p. xii.

13. John E. Mueller, *War, Presidents and Public Opinion* (New York: John Wiley and Sons, 1973); Harlan Hahan, "Dove Sentiment among Blue-Collar Workers," *Dissent*, May–June 1970, pp. 202–5; Andrew Greeley, "Political Attitudes among American White Ethnics," *Public Opinion Quarterly* 26 (1972): 213–20.

14. Kenneth Heineman, "The Silent Majority Speaks: Anti-War Protest and Backlash, 1965–1972," *Peace and Change* 17 (1992): 402–33; Richard Polenberg, *One Nation Divisible* (New York: Viking, 1980); and H. Edward Ransford, "Blue-Collar Anger: Reaction to Student and Black Protest," *American Sociological Review* 27 (1972): 333–46.

15. Frank Parkin, *Middle Class Radicalism* (Cambridge: Cambridge University Press, 1968); Hanspeter Kreisi, "New Social Movements and the New Class in the Netherlands," *American Journal of Sociology* 94 (1989): 1078–1116; Ronald Inglehart, *Culture Shift in Advanced Industrial Society* (Princeton: Princeton University Press, 1990); Stephen Cotgrove and Andrew Duff, "Environmentalism, Middle Class Radicalism and Politics," *Sociological Review* 28 (1980): 333–51; and Steven Brint, "The Political Attitudes of Professionals," *American Journal of Sociology* 90 (1985): 30–71.

16. B. J. Widick, "AFL-CIO Convention: Strong Army of the Status Quo," *Nation*, December 27, 1965, p. 516.

17. For a brash defense of these policies from a CIA participant see Thomas Braden, "I'm Glad the CIA Is Immoral," *Saturday Evening Post*, May 20, 1967. The AFL-CIO has repeatedly denied any involvement with the CIA, a claim contradicted by other CIA agents who have left the service such as Jonathan Stockwell and Philip Agee. See Jonathan Kwitny, *Endless Enemies: The Making of an Unfriendly World* (New York: Congdon and Weed, 1984), pp. 344–45.

18. Daniel Cantor and Juliet Schor, *Tunnel Vision: Labor, the World Economy, and Central America* (Boston: South End, 1987), p. 44. Beth Sims, *Workers of the World Undermined* (Boston: South End, 1992), p. 22, cites the same figure for all of the AFL-CIO's foreign activities in 1987, based on *Perspectives on Labor and the World: The AFL-CIO Abroad*, AFL-CIO Publication No. 182 (Washington, D.C., 1987).

19. The AFL-CIO endorsed an amendment to the defense authorization bill by Representative Samuel Stratton (Dem., N.Y.) to experiment with using military contracts to ease unemployment in particularly depressed areas. AFL-CIO News, October 9, 1982.

20. Labor Action for Peace, untitled brochure [1962?], Swarthmore College Peace Collection.

21. Cantor and Schor, *Tunnel Vision*, p. 3.

22. Walter Reuther, cited in David Elsila, "War, Peace and Jobs," *United Auto Workers Solidarity*, November 1989, p. 12.

23. "Short History of SANE," National Committee for a SANE Nuclear Policy Papers.

24. John Lynch, ed., *Economic Adjustment and Conversion of Defense Industries* (Boulder: Westview, 1987), p. 19.
25. Cited in "Unions Hit Inflated Military Budget," *Dispatcher*, March 24, 1978, p. 2.
26. Ibid.
27. Sane, memorandum, February 1980, National Committee for a SANE Nuclear Policy Papers.
28. William Winpisinger, cited in David Cortright, executive director of Sane, letter in "A Sane Progress Report—Major Unions Endorse Conversion," February 1978. The first sentence is a statement made by Winpisinger himself, the second is Cortright's paraphrasing of Winpisinger's words. The statements were made at a meeting on January 26, 1978.
29. David Gordon, Richard Edwards, and Michael Reich, *Segmented Work, Divided Workers* (New York: Cambridge University Press, 1982); and Michael Piore and Charles Sabel, *The Second Industrial Divide* (New York: Basic, 1984).

CHAPTER 6: THE POLITICAL MOMENT

1. Peter Montague, "The Military Toxics Scandal Deepens," *Rachel's Environmental and Health Weekly*, April 3, 1991.
2. Preamble to the AFL constitution adopted in 1886, as cited in Art Preis, *Labor's Giant Step* (New York: Pathfinder, 1972), pp. 516–17.
3. Cantor and Schor, *Tunnel Vision: Labor, the World Economy, and Central America* (Boston: South End, 1987), p. 14.
4. John Sweeney, as cited in David Glenn, "Adding Brains to Labor's New Political Muscle," *In These Times*, December 14, 1997, p. 23.
5. Riley Dunlap and Rik Scarce, "The Polls—Poll Trends: Environmental Problems and Protection," *Public Opinion Quarterly* 55 (1991): 664.
6. Ibid., p. 670.
7. Dowie, *Losing Ground*, p. 175.
8. Letter from the Southwest Organizing Project and others to the mainstream environmental organizations, March 16, 1990, as cited in Regina Austin and Michael Schill, "Black, Brown, Red and Poisoned," in *Unequal Protection*, edited by Robert Bullard (San Francisco: Sierra Club, 1994), p. 69.
9. Maximo Kalaw, as cited in Dowie, *Losing Ground*, p. 167.
10. Michael Brown, "Peace Movement Takes a New Turn," *National Jobs with Peace Campaign Newsletter*, Summer 1989, p. 3.

CHAPTER 7: COALITION ORGANIZING

1. Council on Economic Priorities, "Vulnerability Index," *Research Report*, June 1990.
2. This organization changed its name from Puget Sound Sane to Washington State Sane/Freeze in 1989.

3. In 1992 the project changed its name to the Economic Conversion Project.
4. See the PEP's newsletter *Peace Economy News*, June 1990.
5. Cited in Pam Smith, "Swords to Plowshares: Economic Conversion at BIW, a Conversation with President Buzz Fitzgerald," *Maine Progressive*, July 1990.
6. Leah Rogne and Bradley Harper, "The Meaning of Civil Disobedience: The Case of the Honeywell Project," in *Peace Action in the Eighties: Social Science Perspectives*, edited by Sam Marullo and John Lofland (New Brunswick, N.J.: Rutgers University Press, 1990).

Chapter 8: Learning in Coalitions

1. Celene Krauss, "Women of Color on the Front Line," in *Unequal Protection: Environmental Justice and Communities of Color*, edited by Robert D. Bullard (San Francisco: Sierra Club, 1994), p. 263.
2. See Steven Lukes, *Power: A Radical View* (London: Macmillan, 1974); John Gaventa, *Power and Powerlessness* (Chicago: University of Illinois Press, 1980).
3. Steve Max, "Four Steps to Developing Leaders," in *Midwest Academy Organizing Manual* (Chicago: Midwest Academy, 1984), p. 112.
4. Paulo Freire, *Pedagogy of the Oppressed* (New York: Seabury, 1970), p. 56.
5. Harry Boyte, *CommonWealth: A Return to Citizen Politics* (New York: Free Press, 1989), p. 12.
6. Dowie, *Losing Ground*; Robert Gottlieb, *Forcing the Spring: The Transformation of the American Environmental Movement* (Washington, D.C.: Island Press, 1993).

Chapter 9: Bridge Builders

1. Eric Mann, "Labor-Community Coalitions," in *Building Bridges: The Emerging Grassroots Coalition of Labor and Community*, edited by Jeremy Brecher and Tim Costello (New York: Monthly Review Press), p. 116.
2. William Gamson, "Democratic Participation in Social Movements" (presidential address to the Eastern Sociological Society, March 24, 1990), p. 23.

Chapter 10: Finding a Common Language

1. Michael Clark, "Message from the President," *Friends of the Earth 1990 Annual Report*, p. 5.
2. Economic Conversion Project of Maine, *Annual Report, 1990–1991*, p. 1.
3. Gary Delgado, *Organizing the Movement: The Roots and Growth of ACORN* (Philadelphia: Temple University Press, 1986), p. 89.
4. Harry Boyte, *The Backyard Revolution* (Philadelphia: Temple University Press, 1980), p. 52.

5. Vladimir Lenin, *What Is to Be Done?* (New York: International, 1929), p. 76.
6. Delgado, *Organizing the Movement*.

CONCLUSION

1. Carol Boggs, "Economic Conversion as a Radical Strategy: Where Social Movements and Labor Meet," in *Building Bridges: The Emerging Grassroots Coalition of Labor and Community*, edited by Jeremy Brecher and Tim Costello (New York: Monthly Review Press, 1990), p. 302.
2. Oil, Chemical and Atomic Workers, "Just Transition for Jobs and the Environment" (New York: Public Health and Labor Institutes, 1998), p. 1.

▲

BIBLIOGRAPHY

American Friends Service Committee. 1951. *Labor Says No to Peacetime Military Con-scription*. Swarthmore College Peace Collection.

Anderson, Michael, and Jeffrey Olson. 1991. *Federal Forests and the Economic Base of the Pacific Northwest*. Washington, D.C.: The Wilderness Society.

Aronowitz, Stanley. 1973. *False Promises*. New York: McGraw-Hill.

——. 1992. *The Politics of Identity*. New York: Routledge.

Baritz, Loren. 1989. *The Good Life: The Meaning of Success for the American Middle Class*. New York: Knopf.

Baumgartner, Mary P. 1985. "Law and the Middle Class." *Law and Human Behavior* 9:3–24.

——. 1988. *The Moral Order of the Suburb*. New York: Oxford University Press.

Bellah, Robert, Richard Madsen, William Sullivan, Ann Swidler, and Steven Tipton. 1985. *Habits of the Heart*. Cambridge: Harper and Row.

Bendix, Reinhard, and Seymour Martin Lipset, eds. 1966. *Class, Status and Power*. New York: Free Press.

Bernstein, Basil. 1971. *Class, Code and Control*, vol. 1. London: Routledge and Kegan Paul.

Bishak, Gregory. 1993. "The Obstacles to Real Security, Military Corporatism and the Cold War State." In *Real Security*, edited by Kevin Cassidy and Gregory Bishak, pp. 133–64. Albany: State University of New York Press.

Bledstein, Burton. 1976. *The Culture of Professionalism: The Middle Class and the Devel-opment of Higher Education in America*. New York: Norton.

Bourdieu, Pierre. 1990 [1977]. *Outline of a Theory of Practice*. New York: Cambridge University Press.

Bourdieu, Pierre, and Jean-Claude Passeron. 1979 [1964]. *The Inheritors, French Stu-dents and Their Relation to Culture*. Chicago: University of Chicago Press.

Boyte, Harry. 1980. *The Backyard Revolution*. Philadelphia: Temple University Press.

——. 1989. *CommonWealth: A Return to Citizen Politics*. New York: Free Press.

Braden, Thomas. 1967. "I'm Glad the CIA Is Immoral." *Saturday Evening Post*, May 20.

Brecher, Jeremy, and Tim Costello, eds. 1990. *Building Bridges: The Emerging Grassroots Coalition of Labor and Community*. New York: Monthly Review Press.

Brint, Steven. 1985. "The Political Attitudes of Professionals." *American Journal of Sociology* 90:30–71.

Bronfenbrenner, Urie. 1972. "Socialization and Social Class." In *The Impact of Social Class*, edited by Paul Blumberg. New York: Crowell.

Brown, Beverly A. 1995. *In Timber Country*. Philadelphia: Temple University Press.

Bullard, Robert, ed. 1994. *Unequal Protection*. San Francisco: Sierra Club.

Burawoy, Michael. 1979. *Manufacturing Consent*. Chicago: University of Chicago Press.

Buttel, Frederick, and William Flin. 1978a. "The Politics of Environmental Concern." *Environment and Behavior* 10:17–36.

———. 1978b. "Social Class and Mass Environmental Beliefs." *Environment and Behavior* 10:433–50.

Cantor, Daniel, and Juliet Schor. 1987. *Tunnel Vision: Labor, the World Economy, and Central America*. Boston: South End.

Carroll, Mathew, and Robert Lee. 1990. "Occupational Community and Identity among Pacific Northwestern Loggers." In *Community and Forestry*, edited by Robert Lee, Donald Field, and William Burch, Jr., pp. 141–55. Boulder: Westview.

Caufield, Catherine. 1990. "A Reporter at Large: The Ancient Forest." *New Yorker*, May 14, pp. 46–84.

Chase, Steve, ed. 1991. *Defending the Earth: A Dialogue between Murray Bookchin and Dave Foreman*. Boston: South End.

Chatfield, Charles, and Peter Van Den Dungen. 1988. *Peace Movements and Political Cultures*. Knoxville: University of Tennessee Press.

Clarke, John, Chas Critcher, and Richard Johnson, eds. 1979. *Working-Class Culture*. New York: St. Martin's.

Clotfelter, James. 1986. "Disarmament Movements in the United States." *Journal of Peace Research* 23:97–101.

Cogan, Morris. 1953. "Toward a Definition of Profession." *Harvard Educational Review* 23:33–50.

Coleman, Richard P., and Lee Rainwater. 1978. *Social Standing in American Society*. New York: Basic.

Commoner, Barry. 1971. *The Closing Circle*. New York: Knopf.

———. 1976. *The Poverty of Power*. New York: Knopf.

Cortright, David. 1978. Letter in "A Sane Progress Report—Major Unions Endorse Conversion." Swarthmore College Peace Collection.

Cotgrove, Stephen, and Andrew Duff. 1980. "Environmentalism, Middle Class Radicalism and Politics." *Sociological Review* 28:333–51.

———. 1981. "Environmentalism, Values and Social Change." *British Journal of Sociology* 32:92–110.

Council on Economic Priorities. 1990. "Vulnerability Index." *Research Report*, June.

Croteau, David. 1995. *Politics and the Class Divide: Working People and the Middle-Class Left*. Philadelphia: Temple University Press.

Davis, Mike. 1986. *Prisoners of the American Dream*. London: Verso.

DeGrasse, Robert W., Jr. 1983. *Military Expansion, Economic Decline*. New York: Council on Economic Priorities.

Delgado, Gary. 1986. *Organizing the Movement: The Roots and Growth of ACORN*. Philadelphia: Temple University Press.

Derber, Charles, William Schwartz, and Yale Magrass. 1990. *Power in the Highest Degree: Professionals and the Rise of a New Mandarin Order*. New York: Oxford University Press.

Dowie, Mark. 1991–92. "American Environmentalism: A Movement Courting Irrelevance." *World Policy Journal* 9:67–92.

———. 1995. *Losing Ground: American Environmentalism at the Close of the Twentieth Century*. Cambridge: MIT Press.

Downey, Gary L. 1986. "Ideology and the Clamshell Identity: Organizational Dilemmas in the Anti-Nuclear Movement." *Social Problems* 33:258–73.

Dunlap, Riley, and Rik Scarce. 1991. "The Polls—Poll Trends: Environmental Problems and Protection." *Public Opinion Quarterly* 55:651–72.

Edelman, Murray. 1988. *Constructing the Political Spectacle*. Chicago: University of Chicago Press.

Ehrenreich, Barbara. 1989. *Fear of Falling*. New York: Pantheon.

Ehrenreich, Barbara, and John Ehrenreich. 1977. "The Professional-Managerial Class." *Radical America* 11:7–31.

Elsila, David. 1989. "War, Peace and Jobs." *United Auto Workers Solidarity*, November, pp. 9, 11–12.

Esping-Andersen, Gøsta. 1985. *Politics against Markets*. Princeton: Princeton University Press.

Esping-Andersen, Gøsta, and Roger Friedland. 1982. "Class Coalitions in the Making of Western European Economies." *Political Power and Social Theory* 3:1–52.

Everhart, Robert. 1983. *Reading, Writing and Resistance: Adolescence and Labor in a Junior High School*. Boston: Routledge and Kegan Paul.

Faber, Daniel, and James O'Connor. 1993. "Capitalism and the Crisis of Environmentalism." In *Toxic Struggles*, edited by Richard Hofrichter, pp. 12–24. Philadelphia: New Society.

Ferree, Myra, and Frederick Miller. 1985. "Mobilization and Meaning: Toward an Integration of Social Psychological and Resource Perspectives on Social Movements." *Sociological Inquiry* 55:38–61.

Findley, Rowe. 1990. "Will We Save Our Own?" *National Geographic*, September, pp. 106–36.

Fisher, Robert, and Joseph M. Kling. 1987. "Leading the People: Two Approaches to the Role of Ideology in Community Organizing." *Radical America* 21:31–45.

Foner, Philip. 1989. *U.S. Labor and the Vietnam War*. New York: International.

Foster, John Bellamy. 1991. "Capitalism and the Ancient Forest." *Monthly Review* 43:1–16.

Fraser, Steve, and Gary Gerstle, eds. 1989. *The Rise and Fall of the New Deal Order, 1930–1980*. Princeton: Princeton University Press.

Freire, Paulo. 1970. *Pedagogy of the Oppressed*. New York: Seabury.

Freudenberg, Nicholas. 1984. *Not in Our Backyards: Community Action for Health and the Environment*. New York: Monthly Review Press.

Fulcher, James. 1994. "The Social Democratic Model in Sweden: Termination or Restoration?" *Political Quarterly* 65:203–13.

Gamson, William. 1964. "Experimental Studies of Coalition Formation." In *Advances in Experimental Social Psychology*, vol. 1, edited by Leonard Berkowitz, pp. 81–110. New York: Academic.

——. 1990. "Democratic Participation in Social Movements." Address to the Eastern Sociological Society, March 24.

Gans, Herbert. 1982 [1962]. *The Urban Villagers*. New York: Free Press.

Gaventa, John. 1980. *Power and Powerlessness*. Chicago: University of Illinois Press.

Gecas, Viktor. 1979. "The Influence of Social Class on Socialization." In *Contemporary Theories of the Family*, vol. 1, edited by Wesley Burr, Reuben Hill, F. Ivan Nye, and Ira L. Reiss, pp. 365–404. New York: Free Press.

Giddens, Anthony. 1979. *Central Problems in Social Theory*. Berkeley: University of California Press.

Gilbert, Dennis, and Joseph A. Kahl. 1993. *The American Class Structure*, 4th ed. Belmont, Calif.: Wadsworth.

Gilkeson, John, Jr. 1986. *Middle Class Providence, 1820–1940*. Princeton: Princeton University Press.

Glenn, David. 1997. "Adding Brains to Labor's New Political Muscle." *In These Times*, December 14, pp. 22–25.

Goffman, Erving. 1974. *Frame Analysis: An Essay on the Organization of Experience*. New York: Harper.

Gordon, David, Richard Edwards, and Michael Reich. 1982. *Segmented Work, Divided Workers*. New York: Cambridge University Press.

Gordon, Suzanne, and Dave McFadden, eds. 1984. *Economic Conversion*. Cambridge, Mass.: Ballinger.

Gottlieb, Robert. 1993. *Forcing the Spring: The Transformation of the American Environmental Movement*. Washington, D.C.: Island Press.

Gouldner, Alvin. 1979. *The Future of Intellectuals and the Rise of the New Class*. New York: Seabury.

Greeley, Andrew. 1972. "Political Attitudes among American White Ethnics." *Public Opinion Quarterly* 26:213–20.

——. 1974. *Building Coalitions: American Politics in the 1970s*. New York: New Viewpoints.

Greider, William. 1992. *Who Will Tell the People: The Betrayal of American Democracy*. New York: Simon and Schuster.

Gup, T. 1990. "Owl vs. Man." *Time*, June 25, pp. 55–56.

Gusfield, Joseph R. 1966. "Functional Areas of Leadership in Social Movements." *Sociological Quarterly* 7:137–56.

Hahan, Harlan. 1970. "Dove Sentiment among Blue-Collar Workers." *Dissent*, May–June, pp. 202–205.

Hall, Stuart. 1994. "Cultural Studies: Two Paradigms." In *Culture/Power/History*, edited by Nicholas B. Dirks, Geoff Eley, and Sherry B. Ortner, pp. 520–38. Princeton: Princeton University Press.

Halle, David. 1984. *America's Working Man: Work, Home and Politics among Blue-Collar Property Owners*. Chicago: Chicago University Press.

Hamilton, Alexander. 1911. *The Federalist*. London: J. M. Dent and Sons.

Harrington, Michael. 1968. *Toward a Democratic Left*. New York: Macmillan.

Hartz, Louis. 1955. *The Liberal Tradition in America*. New York: Harcourt Brace Jovanovich.

Heineman, Kenneth. 1992. "The Silent Majority Speaks: Anti-War Protest and Backlash, 1965–1972" *Peace and Change* 17:402–33.

Herman, Otto. 1991. "Environmentalists Have Natural Link with Labor." Letter to the editor, *Seattle Post Intelligencer*, March 31, p. A5.

Hinckley, Barbara. 1981. *Coalition Politics*. New York: Harcourt Brace Jovanovich.

Hirschman, Albert. 1977. *The Passions and the Interests*. Princeton: Princeton University Press.

Holland, David, and Philip Wandshneider. 1989. "U.S. Military Expenditures: Their Impact on the Washington Economy." Preliminary report to the Washington State Legislature.

Inglehart, Ronald. 1977. *The Silent Revolution*. Princeton: Princeton University Press.

——. 1990. *Culture Shift in Advanced Industrial Society*. Princeton: Princeton University Press.

International Brotherhood of Electrical Workers. n.d. "Tradesman Contact Book."

Jennings, M. Kent. 1987. "Residues of a Movement: The Aging of the American Protest Generation." *American Political Science Review* 81:367–82.

Joyner, Nancy Douglas. 1982. "Coalition Politics: A Case Study of An Organization's Approach to a Single Issue." *Women and Politics* 2:57–70.

Kahn, Mark E. 1986. *Middle Class Radicalism in Santa Monica*. Philadelphia: Temple University Press.

Katz, Milton. 1986. *Ban the Bomb: History of SANE, 1957–85*. New York: Greenwood.

Katznelson, Ira. 1981. *City Trenches*. New York: Pantheon.

Kitschelt, Herbert. 1993. "Class Structure and Social Democratic Party Strategy." *British Journal of Political Science* 23:299–337.

——. 1994. *The Transformation of European Social Democracy*. New York: Cambridge University Press.

Knickerbocker, Brad. 1990. "Oregon's Other Threatened Species: The Timber Worker." *Christian Science Monitor*, August 9, p. 1.

Knoke, David. 1990. *Political Networks: The Structural Perspective*. New York: Cambridge University Press.

Koelble, Thomas. 1991. *The Left Unraveled*. Durham: Duke University Press.

Kohn, Melvin. 1969. *Class and Conformity: A Study of Values*. Homewood, Ill.: Dorsey.

Kohn, Melvin, and Carmi Schooler. 1983. *Work and Personality: An Inquiry into the Impact of Social Stratification*. Norwood, N.J.: Ablex.

Kolko, Gabriel. 1976. *Main Currents in Modern American History*. New York: Harper and Row.

Kolko, Gabriel. 1977. *The Triumph of Conservatism*. New York: Free Press.

Kreisi, Hanspeter. 1989. "New Social Movements and the New Class in the Netherlands." *American Journal of Sociology* 94:1078–1116.

Krauss, Celene. 1994. "Women of Color on the Front Line." In *Unequal Protection: Environmental Justice and Communities of Color*, edited by Robert D. Bullard, pp. 256–71. San Francisco: Sierra Club.

Kriz, Margaret E. 1991. "Jobs v. Owls." *National Journal*, November 30, pp. 2913–16.

Kwitny, Jonathan. 1984. *Endless Enemies: The Making of an Unfriendly World*. New York: Congdon and Weed.

Labor Action for Peace. [1962?]. Untitled brochure. Swarthmore College Peace Collection.

Ladd, Everett. 1978. "The New Lines Are Drawn: Class and Ideology in America," pt. 1. *Public Opinion* 4:48–53.

LaLuz, Jose. 1991. "Creating a Culture of Organizing: ACTWU's Education for Empowerment." *Labor Research Review* 10:61–67.

Landauer, Carl. 1959. *European Socialism: A History of Ideas and Movements*, vols. 1–2. Berkeley: University of California Press.

Lange, Jonathan I. 1993. "The Logic of Competing Information Campaigns: Conflict over Old Growth and the Spotted Owl." *Communication Monographs* 60:239–56.

Larson, Simeon. 1976. *Labor and Foreign Policy: Gompers, the AFL and the First World War, 1913–1918*. Cranbury, N.J.: Associated University Press.

Lash, Scott, and John Urry. 1987. *The End of Organized Capitalism*. Cambridge: Polity.

Lee, Robert. 1990. "Social and Cultural Implications of Implementing 'A Conservation Strategy for the Northern Spotted Owl.' " University of Washington. Mimeographed.

LeMasters, E. E. 1977. *Blue Collar Aristocrats: Life Styles at a Working Class Tavern*. Madison: University of Wisconsin Press.

Lembcke, Jerry, and William Tattam. 1984. *One Union in Wood*. New York: International.

Lenin, Vladimir. 1929. *What Is to Be Done?* New York: International.

Levinson, Andrew. 1974. *The Working Class Majority*. New York: Coward, McCann and Geoghegan.

Levy, Peter B. 1994. *The New Left and Labor in the 1960s*. Urbana: University of Illinois Press.

Lichtenstein, Nelson. 1982. *Labor's War at Home: The CIO in World War II*. New York: Cambridge University Press.

Lichterman, Paul. 1995. "Piecing Together Multicultural Community: Cultural Differences in Community Building among Grass-Roots Environmentalists." *Social Problems* 42:513–34.

——. 1996. *The Search for Political Community*. New York: Cambridge University Press.

Luecke, John. 1937. "Labor's Stake in Peace." Swarthmore College Peace Collection.

Luhan, J. Michael. 1986. "AIFLD's Salvadoran Labor Wars." *Dissent*, Summer, pp. 340–50.

Lukes, Steven. 1974. *Power: A Radical View*. London: Macmillan.

Lynch, John, ed. 1987. *Economic Adjustment and Conversion of Defense Industries*. Boulder: Westview.

MacIntyre, Alasdair. 1981. *After Virtue*. Notre Dame: Notre Dame University Press.

MacGuire, Durmuid. 1990. "New Social Movements and Old Political Institutions: The Campaign for Nuclear Disarmament, 1979–1989." Ph.D. diss., Cornell University.

Mallet, Serge. 1975. *Essays on the New Working Class*. St. Louis: Telos.

Mandelbaum, David. 1973. "The Study of Life History: Gandhi." *Current Anthropology* 14:177–206.

Mannheim, Karl. 1972. "The Problems of Generations." In *The New Pilgrims*, edited by Philip Altbach and Robert Laufer, pp. 101–38. New York: David McKay.

Markusen, Ann, and Joel Yudken. 1992. *Dismantling the Cold War Economy*. New York: Basic.

Marshall, T. H. 1966. "The Nature of Class Conflict," in *Class, Status and Power*, edited by Reinhard Bendix and Martin Lipset. New York: Free Press.

Marullo, Sam, and John Lofland, eds. 1990. *Peace Action in the Eighties: Social Science Perspective*. New Brunswick, N.J.: Rutgers University Press.

Marwell, Gerald, and Patricia Oliver. 1993. *The Critical Mass in Collective Action: A Micro-Social Theory*. New York: Cambridge University Press.

Marx, Karl. 1987 [1848]. "Communist Manifesto." In *Karl Marx: Selected Writings*, edited by David McClellan. New York: Oxford University Press.

——. 1987 [1932]. "The German Ideology." In *Karl Marx: Selected Writings*, edited by David McClellan. New York: Oxford University Press.

Mattasch, John. 1987. "The Sociology of CND." In *The Sociology of War and Peace*, edited by Colin Creighton and Martin Shaw, pp. 199–217. New York: Sheridan House.

Max, Steve. 1984. "Four Steps to Developing Leaders." In *Midwest Academy Organizing Manual*. Chicago: Midwest Academy.

McAdam, Doug. 1982. *Political Process and the Development of Black Insurgency, 1930–1970*. Chicago: University of Chicago Press.

Meier, August, and Elliot Rudwick. 1973. *CORE: A Study of the Civil Rights Movement, 1942–1968*. New York: Oxford University Press.

Melucci, Alberto. 1980. "The New Social Movements: A Theoretical Approach." *Social Science Information* 19:199–226.

Merelman, Richard, and Gary King. 1986. "The Development of Political Activists: Toward a Model of Early Learning." *Social Science Quarterly* 67:473–90.

Meyer, David. 1988. "The Nuclear Freeze Movement in the United States, 1979–1984: Political Opportunities and the Structure of Social Mobilization." Ph.D. diss., Boston University.

Meyer, David, and Nancy Whittier. 1994. "Social Movement Spillover." *Social Problems* 41:277–98.

Mickey, Ross, Chris West, Ralph Saperstein, Bobb Tribble, and Jim McCauley. 1989. "Spotted Owls, Old Growth and the Economy of the Northwest." Portland, Or.: Northwest Forest Resource Council.

Mill, John Stuart. 1882. *Considerations on Representative Government*. New York: Henry Holt.

Moody, Kim. 1988. *An Injury to All*. New York: Verso.

Moore, Barrington. 1966. *The Social Origins of Dictatorship and Democracy*. Boston: Beacon.

Morris, Aldon. 1981. "Black Southern Student Sit-In Movement: An Analysis of Internal Organization." *American Sociological Review* 46:744–67.

Morris, Aldon D., and Carol McClurg Mueller, eds. 1992. *Frontiers in Social Movement Theory*. New Haven: Yale University Press.

Morris, George. 1955. *CIA and American Labor*. New York: International.

Muehlenkamp, Robert. 1991. "Organizing Never Stops." *Labor Research Review* 10:1–5.

Mueller, John E. 1973. *War, Presidents and Public Opinion*. New York: John Wiley and Sons.

Nobel, David. 1986. *Forces of Production*. New York: Oxford University Press.

Offe, Claus. 1980. *Disorganized Capitalism*. Cambridge: MIT Press.

———. 1985. "New Social Movements: Challenging the Boundaries of Institutional Politics." *Social Research* 52:817–68.

Offe, Claus, and Helmut Wiesenthal. 1988. "Two Logics of Collective Action." In *Political Power and Social Theory*, edited by Maurice Zeitlin, pp. 67–115. Greenwich, Conn.: JAI.

Oil, Chemical, and Atomic Workers. 1998. "Just Transition for Jobs and the Environment." New York: Public Health and Labor Institutes.

Olofsson, Gunnar. 1988. "After the Working-Class Movement? An Essay on What's 'New' and What's 'Social' in the New Social Movements." *Acta Sociologica* 31:15–34.

Parkin, Frank. 1968. *Middle Class Radicalism*. Cambridge: Cambridge University Press.

Pateman, Carole. 1970. *Participation and Democratic Theory*. Cambridge: Cambridge University Press.

Peirce, Neal. 1996. "America in Civic Decline? Don't Believe It." *Baltimore Sun*, February 5.

Petrocik, John. 1981. *Party Coalitions: Realignment and Decline of the New Deal Party System*. Chicago: University of Chicago Press.

Piore, Michael, and Charles Sabel. 1984. *The Second Industrial Divide*. New York: Basic.

Pitkin, Hanna. 1981. "Justice: On Relating Private and Public." *Political Theory* 9:327–52.

Piven, Francis Fox, and Richard Cloward. 1977. *Poor People's Movements*. New York: Pantheon.

Plotkin, Sidney. 1990. "Enclave Consciousness and Neighborhood Activism." In *Dilemmas of Activism*, edited by Joseph M. Kling and Prudence S. Posner, pp. 218–39. Philadelphia: Temple University Press.

Polenberg, Richard. 1980. *One Nation Divisible*. New York: Viking.

Preis, Art. 1972. *Labor's Giant Step*. New York: Pathfinder.

Prouty, Andrew. 1985. *More Deadly Than War*. New York: Garland.

Przeworski, Adam. 1985. *Capitalism and Social Democracy*. New York: Cambridge University Press.

Przeworski, Adam, and John Sprague. 1986. *Paper Stones: A History of Electoral Socialism*. Chicago: University of Chicago Press.

Putnam, Robert. 1995. "Bowling Alone: America's Declining Social Capital." *Journal of Democracy* 6:65–78.

Radosh, Ronald. 1969. *Labor and United States Foreign Policy*. New York: Random House.

Ransford, H. Edward. 1972. "Blue-Collar Anger: Reaction to Student and Black Protest." *American Sociological Review* 27:333–46.

Riker, William. 1962. *The Theory of Political Coalitions*. New Haven: Yale University Press.

Rochen, Thomas, and Ray Pierce. 1985. "Coalitions as Rivalries." *Comparative Politics*, July, pp. 437–51.

Rogers, Mary Beth. 1990. *Cold Anger*. Denton: University of North Texas Press.

Rose, Fred. 1995. "Organizing for Conversion." In *The Socio-Economics of Conversion from War to Peace*, edited by Lloyd Dumas, pp. 131–59. Armonk, N.Y.: M. E. Sharpe.

———. 1997. "Towards a Class-Cultural Theory of Social Movements: Reinterpreting New Social Movements." *Sociological Forum* 12:461–94.

Rousseau, Jean-Jacques. 1973 [1762]. *The Social Contract and Discourses*. London: J. M. Dent and Sons.

Rowbotham, Sheila, Lynne Segal, and Hilary Wainwright. 1981. *Beyond the Fragments*. Boston: Alyson.

Rubin, Lillian Breslow. 1976. *Worlds of Pain: Life in the Working-Class Family*. New York: Basic.

Sandel, Michael. 1982. *Liberalism and the Limits of Justice*. New York: Cambridge University Press.

Sapiro, Virginia. 1990. "The Women's Movement and the Creation of Gender Consciousness: Social Movements as Socialization Agents." In *Political Socialization, Citizenship Education, and Democracy*, edited by Orit Ichilov, pp. 266–80. New York: Columbia University Teachers College Press.

"Saving Spotted Owl and Destroying Families." 1992. *USA Today*, May 13, p. A11.

Schmoll, Fritz. 1989. "A 'Red-Green' Coalition in West Berlin: Chances for Left Urban Politics?" Paper presented to the Seventh Urban Change and Conflict Conference, University of Bristol, England.

Scott, Lansing. 1991. "Ancient Forests' 11th Hour." *Seattle Community Catalyst*, September, p. 13.

Shepherd, Susan. 1993. "Need for Union-Community Alliances Setting a Labor Agenda Environment [*sic*]." *News* (Federation for Industrial Retention and Renewal), spring.

Shippee, John. 1977. "Do Movements Learn? A Commentary." *Journal of Peace Research* 14:261–66.

"Short History of Sane." n.d. The National Committee for a SANE Nuclear Policy Papers, Swarthmore College Peace Collection.

Shostak, Arthur B. 1969. *Blue Collar Life*. New York: Random House.

———. 1991. *Robust Unionism: Innovations in the Labor Movement*. Ithaca: ILR Press.

Siegmann, Heinrich. 1985. *The Conflict between Labor and Environmentalism in the Federal Republic of Germany and the United States*. New York: St. Martin's.

Skowroneck, Stephen. 1982. *Building a New American State*. New York: Cambridge University Press.

Staggenborg, Suzanne. 1986. "Coalition Work in the Pro-Choice Movement: Organizational and Environmental Opportunities and Obstacles." *Social Problems* 33:374–90.

Sullivan, William. 1986. *Reconstructing Public Philosophy*. Berkeley: University of California Press.

Tarrow, Sidney. 1995. *Power in Movement*. New York: Cambridge University Press.

Taylor, Richard, and C. Pritchard. 1980. *The Protest Makers: The Nuclear Disarmament Movement of 1958–1965 Twenty Years On*. Oxford: Pergamon.

Thomas, Jack Ward, et. al. 1990. "A Conservation Strategy for the Spotted Owl." Portland, Or.: United States Department of Agriculture.

Thompson, E. P. 1968. *The Making of the English Working Class*. Harmondsworth, Eng.: Penguin.

Thurow, Lester. 1980. *The Zero Sum Society*. New York: Basic.

Tokar, Brian. 1997. *Earth for Sale: Reclaiming Ecology in the Age of Corporate Greenwash*. Boston: South End.

Warren, Donald. 1976. *The Radical Center: Middle Class and the Politics of Alienation*. Notre Dame: Notre Dame University Press.

Weber, Max. 1946. "Class, Status, Party." In *From Max Weber*, edited by H. H. Gerth and C. Wright Mills, pp. 180–95. New York: Oxford University Press.

Wendell, Karen, Daniel Oswald, and Douglas Powell. 1989. *Forest Statistics of the United States, 1987*. Washington, D.C.: United States Department of Agriculture.

Widick, B. J. 1965. "AFL-CIO Convention: Strong Army of the Status Quo." *Nation*, December 27, pp. 516–18.

Williams, Raymond. 1977. *Marxism and Literature*. Oxford University Press.

Williams, William Appleton. 1967. "The Cold War Revisionists." *Nation*, November 13, pp. 492–95.

Willis, Paul. 1977. *Learning to Labour: How Working-Class Kids Get Working-Class Jobs*. New York: Columbia University Press.

Windmuller, John P. 1967. "The Foreign Policy Conflict in American Labor." *Political Science Quarterly* 82:205–34.

Wittner, Lawrence S. 1969. *Rebels against War: The American Peace Movement, 1941–1960*. New York: Columbia University Press.

Wright, Erik Olin. 1985. *Classes*. London: Verso.

Wykle, Lucinda, Ward Morehouse, and David Dembo. 1991. *Worker Empowerment in a Changing Economy*. New York: Apex.

Yergin, Daniel. 1977. *Shattered Peace*. Boston: Houghton Mifflin.

Zald, Mayer, and John McCarthy. 1980. "Social Movement Industries: Competition and Cooperation among Movement Organizations." *Research in Social Movements, Conflicts and Change* 3:1–20.

INDEX

AFL-CIO, 22, 50
conflicts with peace and environmental movements, 28, 30, 41, 43
merger, 82
support for conversion and peace, 87–89, 115
support for military and war, 83, 85–88
Sweeny election, 101–2
Alinsky, Saul, 154, 198, 200
American Federation of Labor (AFL)
alliance with military, 77, 80–81, 85
attacks on progressive unions, 68–69, 81–82
craft unionism, 27–28, 69, 97, 101
development of business unionism, 98
exclusiveness of, 27–28
government attacks on, 84
opposition to war, 78–79
and timber unions, 57, 68
See also AFL-CIO

Bath Iron Works, 121–23, 133–34, 139–40, 144, 175, 184, 202. *See also* Maine: conversion organizing
Bridge builders
defined, 167
generational sources, 168, 215
generational types, 169–76
importance for coalition success, 176–80, 212
risks, 180–84
roles, 176–79, 188
Building trades

environmental ideas of, 188
Seattle and coalitions, 119, 151–54, 170
support for Vietnam War, 4, 83
See also Washington State Building and Construction Trades
Business unionism
in building trades, 149, 153
causes of, 68–69
costs and benefits, 98–99, 149
decline of, 93, 98–100
defined, 69
in International Woodworkers of America, 68–69
as strategy of collaboration, 27–28, 69

Central Intelligence Agency, use of labor movement, 85–86
Class alliances
competing strategies of, 20–23, 51–55, 56–57, 77–78, 210–11
cultural sources of, 23–25, 68–73, 211
political implications, 8–9, 77–78, 90–91
role of bridge builders in, 176–80, 212
See also Working- and middle-class coalitions
Class culture
basis for interpreting interests, 23–25, 56–57, 68–73, 211
and coalitions, 144–45, 167–68, 176
empowering and limiting, 17
and social movement forms, 18–20, 25–26, 63–64, 65–68, 172
and social movement ideology, 32, 162–63, 187–91

and anti-environmental policies, 94–95
and arms trade, 94–95
costs for workers within, 95, 99
and opportunities for coalitions, 111–12
Freese, Jim, 153
Freire, Paulo, 151, 196–99

Generational shifts, 7, 168, 205, 215–16
in environmental movement, 103–7
in labor movement, 81, 92, 99–101,
169–70
in peace movement, 82, 108–11
Gompers, Samuel, 77–78, 80–81

Ideology
characteristics of, 43, 47, 49, 181, 186–87
class origins of, 23–25, 62–63, 65–68,
187–91
in coalitions, 163–64, 187–96
Cold War, 80–82
development of, 161–64, 191–96
development of national agenda, 207,
217–18
of free trade, 94
role of bridge builders, 177–80, 168
in social movements, 149–51, 186–87
in timber conflict, 43–49, 69–72
See also individual movements
Individualism
in the middle class, 19–20, 65–68, 72
in society, 6–7, 155–56, 214
Industrial Workers of the World (IWW),
57, 77, 81, 98
Interest-based organizing, 57–59, 189–91,
196–205, 213
described, 18–19, 63–64, 68–73
See also Working class: culture
Interests
cultural determinants of, 23–24, 56–57,
68–72, 211
hidden, 49–51
middle-class, 19–20, 22, 26–27, 45–46,
72–73
multiple, of classes, 8–9, 20–23, 51–55,
77–78
overemphasis in organizing, 197–98
perceived and misperceived, 43–49, 196
relationship to values, 17–18, 188–91,
196–99, 204–5
role in political education, 6–7, 31,
214–15
working-class experience of, 18–19,
21–22, 43–45, 72–73

International Association of Machinists
(IAM)
Maine Local 6, 122, 133–35, 140, 142–43,
175, 202
national support for conversion, 89–90,
133, 191
See also Maine: conversion organizing
International Brotherhood of Electrical
Workers (IBEW)
Minnesota Local 2047, 125, 127–28,
135–38, 203–4
Washington Local 46, 151–54, 159, 163,
170
See also Minnesota: conversion organizing; Washington state: environmental-construction union coalition
International Woodworkers of America
(IWA)
decline of, 3
history of, 68–69
timber advocacy of, 41

Jay, Maine, labor-environmental coalition,
53–54
Jobs with Peace, 88, 109, 115. See also Minnesota Jobs with Peace
Judd, Ron, 159, 170

Labor and environmental movements
common interests between, 52–53,
100–101, 103
conflicts between, 3–4, 38–43, 146–47,
207–8
cooperation between, 8, 10, 53–54,
147–48, 152–54, 156–59, 167, 182–83
cultural differences between, 68–73
issues confronting, 95–97
See also Timber conflict; Washington
state: environmental-construction
union coalitions
Labor movement
as interest group, 49–51, 198
collaboration with military, 80–88
government attacks on, 81, 84–85,
95–96, 98–99, 147
hierarchy in, 57–60, 68–69, 100
ideology of, 129–30, 189–91
membership, 99, 101
organizing strategies of, 21–22, 27–28,
77–78, 80–82, 90–91, 97–98, 210–
11
perceptions of middle-class movements, 57–59, 135–36

Working- and middle-class coalitions
(*cont.*)
See also Learning: from interclass coalitions; Labor and environmental
movements: cooperation between;
Labor and peace movements: cooperation between; Progressive politics
and coalitions
Working- and middle-class conflict
class cultural causes, 68–73
See also Labor and environmental movements: conflicts between; Labor and
peace movements: conflicts between;
Timber conflict

Working class
activists from, 167, 169–70, 173–76
culture of, 62–63, 72–73, 209
external regulation of, 16, 18, 63, 72–73
ideology of, 18–19, 70, 189–91
logging culture within, 60–64, 68–72
organizing strategies of, 21–22, 27–28,
196
organizing style of, 18–19, 58–60, 63–64
perceptions of middle class of, 57–59,
71–72
size of, 29, 230n. 21
See also Class culture; Interest-based organizing